THE BOER WAR
1899–1902

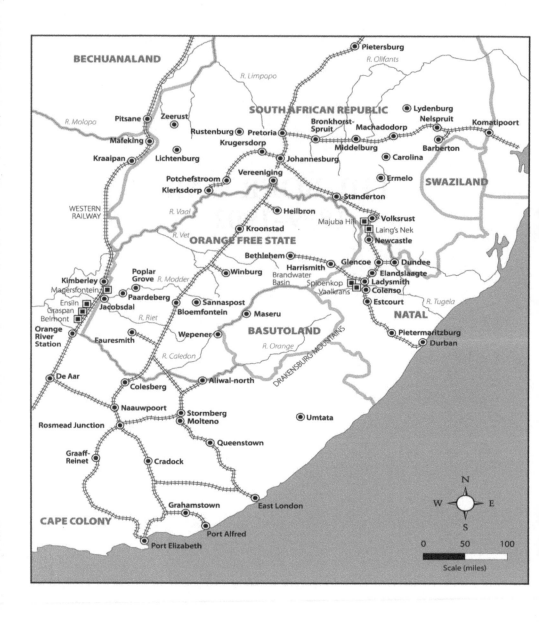

DESPATCHES FROM THE FRONT
The Commanding Officers' Reports from the Field and at Sea

THE BOER WAR 1899–1902

Ladysmith, Magersfontein, Spion Kop, Kimberley, and Mafeking

Introduced and compiled by
John Grehan and Martin Mace

with additional research by
Sara Mitchell and Robert Cager

Pen & Sword
MILITARY

First published in Great Britain in 2014 by
PEN & SWORD MILITARY
An imprint of
Pen & Sword Books Ltd
47 Church Street
Barnsley
South Yorkshire
S70 2AS

Copyright © John Grehan and Martin Mace, 2014

ISBN 978-1-78159-328-8

Typeset by Concept, Huddersfield, West Yorkshire HD4 5JL.
Printed and bound in England by CPI Group (UK) Ltd, Croydon CR0 4YY.

Pen & Sword Books Ltd incorporates the imprints of Pen & Sword Archaeology, Atlas, Aviation, Battleground, Discovery, Family History, History, Maritime, Military, Naval, Politics, Railways, Select, Social History, Transport, True Crime, and Claymore Press, Frontline Books, Leo Cooper, Praetorian Press, Remember When, Seaforth Publishing and Wharncliffe.

For a complete list of Pen & Sword titles please contact
PEN & SWORD BOOKS LIMITED
47 Church Street, Barnsley, South Yorkshire, S70 2AS, England
E-mail: enquiries@pen-and-sword.co.uk
Website: www.pen-and-sword.co.uk

Contents

Introduction

Like so many conflicts that Britain has been involved in, it's Army was ill-prepared for war when the fighting broke out in South Africa in October 1899. The conflict that ensued is commonly referred to as the Boer War, but is more properly named the Second Boer War.

Despite the warnings from many senior figures in South Africa, and threats from the President of the Transvaal, Paul Kruger, Britain had only 14,750 regular soldiers to defend the colonies of Natal and the Cape. The Boers, from the Transvaal and the Orange Free State, could count 50,000 well-armed mounted infantry in their ranks.

The complex origins of the war resulted from more than a century of conflict between the Boers and the British, as well as the deteriorating relationship between the two sides in the years since the end of the First Boer War (was fought from 16 December 1880 until 23 March 1881). That deterioration spilled over into outright war on 11 October 1899.

On that day the Boers mounted a surprise offensive into the British-held Natal and Cape Colony areas. With no regular army units, the Boers had no problems with mobilisation. As with the First Boer War, since they were generally a civilian militia, each Boer wore what he wished, usually his everyday dark-grey, light-grey, neutral-coloured, or earthtone khaki farming clothes – often a jacket, trousers and slouch hat. The exception was the *Staatsartillerie* (Afrikaans for "States Artillery") of the Transvaal and Orange Free State republics which wore light green uniforms.

Moving rapidly across the veldt, the Boers drove the British Natal Field Force into Ladysmith. Other British forces were besieged in Kimberley and Mafeking. The sieges of these places tied down a considerable proportion of the Boer forces. It was a mistake. The great advantage which the Boer troops had over the conventional British soldiers was their speed and manoeuvrability over terrain they knew intimately. By tying down their men in protracted, stagnant sieges the Boers threw away those advantages. Their opportunity to gain a quick victory was lost and gave Britain a second chance.

Nevertheless, when a 47,000-strong British Expeditionary Force reached South Africa it suffered a series of reverses at the hands of the Boers. The British commander, Sir Redvers Buller, divided his army into three columns.

One, under the command of Lord Methuen, was sent to relieve Kimberley, a second under General Gatacre being despatched to the north of Cape Colony, whilst Buller himself marched against the Boers that had invaded Natal. Methuen was repulsed at Magersfontein, Gatacre was beaten at Stormberg and Buller was defeated at Colenso. Buller renewed his offensive but his attacks at Spion Kop and Vaal Krantz were repulsed.

The defeats were a great embarrassment to Britain, and its response was to assemble an overwhelming force to crush the Boers. Britain's top generals, Lord Roberts and Lord Kitchener, were placed in charge of what eventually amounted to over 200,000 regulars and 200,000 militia and irregulars. The full resources of the British Empire were employed with 16,000 volunteers coming from Australia, 6,500 from New Zealand, and others from Canada.

Even with this great deployment of force, the Boers defeated Kitchener at Paardeberg. But eventually the weight of numbers told. Kimberley and Lady-smith were relieved. The Boers at Paardeberg were surrounded and forced to surrender. The Transvaal and the Orange Free State were annexed to the British Crown.

This did not bring an end to the war, but it did alter the nature of the fighting. Unable to stand against the British in open battle, the Boers resorted to guerrilla warfare. They split up into small columns or "Commandos" of about 1,000 men which attacked detached British units or railways.

Kitchener responded by dividing up the country into sections with 3,700 miles of barbed-wire and 8,000 blockhouses. Having isolated each area in this way, the British troops systematically cleared each section of guerrillas. This prevented the fighting Boers from simply melting back into the farming communities only to re-emerge when the British troops had left their sector, the farms were burned and the women and children were herded into concentration camps. Gradually Kitchener's ruthless approach wore the Boers down and on 31 May 1902, the Boers accepted Britain's peace terms.

* * *

The despatches collected in this volume cover the major engagements of the Second Boer War. The First Boer War has not been included. Due to restrictions of space it has not been possible to include all the casualty lists, though where it has been practical this has been done. Lists of individuals considered to be worthy of mentioning by their superior officers have also not been included in every instance for the same reason.

Unlike the despatches of Lord Raglan and his successors in the previous major war of the Victorian era, the Crimean War, the despatches of Redvers Buller, Roberts, Kitchener and their subordinates are highly detailed and comprehensive. This is perhaps most notable with regards to the Siege of Mafeking.

The place was considered to be of considerable strategic importance and Major General Baden-Powell undertook to personally conduct its defence. Mafeking withstood a siege of 217 days and its relief prompted unprecedented scenes of rejoicing across Britain. In his despatch, Baden-Powell provides not only an exciting narrative of the siege but he also details the number of soldiers and civilians in Mafeking, and their composition; the weapons available; the prices paid to native runners to deliver messages (which were high due to the likelihood of them being caught and killed!) and even the quantity of the rations doled out to the various military units.

There are also raw and dramatic accounts from the various officers which draw the reader instantly into the war. After the capture of Spion Kop, the British dug in and thought that their position was secure. Then as we read Lieutenant General Sir Charles Warren's report, a message is received from Colonel Crofton of the Royal Lancaster Regiment: "Reinforce at once or all lost. General dead."

Warren replied immediately, "I am sending two battalions, and the Imperial Light Infantry are on their way up. You must hold on to the last. No surrender." Colonel Thorneycroft, given command on Spion Kop, responded by declaring that unless the enemy artillery could be silenced, his men could not stand another day's shelling. The position was abandoned and Warren demanded, in a public document that would be read by millions, that an inquiry into Thorneycroft's "unauthorized evacuation" of the Kop should be conducted. It is remarkable stuff and, predictably, led to criticism of Warren himself as the senior officer present.

The despatches are reproduced here in the same form as when they were originally published in the UK, though from the time of the action in the heart of Africa to the printing press in London many weeks, or even months, had passed. They have not been modified or interpreted in any way and are therefore the unedited and unique words of the commanding officers as they saw things at the time. The result of this is a variety of styles and in some reports a decided degree of Victorian eccentricity.

A number of words used by the British officers in their despatches will be unfamiliar to present-day readers, though perfectly understandable to the soldiers used to colonial warfare of the 19th century. An example of this is the word "donga", which is a dry ravine with steep sides. Others are the term "bheestie", which was a water-carrier, or a "spruit" which is a small stream. Some, though, have been lost to time and can be found in no modern English dictionary.

By contrast some words from that conflict found their way into the English language, and thus at one time as many as fifteen English football clubs had a kop, which in Afrikaans means hill, where their supporters stood. Likewise, the Boer Commandos were the inspiration for elite fighting troops of the Royal Navy and the British Army.

Any grammatical or spelling errors have also been left uncorrected to retain the authenticity of the documents. These include misspellings such as "troughout" for throughout, "negligeable", "advoid, "harass" and many others. The despatches, then, are presented just as they were when first revealed to the general public more than 100 years ago as the Great Boer War raged.

Abbreviations

AAG – Assistant Adjutant General.
ADC – Aide-de-Camp.
ASC – Army Service Corps.
BA – British Army.
CB – Companion of The Most Honourable Order of the Bath.
CIE – Companion of The Most Eminent Order of the Indian Empire.
CMG – Companion of The Most Distinguished Order of Saint Michael and Saint George.
CRA – Commander Royal Artillery.
DAAG – Deputy Assistant Adjutant General.
DSO – Distinguished Service Order.
GCB – Knight Grand Cross of The Most Honourable Order of the Bath.
GCIE – Knight Grand Commander of The Most Eminent Order of the Indian Empire.
GCSI – Knight Grand Commander of The Most Exalted Order of the Star of India.
KCB – Knight Commander of The Most Honourable Order of the Bath.
KCMG – Knight Commander of The Most Distinguished Order of Saint Michael and Saint George.
LM – Lee-Metford (rifles).
MH – Martini-Henry (rifles).
MVO – Member of The Royal Victorian Order.
pr. prs. –Prisoner of War.
PVO – Provincial Veterinary Officer
QF – Quick Firing (Guns).
RA – Royal Artillery.
RAMC – Royal Army Medical Corps.
RE – Royal Engineers.
RFA – Royal Field Artillery.
RMLI – Royal Marine Light Infantry.
RN – Royal Navy.
VC – Victoria Cross.

1

BATTLES OF TALANA HILL, ELANDSLAAGTE, BELMONT, GRASPAN AND MODDER

FRIDAY, JANUARY 26, 1900.

War Office, January, 26, 1900.

THE following Despatches, with their enclosures, have been received from General, the Right Honourable Sir Redvers Buller, G.C.B., South Africa:-

From the General Commanding-in-Chief the Forces in South Africa to the Secretary of State for War, War Office, London, S.W.

Cape Town,

SIR,   *November* 9, 1899.

I HAVE the honour to forward herewith a report from Lieutenant-General Sir George White, V.C., &c., dated 2nd November, on his operations in Natal, which was handed to me yesterday by Lieutenant-General French on his arrival from Durban. It does not seem to call for any remarks from me.

I have, &c.,
REDVERS BULLER,
General Officer Commanding.

From Lieutenant-General Sir George S. White, V.C., G.C.B., G.C.S.I., G.C.I.E., to the Secretary of State, War Office, London, S.W.

Ladysmith, Natal,

SIR,   *November* 2, 1899.

I HAVE the honour to forward the following report on the military operations in Natal since the date of my arrival in that colony:-

2. I reached Durban and assumed command of the forces in that colony on 7th October, 1899, proceeding direct to Maritzburg. I found the troops, Imperial and Colonial, then in the colony, distributed as under:-

At Pietermaritzburg – 1st Battalion Manchester Regiment, and Mounted Infantry Company, 2nd Battalion King's Royal Rifle Corps.
At Estcourt – Detachment Natal Naval Volunteers, Natal Royal Rifles.
At Colenso – Durban Light Infantry.

At Ladysmith – 5th Lancers, Detachment 19th Hussars, Brigade Division, Royal Artillery; 10th Mountain Battery, Royal Garrison Artillery; 23rd Company, Royal Engineers; 1st Battalion Devonshire Regiment; 1st Battalion Liverpool Regiment, and Mounted Infantry Company; 26th (two sections) British Field Hospital, and Colonial troops.

At Glencoe – 18th Hussars; Brigade Division, Royal Artillery; 1st Battalion Leicestershire Regiment, and Mounted Infantry Company; 1st Battalion King's Royal Rifle Corps, and Mounted Infantry Company; 2nd Battalion Royal Dublin Fusiliers, and Mounted Infantry Company; 6th Veterinary Field Hospital.

With 1 Company, 1st Battalion King's Royal Rifle Corps at Eshowe, and a detachment of the Umvoti Mounted Rifles at Helpmakaar.

3. The information available regarding the positions occupied by the armies of the two Dutch Republics showed the great bulk of the forces of the Orange Free State were massed near the passes of the Drakensberg mountains, west of Ladysmith. The troops of the South African Republic were concentrated at various points west, north, and east of the northern angle of Natal. On 10th October His Excellency the Governor informed me that Her Majesty's Government had received an ultimatum from that of the South African Republic, and that the outbreak of war on the evening of 11th October might be regarded as certain.

4. Since my arrival in the colony I had been much impressed by the exposed situation of the garrison of Glencoe, and on the evening of 10th October I had an interview on the subject with his Excellency the Governor, at which I laid before him my reasons for considering it expedient, from a military point of view, to withdraw that garrison, and to concentrate all my available troops at Ladysmith. After full discussion his Excellency recorded his opinion that such a step would involve grave political results and possibilities of so serious a nature that I determined to accept the military risk of holding Dundee as the lesser of two evils. I proceeded in person to Ladysmith on 11th October, sending on Lieutenant-General Sir William Penn Symons to take command at Glencoe.

5. The Boers crossed the frontier both on the north and west on 12th October, and next day the Transvaal flag was hoisted at Charlestown. My great inferiority in numbers necessarily confined me strategically to the defensive, but tactically my intention was and is to strike vigorously whenever opportunity offers. Up to 19th October the enemy from the north were engaged in moving down on the Biggarsberg – Dundee line in three columns. The main column, under General Joubert, occupied Newcastle, and marched south by

the road leading thence on Glencoe Junction. A second column, under Viljoen, crossed Botha's Pass, and moved south over the Biggarsberg, cutting the railway from Glencoe Junction to Ladysmith on 19th October at Elands Laagte, where they took up a position. A third column, under Lucas Meyer, crossed the Buffalo River, marching west on Dundee, and arrived within striking distance of that place on the night of 19th October. Meanwhile the Free State forces west of Ladysmith contented themselves with occupying the country at the foot of the Drakensberg Range, without approaching within striking distance of Ladysmith, and, though the mounted patrols of both sides were constantly in touch, up to the evening of 19th October, nothing of importance took place in this direction.

6. On the morning of 20th October, at 3.20 A.M., the Mounted Infantry picquet, east of Dundee at the junction of the roads from Landmann's and Vants Drifts, was fired on and compelled to retire. Two companies, 2nd Battalion Royal Dublin Fusiliers, were sent out in support of it by Lieutenant-General Sir W.P. Symons, and at 4.30 A.M. a report was received that the enemy had halted and established themselves at Fort Jones. By 5 A.M. all Sir W.P. Symons' troops were under arms.

7. At 5.50 A.M. the enemy's guns opened fire, from Talana Hill on our camp, at a range of 5,000 yards. Though well directed this fire had but little effect, as the shells, fired with percussion fuzes, buried themselves in the soft earth. Our guns at once returned the fire, but, finding the range too great, the 13th and 69th Field Batteries were moved, at 6 A.M., to a fresh position south of the town of Dundee, with the Mounted Infantry Company of the 1st Battalion King's Royal Rifles as escort. The 67th Field Battery and the 1st Battalion Leicestershire Regiment were detailed to remain in and protect the camp. The 2nd Battalion Royal Dublin Fusiliers and the 1st Battalion Royal Irish Fusiliers were sent through the town to Sand Spruit, the 1st Battalion King's Royal Rifles taking up a position under cover to the east of the town. These preliminary movements were completed by 6.30 A.M.

8. At 7.30 A.M. the Infantry advanced to a small patch of wood, about 1,000 yards beyond Sand Spruit. They moved, in extended order, over open level grass land, the 2nd Battalion Royal Dublin Fusiliers leading, followed in succession by the 1st Battalion King's Royal Rifles and the 1st Battalion Royal Irish Fusiliers. Notwithstanding the open nature of the ground this move-ment was, owing to the accurate fire of our artillery, completed with but slight loss. Sir W.P. Symons' intention was to make a direct attack on the enemy's position under cover of the wood above mentioned, and of some buildings known as Smith's Farm.

9. At 8 A.M. the batteries were brought forward to a range of 2,300 yards, whence the 69th Battery opened fire on Talana Hill, and the 13th Battery on the hill (marked 4,700) south of the road which was also held by the enemy, the guns and escort being under fire from both hills. At the same time Sir W.P. Symons moved the Infantry through the wood to its front edge, on which a very accurate direct fire was opened from the top of Talana Hill, and also from a stone wall which extended half way up and along the side of that hill. The Infantry here were also exposed to an enfilading fire from the hill marked 4,700.

10. At 8.50 A.M. the Infantry Brigade were ordered to advance. The ground was open and intersected by nullahs, which running generally perpendicular to the enemy's position gave very little cover. At 9 A.M. Sir W.P. Symons ordered up his reserves, and advanced with them through the wood at 9.15 A.M. At 9.30 A.M. the Lieutenant-General was, I regret to report, mortally wounded in the stomach, and the command devolved upon Brigadier-General Yule, who directed the 2nd Battalion Royal Dublin Fusiliers on the left, and the 1st Battalion King's Royal Rifle Corps on the right. The latter battalion reached the wall, to which two companies of the 1st Battalion Royal Irish Fusiliers were also brought up, the other six companies being held in reserve. The 2nd Battalion Royal Dublin Fusiliers, however, less favoured by the ground were unable, for some time, to make any progress.

11. About 11.30 A.M., the enemy's guns were silenced, and the Artillery moved into a range of 1,400 yards and opened a very rapid fire on the ridge over the heads of our Infantry. This temporarily brought under the enemy's rifle fire, and enabled our infantry to push on. The ground in places was so steep and difficult that the men had to climb it on hands and knees, but by 1 A.M., the crest was reached, and the enemy, not waiting to come to close quarters, retired in the directions of Landmann's and Vants' drifts. Brigadier-General Yule then ordered the Artillery to the neck on the Dundee – Vants' drift road, on arrival at which point the retreating enemy was seen streaming away in clumps of 50 and 100 men, on which guns could have inflicted great loss. The enemy, however, displayed a white flag, although they do not appear to have had any intention of surrendering, and in consequence the Officer Commanding Royal Artillery refrained from firing.

12. Turning now to our Cavalry, the 18th Hussars received orders at 5.40 A.M. to get round the enemy's right flank and be ready to cut off his retreat. They were accompanied by a portion of the Mounted Infantry and a machine gun. Making a wide turning movement they gained the eastern side

of Talana Hill. Here Lieutenant-Colonel Möller halted with one squadron, 18th Hussars, the machine gun and the Mounted Infantry, sending his other two squadrons further to the east. These two latter squadrons took part in the pursuit of the enemy, who retreated eastward, but Lieutenant-Colonel Möller and the troops with him appear, so far as can be ascertained, to have pursued in a northerly direction, to have come in contact with superior forces not previously engaged, and to have been surrounded and forced to surrender, while endeavouring to return to camp, round the north of the Impati Mountain.

13. The Boer force engaged in this action is computed at 4,000 men, of whom about 500 were killed or wounded. Three of their guns were left dismounted on Talana Hill, but there was no opportunity of bringing them away.

14. Our own losses were severe, amounting to 10 Officers and 31 Non-commissioned officers and men killed, 20 Officers and 165 Non-commissioned officers and men wounded, and 9 Officers and 211 Non-commissioned officers and men missing. The Divisional Staff suffered severely, Lieutenant-General Sir W.P. Symons, K.C.B., being mortally wounded, and both Colonel C.E. Beckett, C.B.. A.A.G., and Major Hammersley, D.A.A.G., being severely wounded. Of the Brigade Staff, Lieutenant-Colonel John Sherston, D.S.O., Brigade Major, was killed, and Captain F.L. Adam, Scots Guards, Aide-de-Camp to Brigadier-General Yule, was severely wounded. Lieutenant-Colonel R. Gunning, commanding 1st Battalion King's Royal Rifle Corps, was killed within a few yards of the crest of the position.

15. Meanwhile, on 20th October, I had pushed a Cavalry reconnaissance to Elands Laagte, and had obtained definite information that a Boer force was in position there, but apparently in no considerable strength. I therefore ordered Major-General French, commanding the Cavalry of the Natal Force, to move out by road at 4 A.M. with five squadrons of Imperial Light Horse and the Natal Field Battery, followed at 6 A.M. by half battalion 1st Battalion Manchester Regiment, with railway and telegraph construction companies by rail. Major-General French's orders were to clear the neighbourhood of Elands Laagte of the enemy, and to cover the construction of the railway and telegraph lines.

16. On arrival near Elands Laagte, the station buildings were found to be in possession of the enemy. Our Artillery opened fire on them, while a squadron of the Imperial Light Horse, under Major Sampson, moved round to the north of them. The enemy at once replied with artillery, and thus disclosed his main position on a commanding group of hills, about one mile south-east of the railway station. This position proving too strong and too strongly held to be dealt with by the force then at Major-General French's disposal, he

retired his troops out of fire, and reported to me by telephone. I sent out to him reinforcements, consisting of one squadron 5th Dragoon Guards, one squadron 5th Lancers, and the 21st and 42nd Batteries Royal Field Artillery, all of which moved by road, and of the 1st Battalion Devonshire Regiment, and five companies Gordon Highlanders, which moved by rail. I also sent out Colonel Ian Hamilton, C.B., D.S.O., to take command of the Infantry portion of the force.

17. As the reinforcements gradually reached him, Major-General French pushed forward again, throwing out one squadron 5th Lancers and four squadrons Imperial Light Horse, under Colonel Chisholme, to the right to clear a ridge of high ground parallel to the enemy's position, from which he considered that an attack could best be developed. This movement was well carried out, the enemy's advanced troops being driven back, and the ridge gained.

18. One squadron 5th Dragoon Guards, one squadron 5th Lancers, and one squadron Natal Mounted Rifles, under Major Gore, 5th Dragoon Guards, were sent forward from our left with orders to turn the enemy's right flank, harass his rear, and be ready to take up the pursuit. At 3.30 P.M. I arrived on the ground in person, but left the executive command of the troops engaged still in the hands of Major-General French.

19. At this hour the ground selected as the first Artillery position having been cleared of the enemy, the Field batteries advanced and opened fire at 4 P.M., at a range of 4,400 yards. After a few minutes the enemy's guns ceased to reply, and our guns were turned on a party of the enemy who were annoying our artillerymen with rifle fire from our right flank at a range of 2,000 yards. This fire quickly drove back the Boers, and the infantry advance commenced.

20. The Infantry had been brought up in preparatory battle formation of small columns covered by scouts. The 1st Battalion Manchester Regiment led with a frontage of 500 yards; the 1st Battalion Devonshire Regiment and the 2nd Battalion Gordon Highlanders followed in succession. Finding the line of advance was leading too much to the south, Colonel Hamilton, C.B., D.S.O. commanding the Infantry Brigade, diverted the Devons more towards the north, while the Gordons remained in reserve between the other two battalions. At 3.30 P.M. the 1st Battalion Devonshire Regiment crested a ridge from which the enemy's position could be clearly seen. The general position of our infantry was then as follows:-

The 1st Battalion Devonshire Regiment, with a frontage of 500 yards, and a depth of 1,300 yards, were halted on the western extremity of a horseshoe shaped ridge, the opposite end of this horse shoe being very rough and broken, and held by the enemy in force. The 1st Battalion Manchester Regiment had struck the ridge fully 1,000 yards to the south-east, just at the point where it begins to bend round northwards. The 2nd Battalion Gordon Highlanders were one mile in rear.

21. The 1st Battalion Manchester Regiment received orders that as soon as the enemy's guns were silenced, they were to work along the crest of the horse shoe and turn the left flank of the enemy. The 2nd Battalion Gordon Highlanders were to support them, and the 1st Battalion Devonshire Regiment were directed to move right across the open grass plain separating them from the enemy, and to hold him in his position as much as possible by their fire. As soon as the 1st Battalion Devonshire Regiment began to move forward, the enemy reopened their artillery fire on them, but owing to the very open formation adopted, the loss at this period was slight. The 1st Battalion Devonshire Regiment pressed on to about 900 yards from the position, opened fire and maintained themselves there, holding the enemy in front of them till 6 P.M.

22. Meanwhile the batteries advanced to a range of 3,200 yards, and again silenced temporarily the Boer guns, while the 1st Battalion Manchester Regiment and the 2nd Battalion Gordon Highlanders, working along the ridge, had a sharp encounter at the point where the horse shoe bends round to the Boer position. The enemy were forced slowly back along the ridge, fighting as they retired.

23. The Manchesters and Gordons, with the Imperial Light Horse on their right, continued to press forward, losing but few men until a point was reached about 1,200 yards from the enemy's camp. Here the ridge became, for 200 yards, flat and bare of stones, while to the north; where the Boers were posted, it was very rocky and afforded excellent cover. Our men, well led by their Officers, and strengthened by their reserves, crossed this open neck of land in brilliant style, but the losses here were heavy, the reserves were all used up and the units were completely mixed. Moreover, the enemy's camp, which was evidently his final position, was still 1,000 yards distant. At this moment the enemy's German contingent, who had been out on the west of the railway trying to capture our trains, reinforced the Boers and Hollanders along the ridge. The enemy became much encouraged, and from this point up to the extreme end of the horse-shoe ridge, where it overlooks the enemy's camp, the struggle was bitter and protracted. Our men worked forward in short rushes of about 50 yards. Many of the Boers remained lying down, shooting from behind stones until our men were within 20 or 30 yards of

them, and then sometimes ran for it and sometimes stood up and surrendered. These latter individuals were never harmed, although just previous to surrendering they had probably shot down several of our Officers and men.

24. At length the guns were reached and captured, and the end of the ridge was gained, from which the whole of the enemy's camp, full of tents, horses, and men, was fully exposed to view at fixed sight range. A white flag was shown from the centre of the camp, and Colonel Hamilton ordered the "cease fire" to be sounded. The men obeyed, and some of them moved a short distance down the hill towards the camp. For a few moments there was a complete lull in the action, and then a shot was heard, which was followed by a deadly fire from the small conical kopje to the east of the camp, and by a determined charge up hill by some 30 or 40 Boers, who effected a lodgment near the crest line within 15 or 20 paces of our men, who fell back for a moment before the fierce suddenness of this attack. Only for a moment, however, for our fire was at once reopened, and, reinforced by a timely detachment of the 1st Battalion Devonshire Regiment, they charged back, cheering, to the crest line, when the remnant of the Boer force fled in confusion towards the north.

25. Meanwhile, the 1st Battalion Devonshire Regiment, who, as already mentioned, had been holding the enemy in front during the first part of the Infantry action, had pushed steadily in as the flank attack began to press on. Our Artillery also had moved in to about 2,200 yards range, whence they kept under the enemy's guns and fired on his infantry position. The 1st Battalion Devonshire Regiment pushed on to 350 yards from the enemy, lay down to recover breath, and then charged with fixed bayonets. Five companies assaulted the detached hill on our left, and three companies the hill on the right, and it was from these latter companies that the detachment referred to in the preceding paragraph joined and assisted the flank attack in the final struggle.

26. The cavalry squadrons on our left, who had been closely watching the progress of events, now charged through and through the retreating enemy, inflicting much loss and capturing many prisoners. The troops bivouacked on the ground, and next morning returned to Ladysmith.

27. The Boer losses were heavy, being estimated at over 100 killed, 108 wounded, and 188 prisoners. Two of their guns were captured, and brought into Ladysmith. Our own losses were also considerable, consisting of 4 Officers and 37 men killed, 31 Officers and 175 men wounded, and 10 men missing. The Imperial Light Horse, and the 2nd Battalion Gordon Highlanders, who

encountered the severest resistance during the progress of the attack, suffered the most severely.

28. Turning now to affairs at Dundee, which I have already described up to the evening of 20th October. On the morning of 21st October, it was ascertained that the enemy had cleared off from the east of that place, but very large bodies were reported to be advancing from the north and north-west. General Yule moved his camp on this day to a more defensible position to the south of the previous camp, but the enemy, bringing up heavy Artillery to the shoulder of the Impati mountain, rendered the site untenable, and another move was made to a site still further south. On 22nd October General Yule decided to effect a junction with the troops at Ladysmith. A reconnaissance in force showed that the Glencoe pass was very strongly held, and that to force it would entail heavy loss. The troops therefore moved off at 9 P.M. by the Helpmakaar – road, reaching Beith on 23rd, and Waschbank Spruit on 24th October, at 9.30 A.M. Knowing of General Yule's approach, I moved out this day to Rietfontein, to cover his flank from attack, and there fought an action, which will be described later. Meanwhile, General Yule, hearing my guns in action, halted his Infantry at Waschbank Spruit, and moved west with his Artillery and mounted troops, in hope of being able to participate in the action. The distance, however, was found to be too great, and he rejoined his Infantry at Waschbank Spruit, halting there for the night. On the morning of 25th October, General Yule's force marched to Sunday's River, whence it reached Ladysmith on 25th October, being joined en route by a force detached by me to meet it. The casualties at Dundee, after 20th October, were very slight, and none whatever were incurred on the march to Ladysmith, where the troops arrived fit and well.

29. Reverting to my action at Rietfontein on 24th October, I may mention in general terms that my object was not to drive the enemy out of any positions, but simply to prevent him crossing the Newcastle road from west to east, and so falling on General Yule's flank. This object was attained with entire success, the enemy suffering severely from our shrapnel fire, which was very successful in searching the reverse slopes of the hills on which he was posted. Our own loss amounted to 1 Officer and 11 men killed; 6 Officers and 97 men wounded, and 2 missing. The details of this action, as well as the various plans and returns, which should accompany a despatch, will be forwarded later; but I am anxious that this report should be sent off at once, as it is very doubtful whether any communications by rail with Pietermaritzburg will remain open after to-day.

30. For the same reason, I have omitted all personal mention of the very many Officers and men who have performed services of the utmost gallantry and

distinction. In a further despatch, I hope to bring those services prominently to your notice.

> I have, &c.,
> GEO. S. WHITE, Lieutentant-General,
> Commanding the Forces in Natal.

General Sir Redvers Buller to Secretary of State for War.

> *Pietermaritzburg, Natal,*
SIR,   *December* 2, 1899.
IN forwarding the enclosed copy of a report from Major-General Hildyard of a night operation on the 23rd ultimo, I have the honour to remark that though, owing to the dreadful weather that night, a complete tactical success was not secured, yet the operation resulted in a strategical success of the greatest value.

A force of the enemy exceeding 7,000 men, fully equipped, and led by the Commandant-General in person, which was intended to overrun the Colony of Natal, was so severely handled by Colonel Kitchener's small force, that they returned at once to Colenso in a manner that was more of a rout than a retreat.

General Hildyard, Colonel Kitchener, and all concerned deserve the greatest credit for the manner in which this operation was planned and executed.

> I have, &c.,
> REDVERS BULLER,
> General.

To General Officer Commanding 2nd Division.

> *Estcourt,*
SIR,   *November* 24, 1899.
ON the 19th November I found it necessary either to reinforce the mounted troops that were posted at Willow Grange, and so divide the forces at my disposal, or to evacuate Willow Grange, which I did. The following day the enemy occupied a position to the west of Willow Grange Station and about six miles south of Estcourt. About halfway between this place and the enemy's position is situated a high hill, marked Beacon Hill on the map. On the afternoon of the 22nd I occupied the slopes of this hill with half 2nd Battalion Queen's, the 2nd Battalion West Yorkshire Regiment, and seven companies 2nd Battalion East Surrey Regiment, and the Durham Light Infantry. A naval 12-pounder gun was placed on the summit of the hill. The 7th Battery Royal Field Artillery was also in position. This force I placed under orders of

Colonel Kitchener, whom I directed to attack the hill during the night of the 22nd–23rd November and seize the enemy's guns and laager. Five companies of the Border Regiment were ordered to march from Estcourt camp in the morning of the 23rd November to assist in the operation. Colonel Kitchener's arrangements for carrying this out were that the 2nd Battalion West Yorkshire Regiment and the seven companies East Surrey Regiment, under his immediate command, should seize the position, and that the rest of the force at his disposal, under Lieutenant-Colonel Hinde, 1st Battalion Border Regiment, should support him as soon as it was daylight.

In taking up the preparatory position on the afternoon of the 22nd November, the exposure of some of the Infantry drew the enemy's artillery fire, which was answered by the Naval gun on Beacon Hill. This led to the enemy being more alert than usual. Early in the night there was a storm of extreme severity, and the men lying out in it amongst the rocks were exposed to its full force.

From the base of the left flank of the enemy's position a wall led right up to the summit, passing over very steep and precipitous ground. On account of the rocky nature of the ground and the absence of beaten tracks the difficulty of assembling the assaulting troops was also very great. These difficulties were eventually surmounted, thanks to the personal energy of Colonel Kitchener, and to the accurate manner in which the column was led by Mr. Chapman, a guide attached to the Staff, who was unfortunately killed.

The position was successfully reached and seized, but some firing occurred on the way up, and when picquets were encountered the enemy's guns (a 12-pounder Creusot and some Hotchkiss quick-firing guns) were not found in position, and it subsequently transpired that they had been withdrawn about 2.30 A.M., the artillery officer in charge of them being uneasy as to their safety.

About 150 Boers were on the hill when it was seized, and these retired precipitately to a second position, on which the bulk of their force was situated, suffering some loss. About 30 horses were captured and the remains of the laager from which the wagons managed to trek. It was not my intention to remain in the position, a course which would have entailed a division of the forces at Estcourt. The rôle of the supporting troops, was, therefore, restricted to covering the withdrawal of the assaulting battalions. Most of the losses occurred during the retirement; they were chiefly in the 2nd Battalion West Yorkshire Regiment, which was the last regiment to retire.

The mounted troops as per margin,* under Lieutenant-Colonel Martyr, were directed to cooperate at daylight by a movement towards Willow Grange Station, and subsequently to patrol towards Highlands. Bethune's Mounted Infantry Regiment was directed to operate on Colonel Kitchener's right flank. The troops under Lieutenant-Colonel Martyr, after holding a party of some 300 Boers south of Willow Grange, moved to the support of Colonel Kitchener's left flank, where they did valuable service in helping him back and assisting to get the wounded of the 2nd Battalion West Yorkshire Regiment down the hill. It was in doing this that Trooper Fitzpatrick, Imperial Light Horse, was killed. The behaviour of Lieutenant Davies, Mounted Infantry Company, King's Royal Rifles, has been specially brought to notice. When under a heavy fire he dismounted, disentangled the reins of a horse he was driving in front of him, and assisted one of his men who had lost his horse to mount and so get away. His conduct on this occasion was very cool, and I consider his services deserve recognition.

Bethune's Mounted Infantry co-operated to the best of their ability on Colonel Kitchener's right flank.

The conduct of all ranks throughout the force engaged was exemplary. Colonel Kitchener led the assaulting force with energy and judgment, and all ranks of the 2nd Battalion West Yorkshire Regiment behaved admirably. Major Hobbs of that battalion was taken prisoner owing to his remaining too long attending to the wounded. He led the first line of the assault with judgment and good sense. The services of Lieutenant Nicholson, 2nd Battalion West Yorkshire Regiment, have been specially brought to my notice for attention to duty and the situation when others were inclined to deal with matters of less importance. I recommend him for special reward. I also recommend Private Montgomery, 2nd Battalion West Yorkshire Regiment, for a distinguished conduct medal. After being wounded in one leg he continued fighting in the firing line until again wounded. Lieutenant-Colonel Harris, 2nd Battalion East Surrey Regiment, commanded the second line, and Major Pearse, 2nd Battalion East Surrey Regiment, the third line of the assaulting force. The behaviour of all ranks of the 2nd Battalion East Surrey Regiment when engaged was satisfactory under great difficulties.

Colonel Hinde, 1st Battalion Border Regiment, commanded the supporting force, which he moved forward by my orders to a supporting position shortly after daylight.

Five companies of the Border Regiment, commanded by Major Pelly, were on the right, and those of the 2nd Battalion Queen's, under Lieutenant-Colonel Hamilton, on the left. The Durban Light Infantry, under Lieutenant-Colonel Meeubin, took up a position in reserve further back. Lieutenant James, Royal Navy, of Her Majesty's ship "Tartar," commanded the Naval 12-pr. gun and did good service, though a Creusot gun, which the enemy brought into action, had the range of him.

Major Ricketts commanded the Bearer Company and did good service both at the time and in connection with the removal of the wounded. My Staff

Officers, Major Munro, Brigade Major, and Lieutenant Blair, Aide-de-Camp, were of good value to me.

The services of the guide, Mr. Chapman, who was so unfortunately killed, were of the greatest value. His intimate knowledge of the ground alone made it possible to carry out the operation. I sincerely trust it may be found possible to bestow on his widow, Mrs. Chapman, of Nottingham Road, some mark of recognition of the distinguished service rendered by her late husband.

I have, &c.,
H. HILDYARD, Major-General,
Commanding 2nd Brigade.

* 1 Company King's Royal Rifles Mounted Infantry, 1 Squadron Imperial Light Horse, Colonel Bethune's Mounted Infantry, Detachment Natal Mounted Police.

From General Sir Redvers Buller to the Secretary of State for War.

Frere Camp,
SIR, *December* 12, 1899.
I HAVE the honour to forward you the enclosed Despatches from Lieutenant-General Lord Methuen, on the operations at Belmont and Enslin.

I have, &c.,
REDVERS BULLER,
General.

Enclosure 1.

Despatch from Lieutenant-General Lord Methuen as to engagement at Belmont, 23rd November, 1899.

Enslin,
SIR, *November* 26, 1899.
ON the morning of 22nd I reconnoitred so far as possible the extensive and very strong position held by from 2,000 to 2,500 Boers, lately strengthened from Mafeking. I could not leave this force on my flank. I enclose sketch by Major Reade, and sketch by Lieutenant-Colonel Verner.* The evening of 22nd we had an artillery duel between our guns and the enemy's large gun. We fired well; they aimed well, but had bad fuzes. We had two wounded, they six killed and wounded.

My orders for the 28th were:- At 3 A.M. Guards Brigade to advance from small white house near railway on Gun Kopje, supported by battery on right, plus Naval Brigade; 9th Brigade on west side of Table Mountain; at same hour, bearing already taken, supported by battery on left, 9th Lancers, two squadrons, one company Mounted Infantry, marching north of Belmont

Station, keeping one to two miles on left flank and advanced; Rimington's Guides, one squadron Lancers, one company Mounted Infantry from Witte Putt to east of Sugar Loaf; one company Mounted Infantry on right of Naval Brigade, protecting right; the force having got over open ground should arrive at daybreak on enemy; 9th Brigade having secured Table Mountain to swing round left and keep on high ground, and then advance east to west on A†; Guards Brigade conform, being pivot; then Guards advance on east edge of Mount Blanc, guns clearing entire advance with shrapnel; Cavalry to get round rear of enemy, securing horses and laager.

The force marched off silently and correctly; I proceeded to a position in rear of the centre of two brigades. Major-General Sir H. Colvile shows the Grenadiers lost direction, and I found myself committed to a frontal attack; sent orders to 9th Brigade to conform to Guards, and having gained first ridge to wait until the guns shrapnelled second line of height. During this assault Lieutenant Fryer was killed leading his men gallantly. The attack was a complete surprise, for they did not know I had moved from Witte Putt to Belmont, and expected an attack in three or four days. It was perfectly timed, and had the Brigadiers allowed daylight to appear before I reached the foot of the position my losses would have been doubled. Lieutenant-Colonel Crabbe was leading with conspicuous courage when he and Lieutenant Blundell were shot by a wounded Boer – the latter Officer has since died. It is not possible to distinguish any officer in khaki, now all badges have been removed, to say nothing of the difficulty of sending a message, the Aides-de-Camp having to bound from boulder to boulder, endeavouring at the same time to keep under cover. I therefore gave the Grenadiers the direction. This was 4.30 A.M., when musketry fire had been opened from the advanced kopjes, and the troops instinctively moved towards the enemy's position. The Scots Guards carried out their instructions to the letter, and gained the heights at the point of the bayonet. The battalion then advanced to the hill east of Mount Blanc, swinging round the left, and advancing up the narrow end. The greatest credit is due to Colonel Paget for the manner in which he carried out his orders, and for the intelligent handling of his battalion when left to his own resources. I note with pleasure the valuable services rendered by Lieutenant-Colonel Pulteney, and the courage displayed by Lieutenant Bulkeley and by Lieutenant Alexander. The 9th Brigade had taken a correct bearing, Lieutenant Festing leading, a duty he performed admirably, and I regret he was wounded. Touch was maintained with Guards. A heavy fire was pouring in from enemy's sangars west of Table Mountain. The Northumberland Fusiliers were ordered to hold their ground whilst the Northamptons were pushed on to some high ground on the right to bring a flanking fire on the sangars. This movement had the desired effect of causing the enemy to quit their defensive position. The line then rapidly advanced on Table Mountain, and occupied it after some slight resistance. At 4.30 A.M. the left battery shelled some Boers enfilading our line from our work by Table Mountain and drove them back. Immediately afterwards the first line of kopjes was crowned by Infantry, at 4.30 the batteries were ordered forward to support the Infantry advance; ten minutes later the Commanding Officer, 9th Brigade, was ordered to slacken his advance until the Boer position had been shelled. It was hard work for this support to come forward because the horses have not recovered five weeks' sea voyage. At 5.45 1st Battalion Coldstreams, being annoyed by heavy firing at 800 yards from Mount Blanc swung their left round, and carried this steep high hill in a brilliant manner, and with slight loss. 1st Battalion Scots Guards now joined the right of the 9th Brigade and continued advance.

I ordered the second line, the 9th Brigade, Yorkshire Light Infantry, and two companies Mounted Infantry, to conform to Guards. Now that the enemy's position was clearly seen, it was clear the original plan of giving the 9th Brigade the lion's share of the day's work was over, nor would it probably have been less costly. The 1st Battalion Coldstream Guards attacked the ridge south-west of Mount Blanc. Colonel Codrington handled his battalion coolly and well. Captain Feilding, Lieutenant the Honourable C. Douglas-Pennant and Lieutenant Price Jones merit praise for coolness and good company leading. The 2nd Battalion Coldstreams were well handled, Major the Honourable A. Henniker's services proving of great value; Major Shute is honourably mentioned. At 5.50 the right battery had shelled some heights to the east of Mount Blanc, and 9th Brigade found itself under a heavy fire from a high ridge south of Table Mountain; the Northamptons and part of Northumberland Fusiliers went forward and held this ridge. At this time Major-General Fetherstonhaugh, to the deep regret of all ranks, was wounded; I cannot exaggerate his loss to myself. Colonel Money took over the command, and the party on the ridge suffered from a distant, but severe, cross fire. The enemy was finally dislodged at the point of the bayonet. A coward's trick now occurred. A white flag was displayed, and when within 50 yards our men ceased firing, and whilst the flag was flying a shot was fired by one of the party at our men. The bearer of the flag, followed by 11 or 12 Boers surrendered.

By 5.30 the left flank of the right attack in advancing up a shallow neck, east of Mount Blanc, received a heavy enfilading fire from the heights on the left front, and edged off towards Mount Blanc. The shells from the Naval Brigade cleared this height, and at 6.10 the situation was as follows:- The last height cleared, the enemy in large numbers galloping into the plain, the enemy's laager trekking across me 3,000 yards off, my mounted troops unable to carry out their orders on one side – left – because the retreat was covered by kopjes, on the other – right – because too far, the Artillery deadbeat, and unable to help me. A Cavalry brigade and a Horse Artillery battery from my right would have made good my success. My losses are no greater than are to be expected; to keep in extended order, covering an enormous front, to get to the enemy's position at daybreak, saves you in the first instance from flanking fire, and in the second from great losses in the plain. There is far too great risk of failure in making flank and front attack in the case of a position such as lay before me at Belmont; the very first element of success is to keep touch between brigades from the first. Nor is there any question of taking the enemy in flank, as on horses he changes front in 15 minutes, as will be shown in my next fight. Shrapnel does not kill men in these kopjes, it only frightens, and I intend to get at my enemy. I have accounted for 83 killed, and have 20 wounded in my hospital, and as their wounded were carried away I may assume their losses were greater than mine. I enclose an extract‡ from the diary of a prisoner holding a high position, which shows the impression made on the enemy. I took more than 50 prisoners, over 100 horses, many dead on the field; have destroyed 64 wagons, and have blown up four large cylinders of gunpowder, taking eight men to lift; 750 shrapnel, 5,000 rounds of small-arm ammunition, a good amount of forage, and as much cattle as I can take with me. Amongst my prisoners are six field cornets, and one German commandant. By 10.30 my division was in camp, by 1 all my wounded were in a comfortable house being carefully tended, by 5 P.M. next day the hospital train conveyed the less severe cases to Orange River, the graver cases to Cape Town. This is the most perfect work I have ever heard of in war, and reflects the highest credit on Colonel Townsend. The wound of the Brigadier of 9th Brigade unfortunately precludes any mention of Officers who distinguished themselves, nor can I help this fine brigade, for I had little occasion for noticing more than the excellent behaviour of the regiments under fire, and can only select one Officer, namely, Major Earle, Yorkshire Light Infantry, whose leading, knowledge, and coolness were noticeable.

Captain Bulfin, the Brigade Major, on whose shoulders a great responsibility rested, did admirable work.

Captain R. Brise is mentioned for good work done, and Captain Nugent's services were of value.

Major-General Sir H. Colvile has already gained my entire confidence, nothing is ever likely to shake his coolness.

The entire force is animated with the best spirit, and my sole regret is that I have lost, and must lose many men whenever I have to fight large numbers of mounted Boers in strong defensive positions.

Their tactics and their courage are indisputable, and it is only to be regretted that they are guilty of acts which a brave enemy should be ashamed of.

Your obedient Servant,
METHUEN, Lieutenant-General.

* Not printed.
† On plan; not printed.
‡ Not printed.

(A.)
From General Officer commanding 1st Brigade
to the Chief Staff Officer, 1st Division.

Belmont Farm Bivouac,
November 23, 1899.

IN accordance with orders received yesterday I marched off the 3rd Battalion Grenadier Guards and the 1st Battalion Scots Guards to rendezvous at the little house on the railway at 3 A.M., whence they were to advance on Gun Hill and assault it. They were guided by my Brigade Major, Captain Ruggles Brise, who led them to the exact spot. Owing to a miscalculation of distance on my part, they did not arrive at the house till 3.30, and owing to the semi-darkness Lieutenant-Colonel Crabbe, Commanding 3rd Battalion Grenadier Guards, mistook the hill appropriated for the Coldstream Guards for the south knoll of Gun Hill, and attacking it on the steep western face, lost heavily; it was during this assault that Lieutenant and Adjutant Fryer, who was leading the men with extraordinary gallantry, was killed. Lieutenant-Colonel Crabbe, who was also leading with great gallantry, was not hit in the assault, but by a wounded Boer, as was Lieutenant Blundell. Second Lieutenant Powell's leading was very noticeable during this assault.

After the capture of this position, the Grenadiers were re-formed and ordered to proceed in a southerly direction along the ridge by the General Officer commanding. This they did, and crossing the intervening valley between the ridge and Mount Blanc, took the valley. The Scots Guards advanced straight to Gun Hill from the rendezvous, and took it at the point of the bayonet, remaining there till ordered by me to form up in the saddle between Gun Hill and the hill which should have been taken by the Coldstream Guards; they advanced along this, then crossed the valley between it and the hill to the north of Mount Blanc, swinging round their left and advancing up the narrow end. I consider the greatest credit is due to Colonel Paget for the manner in which he carried out my instructions, and for the very intelligent handling of his battalion when left to his own resources. He wishes to draw attention to the valuable services rendered by Lieutenant-Colonel

Pulteney, and to the pluck displayed by Lieutenants Bulkeley and Alexander, both of whom insisted on going on after they were wounded.

I remained with the reserve (the 1st and 2nd Battalions Coldstream Guards) during the assault on Gun Hill, and, as soon as that appeared to be taken, directed them to advance from the railway, and, leaving it on their right, take the hill assigned to them. Owing, however, partly to too great extension to the right, and partly to an initial error in direction in the semi-darkness, the 1st Battalion Coldstream Guards came under fire from Mount Blanc, at about 800 yards, and Lieutenant-Colonel Codrington swinging his left slightly round to meet this, became committed to a frontal attack on Mount Blanc, which his battalion accomplished in a very brilliant manner, with remarkably little loss.

Our 2nd Battalion Coldstream Guards had a tendency to conform with the 1st Battalion, and thus also got too much to the right, but I was able to secure half the battalion to advance to the right of the Scots Guards along the ridge. This half battalion co-operated with the Scots Guards in the assault of the hill to the south-west of Mount Blanc. In spite of his error of direction, Lieutenant-Colonel Codrington's battalion was well and correctly handled. He draws particular attention to the skilful handling of his company by Captain Feilding, the coolness displayed by Lieutenant the Honourable C. Douglas-Pennant, and the complete control exercised over his company by Second Lieutenant Price Jones.

Lieutenant-Colonel Stopford's battalion had less severe work than the others of my brigade, but I consider its advance under fire was distinctly well performed. Lieutenant-Colonel Stopford particularly calls attention to the services of Major the Honourable A. Henniker-Major and Captain Shute.

I should like to draw the attention of the General Officer Commanding to the assistance rendered me by my Aide-de-Camp, Captain G. Nugent, and my Brigade Major, Captain Ruggles Brise. The latter was entrusted with leading the two battalions to Gun Hill, a task in which he was handicapped by never having seen the ground by daylight.

H.S. COLVILE, Major-General,
Commanding 9th Brigade.

(B.)
From General Officer Commanding 9th Brigade
to Chief Staff Officer, 1st Division.

Belmont,
November 23, 1899.

SIR,
I HAVE the honour to submit the following report of the part taken by the Brigade under my command in the action which took place to-day. The

rendezvous was left at 3.7 A.M. in the following formation:- Northumberland Fusiliers, in column of companies, on the left, directing, and 50 paces from them moved the Northamptonshire Regiment in similar formation, and parallel to them. In rear of both these battalions was the 2nd Battalion King's Own Yorkshire Light Infantry and two companies Munster Fusiliers.

The advance was made on a bearing 94 degrees from the point of rendezvous, Lieutenant Festing, Northumberland Fusiliers, acting as guide. This duty was performed admirably by him, and I deeply regret to notice the name of this promising young Officer among the list of wounded.

On crossing the railway line the enemy were observed in small parties on the high ground to our front. Two companies of the Northumberland Fusiliers extended to the left and two companies of the Northamptons prolonged the line to the right. Two companies of the Northumberland Fusiliers were further extended in echelon on our left, while on our right moved the Guards Brigade, which could be heard distinctly. In this formation the advance was steadily continued – still directed by Lieutenant Festing – on Table Mountain, until the Northumberland Fusiliers were checked by a heavy fire from some sangars south of Table Mountain. The Northumberland Fusiliers were directed to hold their ground, while the Northamptons were pushed on to some high ground on the right in order to bring a flanking fire on the sangars. This movement had the desired effect of causing the enemy to quit their defensive position. The line then rapidly advanced on Table Mountain, and occupied it after some slight resistance. A battalion of the Guards was then on our right, and during the next advance joined on to our line.

About this time the second line of the brigade, composed of the Yorkshire Light Infantry and two companies Munster Fusiliers, were detached to some other part of the field by order of the General Officer Commanding the Division. Meanwhile, finding the steady fire coming from a high ridge south of Table Mountain prevented the swinging round of our left flank as had been arranged, the Northamptons, with part of the Northumberland Fusiliers, were sent forward and occupied this ridge; but the smallness of this force and the lack of support rendered it undesirable to do more than merely hold this ridge. About this time I received a bullet in the right shoulder, and handed over the command of the 9th Brigade to Colonel Money, C.B., commanding the Northumberland Fusiliers. I subsequently learnt that the party on this ridge suffered severely from a cross fire directed on them from the high ground about a thousand yards to our front (east), as well as from a still more dangerous close-range fire from a party of the enemy, which had established itself on the northern edge of the crest. This party was finally dislodged at the point of the bayonet, and "independent fire" poured into them at a distance of

50 yards, when a white flag was hoisted by the party. On our men ceasing fire, the white flag still being displayed, a shot was fired by this party at our men; but the actual bearer of the flag of truce, followed by some eleven or twelve unarmed Boers, surrendered themselves to Colonel Money and were made prisoners. The wounded, some twelve in number, were attended to by our Medical Officers. Five dead Boers were found inside the sangar, while a little lower down the slope seven more dead bodies of the enemy were discovered.

All resistance now having ceased the 9th Brigade returned to the bivouac ground, bringing in their dead and wounded. The bivouac ground was reached at 10.30 A.M.

Signed for Major-General Fetherstonhaugh,
EDWARD S. BULFIN, Captain,
Brigade Major, 9th Brigade.

Enclosure 2.

Despatch from Lieutenant-General Lord Methuen as to engagement at Enslin, 25th November, 1899.

SIR,

I RECEIVED information on afternoon of 24th that a force of 400 Boers and two guns prevented my train from proceeding near Grass Pan, about 7 miles from Belmont. It seemed to me that it would be best to march the division at once to Swinks Pan, which would place me on the left front of the enemy's position, and that if I worked one battery round each flank, sent my Cavalry and Mounted Infantry well forward, the greater part of the Cavalry being on the eastern side, I ought to capture the eastern force. The Naval Brigade and 9th Brigade I left for protecting the guns, or assaulting a position, if necessary. The Guards Brigade I left with the baggage to march to Enslin, where I had my next camp. The brigade could always give a hand if wanted. I had left 1st Battalion Scots Guards at Belmont Station, also 2 companies, Munster Fusiliers, because there were 500 Boers and a gun, so it was said, threatening Belmont. I made this my divisional battalion, marching straight from Belmont to Enslin. The armoured train with Infantry was to give me a help from the line. I started at 3.30 A.M., and was in action at 6.30, my troops being in the position assigned. Major-General Sir H. Colvile describes the action of the Guards, but might have said I gave the brigade rather a longer march than necessary, because I heliographed the brigade should march south-east, the direction the enemy was advancing from. I had better have said: "Come to my support."

My position at 7 A.M., was full of interest, for, instead of 400, I have since ascertained I had 2,500 Boers (300 from Transvaal, six guns, one Hotchkiss, one Maxim), and at the same moment I had reliable information from Major Rimington that 500 fresh Boers, plus a laager behind them, were behind some kopjes two miles off, and in my rear. I then heliographed to the Guards, and continued my attack.

The fighting was far harder than on Thursday, and I would not let a man go forward until I had covered the two high hills with shrapnel. The manner in which the batteries were handled, their accuracy in firing, is beyond all praise, and why this action is, to my mind, interesting is that you can compare it to Belmont. In the battle of Belmont you have a surprise and one battalion losing direction and suffering heavy loss; in the battle of Enslin you have a position well prepared by shrapnel, the right battery fires 500 rounds; and you have the Naval Brigade behaving splendidly, but not taking advantage enough of cover and suffering accordingly. The loss was great in both cases, and convinces me that if an enemy has his heart in the right place he ought to be able to hold his own against vastly superior forces, and it does our men great credit that nothing stops them.

The 9th Brigade consisted of the Northumberland Fusiliers, 2nd Battalion Northamptons, half Battalion Loyal North Lancashires, 2nd Battalion King's Own Yorkshire Light Infantry. The Naval Brigade was attached to this brigade, and was commanded by Captain Prothero. The brigade was distributed as follows:- 5 companies Northumberland Fusiliers, remained as a containing line in front of right of the enemy's position, and did not advance until the end of the engagement; 2 companies Northumberland Fusiliers, escort to guns; the remainder of the brigade attacked the kopjes on left of the Boer position. The fire from here was very heavy, and the Naval Brigade suffered severely, keeping in too close formation. The Officers, petty officers, non-commissioned officers led their men with great gallantry, and I have great pleasure in bringing to your notice the plucky conduct of Lieutenant W.T.C. Jones, Royal Marine Light Infantry, who although he had a bullet in his thigh, led his men to the top of the kopje, and only had his wound dressed at the conclusion of the action. The command of the Naval Brigade devolved on Captain A.E. Le Marchant, Royal Marine Light Infantry, when his senior officers were killed or wounded, and he led the remnant of the Naval Brigade up the kopje, with great coolness and ability. The kopje gained, it was found evacuated, and the enemy having gone to the right, their position was enfiladed. The position was taken by the Naval Brigade, Marines, Yorkshire Light Infantry, and Loyal North Lancashires. The attack was ably supported by the fire of the Field Artillery Battery on the right. I beg to bring to your notice No. 1843 Colour-Sergeant Waterhouse, King's Own Yorkshire Light Infantry, who at a critical moment acted with great coolness in shooting down an enemy who had been doing great execution on our men at 1,150 yards.

Lieutenant Taylor, Aide-de-Camp, is favourably mentioned. The heights gained, I found I had taken the whole Boer force in flank, and had entirely cut them off from their line of retreat. My guns played on the masses of horse-men, but my few cavalry, dead beat, were powerless, and for the second time I longed for a Cavalry Brigade and a Horse Artillery Battery to let me reap the fruits of a hard fought action. I buried 21 Boers; there were 50 horses dead in one place. I found over 30 wounded in the Boer hospital here, and I have fought distinctly different Boers on the two days.

My casualties were as follows:-

Officers.

Naval Brigade. – Killed, 3; wounded, 3.
King's Own Yorkshire Light Infantry. – Wounded, 3.
Total. Killed, 3; wounded, 6.

Rank and File.

Naval Brigade. – Killed, 6; wounded, 89.
King's Own Yorkshire Light Infantry. – Killed, 7; wounded, 34; missing, 4.
Royal Marine Light Infantry. – Wounded, 2.
Northumberland Fusiliers. – Wounded, 2.
2nd Battalion North Lancashire. – Killed, 1; Wounded, 6; missing, 2.
Northamptons. – Killed, 1; wounded, 4; missing, 1.
Total. Killed, 15; wounded, 137; missing, 7.

I am, &c.,
METHUEN, Lieutenant-General.

P.S. – I enclose an interesting account of work performed by the Naval Brigade near the line. Their guns were of great value, and the work performed was of great interest. Lieutenants Campbell and L.S. Armstrong displayed great coolness in conducting the fire of their guns. Petty Officers Ashley, "Doris," and Fuller, "Monarch," laid their guns with great accuracy under fire.

I again draw attention to the exceptional organizing power of Colonel Townsend at Swink's Pan at 11.30 P.M. I was informed that owing to all the ambulances having been used for taking the wounded to the train at Belmont, I had scarcely a field hospital mounted officer, only three ambulances, and three stretchers. I knew I had to fight next morning, so got together 50 blankets in order to carry wounded with help of rifles. I also sent to Colonel Townsend to make arrangements for wounded by 3 A.M., a messenger having to ride 7 miles to him. He met me on the field with full supply of ambulances, and I never saw anything more of him or the wounded because he had a train ready for them between Grass Pan and Belmont. His only complaint is that there is not much of his mules left, an observation which applies equally to men and animals.

METHUEN,
Lieutenant-General.

(A.)
From General Officer Commanding 1st Brigade to
Chief Staff Officer 1st Division.

Enslin,
SIR, *November* 25, 1899.
IN accordance with orders received last night the Guards Brigade fell in as escort to the baggage train at 4 A.M. to-day; it was, however, 6.30 before the whole train was ready to start. We followed the guide of Rimington's Horse to within a mile and a half of Grass Pan Station. I saw firing to the north-west and decided to advance, giving orders to Lieutenant-Colonel Codrington to protect the baggage column with the 1st Battalion Coldstream Guards, and extending the 2nd Battalion Coldstream Guards, and the 3rd Battalion Grenadiers, facing north. During the extension a few blind shells fell near the firing line doing no damage. At this time (7.30) the 1st Battalion Scots Guards came up from Belmont, and with them I prolonged the line to the left, but soon afterwards received a telegram from the General Officer Commanding, informing me that the Scots Guards were taken as a divisional battalion. I therefore advanced with the Grenadiers and 2nd Battalion Coldstreams, arriving at the east of the Rooi Laagte position as the 9th Brigade was forming up.

There were no casualties in my Brigade to-day, and no ammunition expended.

H.E. COLVILE, Major-General,
Commanding 9th Brigade.

(B.)
From Lieutenant-Colonel Money, C.B,, 1st Battalion Northumberland Fusiliers, Acting Officer Commanding 9th Brigade, to Chief Staff Officer, 1st Division.

Enslin,
SIR, *November* 26, 1899.
I HAVE the honour to report that, in the action of Enslin, on the 25th November, the Brigade consisted of:- the Naval Brigade, under Captain Prothero, Royal Navy; the Northumberland Fusiliers, 2nd Battalion Northamptonshire Regiment, one-half battalion Loyal North Lancashire

Regiment, and the 2nd Battalion King's Own Yorkshire Light Infantry. During the main attack the Brigade was distributed as follows:- Five companies Northumberland Fusiliers remained as a containing line in front of right of enemy's position, and did not advance until near the conclusion of the engagement; two companies Northumberland Fusiliers escort to guns. With the remainder of the Brigade I attacked the kopje on left of Boer position. The fire from this was very hot, and the troops suffered severely during the attack until they reached the dead ground at the foot of the kopje. The Naval Brigade suffered most heavily, owing, I think, to their keeping in too close formation. The Officers, petty officers, and non-commissioned officers led their men with great gallantry, and I wish especially to bring to the notice of the General Officer Commanding, 1st Division, the plucky conduct of Lieutenant W.T.C. Jones, Royal Marine Light Infantry, who, although having a bullet in his thigh, led his men to the top of the kopje, and only had his wound dressed at the conclusion of the operations. The command of the Naval Brigade devolved on Captain A.E. Marchant, Royal Marine Light Infantry, when his senior Officers were killed or wounded, and he led the remnant of the Naval Brigade up the kopje with great coolness and ability.

On reaching the top of this kopje it was found the enemy had just left it, and had gone more towards the right of their position. I was now able to enfilade their position on the right, but was also subject to a heavy enfilading fire from portions of the Boer position between the two kopjies. I saw the enemy clearing off with as many horses as were not wounded (there were a considerable number of wounded horses in rear of the position), and eventually ceased firing about 10 A.M., and reported to the Artillery on the right that they might effectually fire on the retreating Boers if they came up at once, which they did.

I beg to bring to the notice of the General Officer Commanding, for distinguished conduct in the field, No. 1843, Colour-Sergeant Waterhouse, King's Own Yorkshire Light Infantry, who at a critical moment acted with great coolness, and shot down one of the enemy's sharpshooters who had been doing great execution to our men advancing at a range of 1,150 yards.

My Staff, Captain Bulfin and Lieutenant Taylor, rendered me great assistance, and were near me at the final assault.

I have, &c.,
C.G.C. MONEY,
Lieutenant-Colonel, Commanding 9th Brigade.

From the General Commanding-in-Chief the Forces in South Africa to the Secretary of State for War.

Chieveley Camp,

SIR, *December* 16, 1899.

I HAVE the honour to bring the following cases of Distinguished Service in the Field to your notice.

At Colenso, on the 15th December, the detachments serving the guns of the 14th and 66th Batteries, Royal Field Artillery, had all been either killed, wounded, or driven from their guns by Infantry fire at close range, and the guns were deserted.

About 500 yards behind the guns was a donga, in which some of the few horses and drivers left alive were sheltered. The intervening space was swept with shell and rifle fire.

Captain Congreve, Rifle Brigade, who was in the donga, assisted to hook a team into a limber, went out and assisted to limber up a gun; being wounded he took shelter, but seeing Lieutenant Roberts fall badly wounded he went out again and brought him in. Some idea of the nature of the fire may be gathered from the fact that Captain Congreve was shot through the leg, through the toe of his boot, grazed on the elbow and the shoulder, and his horse shot in three places.

Lieutenant the Honourable F. Roberts, King's Royal Rifles, assisted Captain Congreve. He was wounded in three places.

Corporal Nurse, Royal Field Artillery, 66th Battery, also assisted. I recommend the above three for the Victoria Cross.

Drivers H. Taylor, Young, Petts, Rockall, Lucas, and Williams, all of the 66th Battery, Royal Field Artillery, rode the teams, each team brought in a gun. I recommend all six for the Medal for Distinguished Conduct in the Field.*

Shortly afterwards Captain H.L. Reed, 7th Battery, Royal Field Artillery, who had heard of the difficulty, brought down three teams from his battery to see if he could be of any use. He was wounded, as were five of the 13 men who rode with him; 1 was killed, his body was found on the field, and 13 out of 21 horses were killed before he got half-way to the guns, and he was obliged to retire.

I recommend Captain Reed for the Victoria Cross, and the following non-commissioned officers and men, 7th Battery, Royal Field Artillery, for the Medal for Distinguished Service in the Field:-

86208 Corporal A. Clark, wounded.
87652 Corporal R.J. Money.
82210 Acting Bombardier J.H. Reeve.

28286 Driver C.J. Woodward.
22054 Driver Wm. Robertson, wounded.
22061 Driver Wm. Wright, wounded.
22051 Driver A.C. Hawkins.
26688 Driver John Patrick Lennox.
22094 Driver Albert Nugent, killed.
23294 Driver James Warden.
32067 Driver Arthur Felton, wounded.
83276 Driver Thomas Musgrove.
26523 Trumpeter William W. Ayles, wounded.

I have differentiated in my recommendations, because I thought that a recommendation for the Victoria Cross required proof of initiative, something more in fact than mere obedience to orders, and for this reason I have not recommended Captain Schofield, Royal Artillery, who was acting under orders, though I desire to record his conduct as most gallant.

Several other gallant drivers tried, but were all killed, and I cannot get their names.

I have, &c.,
REDVERS BULLER,
General.

*I cannot get their numbers, but am told they are the only ones of their names in the battery.

From the General Commanding-in-Chief the Forces in South Africa to the Secretary of State for War.

Chieveley Camp,
SIR,   *December* 17, 1899.
I HAVE the honour to report that I moved off from Chieveley and Dornkop Spruit Camps at 4 A.M. on the 15th instant.

Force as in attached list.

I attach a copy of the orders that were by my direction issued by the General Officer Commanding Natal Field Force.

I enclose a reconnaissance sketch of the Colenso position.*

Colenso Bridge is the centre of a semicircle surrounded by hills, the crests of which dominate it by about 1,400 feet at a distance of about four and a half miles.

Near the bridge are four small lozenge-shaped, steep-sided, hog-backed, hills, each, as it is further from the river, being higher and longer than the next inner one. These hills, the first of which is known as Fort Wylie, were very strongly entrenched with well-built, rough, stone walls along every crest line that offered; in some cases there were as many as three tiers. It was a very awkward position to attack, but I thought that if I could effect a lodgement under cover of Fort Wylie, the other hills would to a great extent mask each other, and shell fire and want of water would clear them out in time.

All visible defences had been heavily shelled by eight Naval guns on the 13th and 14th, but though some of the defences were damaged and accurate ranges obtained, we failed to induce the enemy to disclose his own position, or to reply in any way to our fire.

My idea was to try and cross the Bridle Drift first; if we got over, the troops would move down the river and help the crossing at the main drift; if we did not get over, the troops there would contain all the enemy on the western side, and would so cover the flank of the attack on the main drift by the bridge.

General Hart advanced to the attack of the Bridle Drift, but did not find it. (I heard afterwards that a dam had been thrown below it, and the water made deep.) Watching his advance, I saw his troops pressing on into the salient loop of the river. I saw at once that if he got there he would be under a severe cross fire, and sent to tell him to recall them. In the interval, he had become heavily engaged, and I sent two battalions of General Lyttelton's Brigade and Colonel Parsons' Brigade Division, Royal Field Artillery (two batteries), to help extricate him.

This they did, and subsequently, as ordered, came to the right to support the main advance. At the same time General Hildyard was advancing on the bridge, and as I was proceeding in that direction to superintend the attack, and also to ascertain what Colonel Long's Brigade Division, which was very heavily engaged on the right, was doing, I received a message, that he had been driven from his guns by superior Infantry fire.

I believed at the moment that the six Naval had shared the same fate, and I at once decided that without guns it would be impossible for me to force the passage.

I directed General Hildyard to divert the right of his two leading battalions to the east of the railway and direct it upon the guns, his left battalion to advance on Colenso, but not to become too hotly engaged.

These orders were admirably carried out by the Royal West Surrey and the Devonshire Regiments, but Fort Wylie, which had been silenced by the fire of the 14th and 66th Batteries, was reoccupied, and the fire was so heavy that no troops could live in the open by the guns. At the first attempt to withdraw them, Captain Schofield, Royal Artillery, Captain Congreve, Rifle Brigade, and Lieutenant the Honourable F. Roberts, King's Royal Rifles, with Corporal Nurse, and Drivers H. Taylor, Young, Petts, Rockall, Lucas, and Williams, all of the 66th Battery, brought off two guns, but the enemy then found out what was being done, and such a deadly fire was kept up that although several attempts were made to cover the fatal 500 yards either horses or men, or both, were killed before they got to the guns.

A final most gallant attempt was made by Captain H.L. Reed, of the 7th Field Battery, who came down with three teams to see if he could help. He and five of the 13 men were wounded, and one killed, and 13 horses killed out of 22 before they got half-way up to the guns. After that I would not allow another attempt and the guns were abandoned.

I am making another representation regarding the Officers and men concerned in these attempts.

Fortunately the Naval guns had not reached the position taken up by the 14th and 66th Batteries when fire was opened; their drivers however bolted, and their oxen were stampeded, or killed; but by dint of hard work all the guns and the ammunition wagons were hauled out of range. All worked well, and Lieutenant Ogilvy, Her Majesty's ship "Tartar," and Gunner Wright, Her Majesty's ship "Terrible," particularly rendered excellent service. These guns, however, had been rendered immobile for the day.

During all this time, and throughout the day, the two 4.7-inch and four 12-pounder Naval guns of the Naval Brigade, and Durban Naval Volunteers, under Captain E.P. Jones, Royal Navy, were being admirably served and succeeded in silencing every one of the enemy's guns they could locate.

Colonel Long, Royal Artillery, has been dangerously wounded, and I am unable to obtain his explanations. His orders were to come into action covered by the 6th Brigade, which Brigade was not, as he knew, intended to advance on Colenso. I had personally explained to him where I wished him to come into action, and with the Naval guns only, as the position was not within effective range for his field guns. Instead of this he advanced with his batteries so fast that he left both his Infantry escort and his oxen-drawn Naval guns behind, and came into action under Fort Wylie, a commanding trebly entrenched hill, at a range of 1,200 yards and I believe within 300 yards of the enemy's rifle pits.

The men fought their guns like heroes and silenced Fort Wylie, but the issue could never have been in doubt, and gradually they were all shot down. I am told that Second Lieutenant Holford, 14th Field Battery, displayed particular gallantry when all were good.

After this, I directed a withdrawal to our camps. It was accomplished in good order. There was no pursuit, and the shell fire was negligeable and controlled by our Naval guns. The day was fearfully hot, the sky cloudless, the atmosphere sultry and airless, and the country waterless in most parts.

Colonel Bullock, 2nd Devons, behaved with great gallantry; he did not receive the orders to retire; his party defended themselves and the wounded of the two batteries till nightfall, inflicting considerable loss on the enemy, and it was only when surrounded that he consented to surrender, because the enemy said they would shoot the wounded if he did not.

During the progress of events that I have been describing, the mounted men under Lord Dundonald, supported by two guns of the 7th Battery, Royal Field Artillery, and two battalions, 6th Brigade, were heavily engaged with a considerable force that attacked my right flank, and which they repulsed. The other four guns, 7th Battery, Royal Field Artillery, were enfilading the Colenso position.

I cannot speak too highly of the manner in which the Mounted Volunteers behaved.

I attach a list of casualties. It is, I regret to say, heavy, though luckily a large proportion are slight.

We were engaged for eight hours with an enemy occupying commanding selected and carefully prepared positions – positions so carefully prepared that it was almost impossible for Infantry to see what to aim at, and I think the force opposed to us must altogether have equalled our own. We had closed on the enemy's works, our troops were in favourable position for an assault, and had I, at the critical moment, had at my disposition the Artillery I had, as I believed, arranged for, I think we should have got in. But without the immediate support of guns, I considered that it would be a reckless waste of gallant lives to attempt the assault.

Considering the intense heat, the conduct and bearing of the troops was excellent. I especially noticed the Royal West Surrey, the Devonshire and the Border Regiments, but all were good.

I am unable to give an estimate of the enemy's loss. They were extremely well concealed, but, judging from their fire in places, their trenches must have been very full of men, and our shell fire was constant and very accurate. Among the many conflicting accounts I have received, I incline to believe those, and they are the majority, which state that the enemy's losses were heavier than they had thought possible.

I have, &c.,
REDVERS BULLER,
General.

*Not printed.

List of Casualties.
Action at Colenso on 15th December, 1899.

KILLED.

Imperial Light Horse – Other ranks, 3.
South African Light Horse – Other ranks, 4.

Natal Carbineers – Other ranks, 4.
7th Battery, Royal Field Artillery – Other ranks, 1.
14th Battery, Royal Field Artillery – Officers, 1. Other ranks, 5.
66th Battery, Royal Field Artillery – Officers, 1. Other ranks, 3.
Thorneycroft's Mounted Infantry – Officers, 1. Other ranks, 4.
1st Battalion Border Regiment – Other ranks, 6.
1st Battalion Connaught Rangers – Other ranks, 24.
2nd Battalion Devonshire Regiment – Other ranks, 9.
2nd Battalion Royal Dublin Fusiliers – Officers, 2. Other ranks, 38.
1st Battalion Royal Inniskilling Fusiliers – Officers, 1. Other ranks, 17.
2nd Battalion Royal Irish Fusiliers – Other ranks, 2.
2nd Battalion Royal Scots Fusiliers – Other ranks, 12.
2nd Battalion East Surrey Regiment – Other ranks, 1.
2nd Battalion Royal West Surrey Regiment – Other ranks, 3.
Royal Army Medical Corps – Officers, 1.
Total – Officers, 7. Other ranks, 136.

WOUNDED.

Royal Navy – Other ranks, 3.
13th Hussars – Other ranks, 2.
Imperial Light Horse – Other ranks, 7.
South African Light Horse – Officers, 2. Other ranks, 19.
Natal Carbineers – Officers, 2. Other ranks, 6.
C.R.A. – Officers, 1.
1st Brigade Division Staff, Royal Artillery – Officers, 2.
7th Battery, Royal Field Artillery – Officers, 1. Other ranks, 8.
14th Battery, Royal Field Artillery – Officers, 1. Other ranks, 16.
64th Battery, Royal Field Artillery – Officers, 1. Other ranks, 2.
66th Battery, Royal Field Artillery – Officers, 2. Other ranks, 11.
73rd Battery, Royal Field Artillery – Other ranks, 5.
1st Division Ammunition Column – Other ranks, 1.
Thorneycroft's Mounted Infantry – Officers, 3. Other ranks, 27.
5th Brigade Staff – Officers, 1.
1st Battalion Border Regiment – Officers, 3. Other ranks, 42.
1st Battalion Connaught Rangers – Officers, 2. Other ranks, 103.
2nd Battalion Devonshire Regiment – Officers, 6. Other ranks, 60.
2nd Battalion Royal Dublin Fusiliers – Officers, 3. Other ranks, 148.
1st Battalion Durham Light Infantry – Other ranks, 2.
1st Battalion Royal Inniskilling Fusiliers – Officers, 10. Other ranks, 76.
2nd Battalion Royal Irish Fusiliers – Officers, 1. Other ranks, 20.
King's Royal Rifle Corps – Officers, 1.*

Rifle Brigade – Officers, 2. Other ranks, 6.
2nd Battalion Royal Fusiliers – Other ranks, 2.
2nd Battalion Royal Scots Fusiliers – Other ranks, 20.
2nd Battalion East Surrey Regiment – Other ranks, 31.
2nd Battalion Royal West Surrey Regiment – Officers, 2. Other ranks, 89.†
1st Battalion Royal Welsh Fusiliers – Other ranks, 3.
2nd Battalion West Yorkshire Regiment – Officers, 1.
Total – Officers, 47. Other ranks, 709.

MISSING.

South African Light Horse – Officers, 2. Other ranks, 11.
14th Battery, Royal Field Artillery – Officers, 3. Other ranks, 40.
66th Battery, Royal Field Artillery – Officers, 2. Other ranks, 24.
1st Battalion Border Regiment – Other ranks, 1.
1st Battalion Connaught Rangers – Officers, 2. Other ranks, 23.
2nd Battalion Royal Dublin Fusiliers – Other ranks, 28.
1st Battalion Royal Inniskilling Fusiliers – Other ranks, 8.
2nd Battalion Royal Irish Fusiliers – Other ranks, 13.
2nd Battalion Royal Scots Fusiliers – Officers, 6. Other ranks, 39.
Total – Officers, 15. Other ranks, 187.

PRISONERS.

1st Brigade Division Staff, Royal Artillery – Officers, 1.
2nd Battalion Devonshire Regiment – Officers, 4. Other ranks, 33.
Total – Officers, 5. Other ranks, 33.

List of Troops engaged in attack on the Boer position at Colenso on the 15th December, 1899:-

Mounted Troops.

1st Royal Dragoons.
13th Hussars.
South African Light Horse.
Natal Carbineers.
Imperial Light Horse.
Bethune's Mounted Infantry.
Thorneycroft's Mounted Infantry.
1st Battalion King's Royal Rifle Corps Mounted Infantry.
Royal Dublin Fusiliers Mounted Infanty.

Artillery.

Two 4.7-inch Naval guns, manned by crews from Her Majesty's ship "Terrible" and Natal Naval Artillery Volunteers.

Two 12-pounder Naval guns, manned by crews from Her Majesty's ship "Tartar."

Ten 12-pounder Naval guns, manned by crews from Her Majesty's ship "Terrible" and Naval Volunteers.

7th Battery, Royal Field Artillery.

14th Battery, Royal Field Artillery.

16th Battery, Royal Field Artillery.

64th Battery, Royal Field Artillery.

73rd Battery, Royal Field Artillery.

Royal Engineers.

17th Company, Royal Engineers.

"A" Pontoon Troop.

Infantry.

2nd Brigade. – Major-General Hildyard, C.B.

2nd Battalion Royal West Surrey Regiment.

2nd Battalion Devonshire Regiment.

2nd Battalion West Yorkshire Regiment.

2nd Battalion East Surrey Regiment.

4th Brigade.

Major-General the Honourable N. Lyttelton, C.B.

2nd Battalion Scottish Rifles.

3rd Battalion King's Royal Rifle Corps.

1st Battalion Durham Light Infantry.

1st Battalion Rifle Brigade.

5th Brigade.

Major-General Hart, C.B.

1st Battallion Inniskilling Fusiliers.

1st Battalion Connaught Rangers.

1st Battalion Royal Dublin Fusiliers.

2nd Battalion Border Regiment.

6th Brigade.

Major-General Barton, C.B.

2nd Battalion Royal Fusiliers.

2nd Battalion Royal Scots Fusiliers (four companies).

1st Battalion Royal Welsh Fusiliers.

2nd Battalion Royal Irish Fusiliers.

*Since dead.

†Four since dead.

ORDERS by Lieutenant-General Sir F. Clery, K.C.B., Commanding South Natal Field Force.

Chieveley,
December 14, 1899, 10 P.M.

1. THE enemy is entrenched in the kopjes north of Colenso Bridge. One large camp is reported to be near the Ladysmith Road, about 5 miles north-west of Colenso. Another large camp is reported in the hills which lie north of the Tugela in a northerly direction from Hlangwane Hill.

2. It is the intention of the General Officer Commanding to force the passage of the Tugela to-morrow.

3. The 5th Brigade will move from its present camping ground at 4.30 A.M. and march towards the Bridle Drift, immediately west of the junction of Dornkop Spruit and the Tugela. The Brigade will cross at this point, and after crossing move along the left bank of the river towards the kopjes north of the iron bridge.

4. The 2nd Brigade will move from its present camping ground at 4 A.M., and passing south of the present camping ground of No. 1 and No. 2 Divisional Troops, will march in the direction of the iron bridge at Colenso. The Brigade will cross at this point and gain possession of the kopjes north of the iron bridge.

5. The 4th Brigade will advance at 4.30 A.M. to a point between Bridle Drift and the railway, so that it can support either the 5th or the 2nd Brigade.

6. The 6th Brigade (less a half battalion escort to baggage) will move at 4 A.M. east of the railway in the direction of Hlangwane Hill to a position where he can protect the right flank of the 2nd Brigade, and, if necessary, support it or the mounted troops referred to later as moving towards Hlangwane Hill.

7. The Officer Commanding Mounted Brigade will move at 4 A.M. with a force of 1,000 men and one battery of No. 1 Brigade Division in the direction of Hlangwane Hill; he will cover the right flank of the general movement, and will endeavour to take up a position on Hlangwane Hill, whence he will enfilade the kopjes north of the iron bridge.

The Officer Commanding mounted troops will also detail two forces of 300 and 500 men to cover the right and left flanks respectively and protect the baggage.

8. The 2nd Brigade Division, Royal Field Artillery, will move at 4.30 A.M. following the 4th Brigade, and will take up a position whence it can enfilade the kopjes north of the iron bridge. This Brigade Division will act on any orders it receives from Major-General Hart.

The six Naval guns (two 4.7-inch and four 12-pounder) now in position north of the 4th Brigade, will advance on the right of the 2nd Brigade Division, Royal Field Artillery.

No. 1 Brigade Division, Royal Field Artillery (less one battery detached with Mounted Brigade), will move at 3.30 A.M. east of the railway and proceed under cover of the 6th Brigade to a point from which it can prepare the crossing for the 2nd Brigade.

The six Naval guns now encamped with No. 2 Divisional Troops will accompany and act with this Brigade Division.

9. As soon as the troops mentioned in preceding paragraphs have moved to their positions, the remaining units and the baggage will be parked in deep formation, facing north, in five separate lines, in rear of to-day's Artillery position, the right of each line resting on the railway, but leaving a space of 100 yards between the railway and the right flank of the line.

In first line (counting from the right):-

> Ammunition Column, No. 1 Divisional Troops.
> 6th Brigade Field Hospital.
> 4th Brigade Field Hospital.
> Pontoon Troop, Royal Engineers.
> 5th Brigade Field Hospital.
> 2nd Brigade Field Hospital.
> Ammunition Column, No. 2 Divisional Troops.

In second line (counting from the right):-

> Baggage of 6th Brigade.
> Baggage of 4th Brigade.
> Baggage of 5th Brigade.
> Baggage of 2nd Brigade.

In third line (counting from the right):-

> Baggage of Mounted Brigade.
> Baggage of No. 1 Divisional Troops.
> 1 Baggage of No. 2 Divisional Troops.

In the fourth and fifth lines (counting from the right):-

> Supply Columns, in the same order as the Baggage Columns in second and third lines.

Lieutenant-Colonel J. Reeves, Royal Irish Fusiliers, will command the whole of the above details.

10. The position of the General Officer Commanding will be near the 4.7-inch guns. The Commanding Royal Engineer will send two sections

17th Company, Royal Engineers, with the 5th Brigade, and one section and headquarters with the 2nd Brigade.

11. Each Infantry soldier will carry 150 rounds on his person, the ammunition now carried in the ox wagons of regimental transport being distributed. Infantry greatcoats will be carried in two ox wagons of regimental transport, if Brigadiers so wish; other stores will not be placed in these wagons.

12. The General Officer Commanding 6th Brigade will detail a half battalion as Baggage Guard. The two Naval guns now in position immediately south of Divisional Head-quarter Camp will move at 5 A.M. to the position now occupied by the 4.7-inch guns.

By order,
B. HAMILTON, Colonel,
Assistant Adjutant-General,
South Natal Field Force.

From the General Commanding-in-Chief the Forces in South Africa to the Secretary of State for War.

Frere Camp,

SIR, *December* 21, 1899.

I HAVE the honour to forward you the enclosed Despatch from Lieutenant-General Lord Methuen on the operations at Modder River.

I have, &c.,
REDVERS BULLER,
General.

From the Lieutenant-General Commanding the 1st Division to the Chief Staff Officer.

Modder River,

SIR, *December* 1, 1899.

I HAVE the honour to report to you that on my arrival at Witkop on November 27 I proceeded to reconnoitre the Modder River, and, from the information I had received, came to the conclusion that the entire force of the enemy had assembled at Spytfontein, and that I should not meet with any determined resistance on the Modder.

I therefore, decided the next morning, under cover of my Artillery, and protected by my Cavalry and Mounted Infantry, to throw up proper protection for my railway, leaving the Northamptonshire Regiment, 300 Engineers, the Naval Brigade, and three guns. I intended next day to have taken my force, with five days' rations, via Jacobsdal, Modder River, to some dams east of Spytfontein, and to have thence delivered my attack.

On the morning of 28th November information reached me through a native that Modder River village was strongly occupied, and I therefore did not feel justified in running any risk regarding the railway, and decided to establish myself on Modder River before proceeding any further.*

I proceeded at 4 A.M. with the mounted troops, the guns coming on so soon as sufficiently protected by the Infantry. In the village itself we could not see any signs of men, guns, or wagons, but to the east of the village we found the enemy in strong force, and aggressive.

I had arranged with the Officer Commanding Royal Artillery to prepare the Infantry attack with both batteries from the right flank, and the Infantry Division being still some miles distant, I gave them two distinct points to march on, which allowed of the brigades keeping in extended order and covering a very wide front.

As will be seen in the report of the Officer Commanding Royal Artillery, the guns were soon engaged with the enemy on our right flank, the 9th Lancers and Mounted Infantry co-operating with the guns in protecting this flank. The enemy brought three guns into action under perfect cover, and fired with great accuracy. Our guns, 75th and 18th Batteries, eventually disabled one gun, and with a stronger force of the Cavalry it might have been possible for me to have secured it.

The enemy appeared to be retiring, and there were no signs that the village was held in strength. We all believed the force in our front was fighting a retiring action, and had no idea 8,000 Boers had been brought from Spytfontein to oppose us.

In no case is it a position to be turned by a wide detour, and I felt sure my right course was to keep my two brigades in touch, widely extended, and trust to their gaining the opposite bank, as was done. Any other course must be attended with great risk when opposite 8,000 horsemen with a river to assist them. In any case the Modder village is not a position I could turn by making a wide detour.

The Guards Brigade had orders to develop their attack first, which they did with the 1st Battalion Scots Guards on the right, with orders to swing their right well round in order to take the enemy in flank, the 2nd Battalion Coldstreams and the 3rd Battalion Grenadiers making the frontal attack, the former on the left to keep touch with the 9th Brigade. The 1st Battalion Coldstreams in reserve in the right rear.

At 8.10 A.M. a sudden and very heavy fire announced that the enemy held the river in great strength, and perfectly concealed. Many casualties now occurred, and the Scots Guards Maxim detachment were completely wiped out. The two companies pushed on until they suffered again heavily from enfilade fire, Colonel Paget's horse, hit in five places, being killed. At 8.10 A.M. the 1st Battalion Coldstreams extended, and swinging the right round, prolonged the line of the Scots Guards to the right. The Riet River prevented any further advance. The troops then lay down, being fairly under cover in that position. Two companies Scots Guards fell back by order of the Brigadier to a reservoir, to secure the right flank, which I think was quite secured, as a matter of fact, by my mounted troops. The 3rd Battalion Grenadiers and 2nd Battalion Coldstreams advanced to within 1,100 yards of the enemy, lay down, and held their own. Captain Heneage tried to advance further, and lost four sergeants.

Meanwhile the 9th Brigade had advanced the Northumberland Fusiliers along the east side of the railway line, supported by half a battalion of the Argyll and Sutherland Highlanders. The Yorkshire Light Infantry advanced along the west side of the railway, supported by the remaining half battalion of Argyll and Sutherland Highlanders. The half battalion Loyal North Lancashire prolonged the line to the left, and endeavoured to cross the river and threaten the enemy's right flank. The six companies Northamptons acted as a baggage guard.

The 9th Brigade had the same hard task before it that faced the Guards Brigade – on the extreme left an outcrop of rocks and small kopjes on the left bank of the river, considerably in advance of the enemy's main position, were strongly held by the enemy, and checked the advance of the Loyal North Lancashire. Some 600 yards east, the same side of the river, a farm house and kraal on a slight eminence covering the dam and drift at the west end of village, also strongly occupied, checked the advance. A withering fire from these buildings checked the advance of the Brigade. They were, however, carried, early in the afternoon by two companies of the Yorkshire Light Infantry, under Lieutenant-Colonel Barter, together with some Highlanders and Northumberland Fusiliers. Lieutenant Fox, Yorkshire Light Infantry, gallantly led this assault; he was severely wounded. Almost at the same moment the rocks and kopjes on the extreme left were carried by the Loyal North Lancashire. We had now won the river and west side of village, out of which the enemy were soon chased. Major-General Pole-Carew led his men in a gallant manner for three-quarters of a mile up the bank, when he was forced back, and had to content himself with holding a fairly good position he had gained on the right bank.

I had promised Major-General Pole-Carew to send him what troops I could get, and it was in this successful endeavour that Lieutenant-Colonel Northcott, who never left me, fell mortally wounded. The Army has lost one of the ablest Officers in Her Majesty's Service, and I cannot express the grief his death has caused me. He was beloved by every one who knew him. I received a flesh wound shortly after 5.30, and told Major-General Sir H. Colvile to take over the command.

During the entire action, the 75th and 18th Batteries had vied with one another in showing gallantry and proficiency. I dare not write more than Colonel Hall has written, his modest account scarcely doing justice to the splendid conduct of our gunners. The 62nd Battery, marching from Belmont, came straight into action, and were of great service.

Colonel Paget, having taken over command of the Guards Brigade, Major-General Sir H. Colvile quite rightly did not care to rush the passage of the river with tired troops. Colonel Hall points out it would have been better that he should have known the point of attack, but the truth is that when no one can get on a horse with any safety within 2,000 yards of the enemy, orders cannot be conveyed, and, personally, I am first to admit I was for most of the day in positions I had no right to be in, because I could only see how the fight was progressing by going to the front.

I have much pleasure in bringing to your notice the names of the following Officers and rank and file who distinguished themselves during the day:-

Major Count Gleichen, C.M.G., for the coolness shown by him throughout the engagement, especially in attending to the wounded under a heavy fire.

Sergeant Brown and Private Martin, 3rd Battalion Grenadier Guards, who helped him, were both shot.

Sergeant-Major Cooke, 3rd Battalion Grenadiers, displayed remarkable coolness under fire.

Lieutenant the Honourable A. Russell showed great coolness in working the machine gun, which he did with marked success.

Major Granville Smith, Coldstream Guards, in volunteering to find a ford, which he did in dangerous mud and a strong river.

Captain and Adjutant Steele, Coldstream Guards, for excellent service during the day.

Sergeant-Major S. Wright, Coldstream Guards, showed great coolness when a change of ammunition carts was being made, and was of great value at a critical time.

Native Driver Matthews for making the other natives stick to their carts, when they would otherwise have bolted.

Drill and Colour-Sergeant Price, Coldstream Guards, at Belmont, and at Modder River, rendered excellent service whilst commanding half a company.

Drill and Colour-Sergeant Plunkett, Coldstream Guards, collected 150 men, and helped the 9th Brigade crossing the river under Captain Lord Newtown Butler.

No. 1825 Lance-Corporal Webb, Coldstream Guards, twice asked leave to go into the open to bind up the wounds of a Grenadier; under a heavy fire, he succeeded in his object.

Captain Hervey Bathurst, Grenadier Guards, was of great value in rallying a number of Grenadiers and Coldstreams shaken by the fire.

I again call attention to Colonel Paget's cheerfulness and intelligence under the most trying surroundings.

He draws attention to Captain Moores, Royal Army Medical Corps, who, although wounded in the hand, said nothing, but continued his duties. Also, he draws attention to the good services of the Master of Ruthven, Scots Guards. The valuable services of Captain Nugent, Aide-de-Camp and Captain Ruggles-Brise are again noted.

The names of Lieutenant-Colonel Barter, King's Own Yorkshire Light Infantry, and Major the Honourable C. Lambton, Northumberland Fusiliers, are mentioned for having rendered invaluable assistance to their Brigadier. Captain Bulfin, Yorkshire Regiment, did his duty admirably.

Lieutenant Percival, Northumberland Fusiliers, managed with great difficulty to establish himself with a small party on a point near the railway, from which, by his judgment and coolness, he was able to keep down the fire of the enemy, many of his small party being killed.

3499 Lance-Corporal R. Delaney,

4160 Private J. East,

4563 Private Segar,

4497 Private Snowdon,

Northumberland Fusiliers, under a very heavy fire picked up and brought in a wounded man of the Argyll and Sutherland Highlanders, No. 3955 Private Smarley, Northumberland Fusiliers, No. 1 of a Maxim detachment, who showed great coolness and judgment when wounded.

Major Lindsay, Royal Artillery, 75th Battery, ignored a painful wound, and continued in command of his battery. Lieutenant Begbie, Royal Artillery, suddenly placed in command of his battery, led it, and brought it into action with great coolness.

Captain Farrell wounded a second time, continued to do his duty, having first placed a wounded man on one of the gun carriages. Wounded gunners and drivers continued at their duty.

Lieutenant Rochford Boyd, Royal Artillery, on this, as on former occasions, showed himself reliable and capable of acting without orders.

I personally bring to notice the value of Lieutenant-Colonel Rhodes' service and Major Streatfield's service in sending forward reinforcements to Major-General Pole-Carew, for on this movement the result of the evening's success depended.

I cannot too highly commend the conduct of the troops, ably assisted by the Naval Brigade, for on them the whole credit of our success rests. The next morning we found the enemy had quitted the position, which I understand was one of very great strength. As regards the losses of the enemy, 23 bodies have been found, and the inhabitants informed me that the dead were buried at once in the gardens, and the wounded conveyed away to Jacobsdal. I have had to bury nearly 200 horses.

All evidence tends to show that at 2 a certain number began to clear, and that at 4 a good number more moved off; that the leaders lunched in the hotel I am now writing from, and were utterly disheartened at our stubbornness. I expect one more fight at Spytfontein will convince a great number of the Orange Free Staters that it is better not to continue fighting. I am thankful the list of casualties is no greater than it is, for many of the cases are slight.

Again I call attention to the splendid hospital arrangements, for at 4.45 P.M. on the day after the fight all my wounded were on their way to Cape Town.

I am glad to have been slightly wounded, because in no other way could I have learnt the care taken of the wounded, and there was nothing Officer or private soldier required that was not provided at once, and the Medical Officers never tired in their endeavour to alleviate suffering.

I have, &c.,
METHUEN,
Lieutenant-General.

* All my information was to the effect that the Modder and Riet Rivers were fordable anywhere, information which proved quite incorrect.

From the General Commanding-in-Chief the Forces in South Africa to the Secretary of State for War.

Frere Camp,

SIR,   *December* 28, 1899.

I HAVE the honour to forward herewith a report by Colonel H.S.G. Miles on the action at Zoutspans Drift, which took place on the 13th instant. I suppose our Officers will learn the value of scouting in time, but in spite of all one can say, up to this, our men seem to blunder into the middle of the enemy, and suffer accordingly.

I have, &c.,
REDVERS BULLER,
General.

From Colonel H.S.G. Miles, Commanding, De Aar – Belmont, to the Chief Staff Officer, Cape Town.

Orange River,

SIR, *December* 15, 1899.

I HAVE the honour to forward here with reports* on the action at Zoutspans Drift, which took place in the afternoon of the 13th instant.

For some days information had been received that a party of Boers was at Dalton's Pont, some 20 miles up the river, and a guide informed us that, from this body, another party was at Zoutspans Drift (the next above Orange River Bridge). Other parties of Boers were believed to be moving on the north bank of the river, from 20 to 30 Boers in each, all found, it is understood, from a Boer laager at Goemansberg.

In these circumstances it was deemed advisable to strengthen the ordinary patrol which proceeds daily from here to the drift. Half the company of Mounted Infantry (South-Eastern Company), under Captain Bradshaw (54 men) and a party of Remington's Guides (16 men), under Lieutenant Macfarlane were detailed for the duty, and Captain Bradshaw was instructed to proceed to the drift to reconnoitre carefully, and to report strength and position of the enemy.

The party appears to have come upon the enemy somewhat suddenly, and from verbal accounts it appears that their attack was in the nature of a surprise. The attack was pushed on very rapidly, and, unfortunately, Captain Bradshaw was killed early in the action.

The Boers retired after about an hour's action: they removed their wounded in carts. Our wounded were, in the same manner, taken to Mr. Attewell's farm at Ramah, who treated them with the greatest kindness and attention. I sent out the next morning, 13th instant, and brought all in, including the bodies of those killed.

Native reports say that one of the Free State Commandants was killed, but these reports are very unreliable.

Captain Bradshaw was an energetic and valuable Officer, and I deeply regret his loss.

I have, &c.,

H.G. MILES, Colonel,

Commanding Line, De Aar – Belmont.

*Not printed.

2

BATTLE OF GRASPAN, NAVAL DESPATCHES

Admiralty, March 28, 1900.

DESPATCHES, of which the following are copies, have been received from Rear-Admiral Sir Robert H. Harris, K.C.M.G., Commander-in-Chief on the Cape of Good Hope and West Coast of Africa, reporting proceedings of Naval Brigade from the time of reaching Lord Methuen's Headquarters to the Battle of Graspan:-

H.M.S. "Doris," Simon's Bay,
SIR,   4th December, 1899.

IN accordance with your orders I left Simon's Bay on Sunday the 19th November, and arrived with the Naval Brigade at Lord Methuen's Headquarters at about 1 o'clock on the 22nd. On reporting myself to Lord Methuen I received orders to accompany him that afternoon to Belmont. Having to wait for transport from Orange River, which arrived very late in the evening, I could not manage to leave until the brigade had already marched some hours. Having packed waggons and harnessed mules I marched at 8.30 to Belmont. Being a long column it was necessarily a very slow march, and the mules were troublesome.

2. On arriving within one mile of Belmont I received orders through a staff officer to go back along the road, and to be in Belmont by 3 o'clock next morning to report myself to the General. On arriving at headquarters at 3 A.M., I received orders to communicate with Colonel Hall, commanding Royal Artillery; having met him, I marched out of Belmont by road in company with Colonel Hall's battery of field artillery. After clearing Belmont kopjes we turned off the road on the open veldt; day was just dawning, and we could see the top of the line of kopjes held by the enemy. We were then advancing towards the centre of his position, over very rough ground intersected with dykes. This tried our gun-mountings very severely.

Unfortunately one gun capsized, but was soon righted, and I was relieved to find that there was no damage done, and that the dockyard work stood the test so well.

On proceeding to higher ground a view of the Boers' position was then obtained. A long line of kopjes, which looked very much higher at dawn of day than they really were, the light being very bad indeed, and the sun coming up behind the kopjes cast dark shadows, which made it very hard to distinguish any objects. In addition to this there was a mist round the lower part of the kopjes.

3. Firing was now going on in our front, the Boers evidently having been repulsed. Colonel Hall here turned away to his left, and to the left of the Boer position, on the understanding that I should take up a position across the railway line on higher ground, and he would soon communicate with me. This I did, but had great difficulty in taking my heavy ammunition waggons and guns across the railway-line, finally succeeding. I here brought the battery into action to try the range of the extreme depth of the Boer position, but after firing a range-finding shot and not seeing it pitch, I limbered up.

4. Hearing heavy firing on the right of the position, and not having had any communication from Colonel Hall, I determined, if possible, to get the battery in range of the large kopje, which a battery of the Royal Artillery were shelling. The guns not being mobile, and having to cover heavy ground I was unfortunately too late to take part in shelling the top of the kopje, which the Guards carried.

5. I then turned to the left between two kopjes, and found the Boers on the rear kopje firing upon advancing infantry. I immediately got the battery into action, and at 1,700 yards shelled the Boers who were firing on our troops, the practice being excellent. The Boers were very soon silenced and retreated.

6. I received orders from the General to take my guns, if possible, on to a low kopje about 800 yards from my front, so as to shell the retreating Boers from their position. I limbered up and advanced as quickly as possible over very rough ground, and advancing well ahead myself to survey the kopje. I found, when I arrived on top, that it was impossible to take wheels over it, so reluctantly had to give it up. Here my officers, men, and mules were almost dead beat and the battle over. Having watered my mules I returned to camp with the remainder of the troops.

7. At 3 P.M. next day the whole Brigade marched out of Belmont to the railway station, where our guns were entrained. The gun mules were handed over to Colonel Hall to save his horses. The guns and ammunition were left entrained under command of Lieutenant Dean, with his half-battery and officers to guard them. The remainder of the Naval Brigade marched at the head of the column to the next bivouac. At 10.30 P.M. I received orders from General Methuen that next morning the Naval Brigade would lead the attack on the enemy's position, supported by the Yorkshire Light Infantry, the attacking force being under the command of Brigadier-General Money. We paraded at 3 A.M., and marching at the head of the column, came up to the left of the enemy's position at daylight, the Field Artillery engaging the right and left of the enemy's position and shelling the top of the kopjes.

The armoured train with naval guns in rear was steaming up on the left of our advance. I observed one of our guns in action firing at the extreme left of the Boer position, which rested on the railway line. The infantry marching away to the right I had no further opportunity of observing the action of the guns after that.

8. The Brigade was deployed into line single rank four paces interval, and advanced on the enemy's position. The disposition of officers was as follows:-

Major Plumbe, R.M.L.I., in command of the left;
Commander Ethelston, in command of the right;
Myself in the centre.

When in front of the kopje to be attacked the line was wheeled, the right brought up, and the Brigade advanced to the attack immediately. The enemy opened fire on the Brigade at about 600 yards, a very heavy front fire. The Brigade still advanced steadily by rushes, and in a short time a very heavy cross fire was opened from our left flank, but in spite of the murderous fire the behaviour of our officers and men was beyond all praise. They all showed great courage and cool determination. Although losing heavily both in officers and men, I had the satisfaction of seeing, after being wounded and being carried to the rear, our bluejackets and marines in possession of the enemy's position. To give some idea of the heavy fire, several times I saw a man hit three times before he reached the ground, but there was never the slightest hesitation in the advance from beginning to end.

9. After the death of Commander Ethelston, Lieutenant Boyle led his blue-jackets into the enemy's position. Captain Marchant also, after the death of Major Plumbe, led his marines into the enemy's position. When the conduct of all officers is of such a quality it is impossible to single out any particular instance, but I may mention Lieutenant Jones, R.M.L.I., who, although wounded in the thigh, did not stop until he led his men into the enemy's position.

10. I herewith embody two reports: the first from Captain Marchant, R.M.L.I.; the second from Lieutenant Dean of his action on the left of the position, which I did not see, as he was some miles off, but he and his officers and men must have behaved excellently to have done what they did.

I have the honour to be, Sir,
Your obedient Servant,
R. PROTHERO,
Captain and O.C. R.N. Brigade.

Rear-Admiral Sir R.H. Harris, K.C.M.G.,
Commander-in-Chief.

Royal Naval Brigade,
In Camp at Esland Station,
SIR,   26th November, 1899.

I HAVE the honour to report that the Naval Brigade was in action yesterday morning at the battle of which you have had telegraphic information.

2. The officers, petty officers, non-commissioned officers, and men behaved with conspicuous gallantry, but I regret to inform you that the losses in killed and wounded were exceptionally heavy for the small number of men forming the Naval Brigade.

3. I enclose a report from Lieutenant F. Dean, who was in command of the guns during the action, as I did not see what the movements of the guns were during that stage of the action.

4. The remainder of the bluejackets who were not with the guns and all the marines formed part of the firing line, and were under the command of Captain Prothero.

They advanced with other troops, and attacked a very strong position held by the Boers, who were in large force and had large guns with them. About 400 yards from the foot of an almost inaccessible hill, from which the enemy had to be driven, the line was fired on from two positions, and it was here that so heavy a loss was sustained.

I regret to inform you that at this point Commander A.P. Ethelston, Major J.H. Plumbe, R.M.L.I., and Captain Guy Senior, R.M.A., were killed whilst gallantly leading their men, and Midshipmen C.A.E. Huddart was mortally wounded. Captain Prothero, both before and after he was wounded, behaved with great gallantry and coolness.

Lieutenant W.T.C. Jones, R.M.L.I., who was wounded in the hip by a bullet which has not yet been extracted, was also wounded at this stage, but undeterred charged to the top of the hill, where his wound was dressed. The conduct of this officer is deserving of the highest praise, and I strongly recommend him to your notice. Midshipman Wardle also showed great gallantry, and remained with Major Plumbe and several dead and wounded men, and attended to them and dressed their wounds under a heavy fire.

5. Lieutenant the Hon. E.S.H. Boyle and Lieutenant F.J. Saunders, R.M.L.I., Gunner

Lowe, R.N., and Midshipman W.W. Sillem, also charged to the top of the hill, gallantly leading their men all the time under a very heavy fire, and are all deserving of special mention.

6. At the top of the hill I collected as many men as possible and advanced to the farthest position, driving the enemy before us until the position was finally captured and the Boers in full retreat with their horses and waggons.

7. Lieutenant F. Dean, Lieutenant G.W. McO. Campbell, Sub-Lieutenant White (who was in charge of the ammunition supply), and Midshipman Armstrong, who were with the guns, behaved with great gallantry in a very exposed position, which was commanded by the enemy's guns, and where they were subjected to a heavy artillery fire, which proved so accurate as to wound six men of the guns' crews.

8. Fleet Surgeon James Porter, who was with the firing line, and Surgeon Beadnell with the guns did gallant and most excellent service under trying conditions, under fire nearly the whole time.

9. It is with deep regret that I have to report the death of Midshipman Huddart, who behaved magnificently, and still advanced after he had been twice wounded until he was finally struck down mortally wounded.

10. Midshipman Sillem was stunned half-way up the hill and remained unconscious for some time.

11. General Lord Methuen came specially to see me, and ordered the men to fall in, and complimented them on their behaviour, and expressed his regret at the heavy losses we had sustained in officers and men.

12. After the action was over, being the senior officer present, I collected the men, marched into camp, and took command of the brigade.

I have the honour to be, Sir,
Your obedient Servant,
A.E. MARCHANT,
Captain, R.M.L.I.,
Commanding Royal Naval Brigade.

The Commander-in-Chief,
H.M. Ships,
Cape of Good Hope.

Gras Pan,

SIR,   26th November, 1899.

IN compliance with your orders of this date, I have the honour to submit for the information of the Commander-in-Chief a report of my proceedings with the four naval guns and four half guns' crews under my command yesterday.

2. Arrived at Gras Pan at 5.45 a.m., and observing the enemy in an apparently strong position, 5,000 yards in advance, I detrained two guns – not having enough men to handle more – and at 5.55 a.m. fired one round to test range. I then waited till the Royal Artillery with six guns took up a position on my right front and opened fire on the enemy. I did the same, and subsequently

advanced to ranges of 4,000 and ultimately 2,800 yards, acting from time to time on requests I received from the officer commanding Royal Artillery, who was attacking the same position, viz., two strongly fortified kopjes on either side of the railway with a well protected gun in each.

3. About 8 a.m. I received verbal orders to retire from my position, as the Royal Artillery were about to move away to the right, and it would then be untenable for my two guns. The Royal Artillery were already moving off when I got the order, and the Boer guns, having got our range accurately, were pouring on us such an effective shrapnel fire, that I judged it impossible to carry out the order without either leaving the guns or suffering very heavy losses, both amongst our own men and the company of Royal Engineers who were helping us, if we attempted to retreat with them.

I, therefore, continued to fire as briskly as possible at the Boer guns, with such effect that we continuously put them out of action, first one and then the other, for as much as 15 or 20 minutes at a time. Their shells burst with utmost accuracy, and both our guns and ammunition trolly were spattered all over with shrapnel balls; but, owing to my system of making all hands lie down when we saw their guns flash and remain till the shell burst and the balls flew by, we had only six men wounded when, at 9.30 a.m., the Boers finally ceased firing and abandoned their position.

4. I beg that you will submit to the Commander-in-Chief that Lieut. Campbell and Mr: Armstrong, midshipman, displayed marked coolness and courage in controlling the fire of their guns and inspiriting the men, who all worked splendidly. I would recommend for favourable consideration Petty Officers 1st class Ashley (H.M.S. "Doris") and Fuller ("Monarch"), who under the trying circumstances laid their guns with the greatest accuracy. I am confident that, had the Boer guns been exposed as ours were, we should have not only silenced but captured them.

5. On Friday night I found Surgeon Beadnell at Belmont Station; he had been invalided by a medical board that day and was waiting for the hospital train. Though in bad health he gladly accepted my order to remain with the guns in view of the pending engagement, and on Saturday he rendered invaluable aid to our wounded, working close up to the guns where shrapnel balls were showering every other minute.

I am, Sir, your obedient Servant,
F.W. DEAN,
Lieutenant, R.N.

Captain Marchant, R.M.L.I.,
Commanding Naval Brigade.

3

BATTLE OF LADYSMITH

SECTION II. – NATAL FIELD ARMY.
No. 1.
From General Sir Redvers Buller to the
Secretary of State for War.
(Through the Field-Marshal Commanding-in-Chief, Cape Town.)

Spearman's Hill Camp,
Sir,   Sir, 2nd February, 1900.
I have the honour to forward a despatch from Lieut.-General Sir George White, which I have only just received by runner. It is in continuation of his despatch of the 2nd November, 1899,* and it will be seen by paragraph 12 that it deals only with his operations up to 30th October, 1899.

It may, therefore, I think, be inferred that the services of the Officers, non-commissioned officers and men which he brings to notice were rendered by them prior to that date.

I have &c.,
REDVERS BULLER, General.
Jacobsdal,
18th February, 1900.

Secretary of State for War.
Forwarded.
ROBERTS, Field-Marshal,
Commanding-in-Chief, South Africa.

From Lieut.-General Sir George White, V.C., G.C.B., G.C.S.I., G.C.I.E., Commanding the British Forces in Natal, to the Secretary of State for War. (Through the General Officer Commanding in South Africa.)

Ladysmith, Natal,
Sir,   2nd December, 1899.
In continuation of my despatch of 2nd November, 1899, I have now the honour to report the occurrences of 24th October, referred to briefly in the last paragraph of my above-mentioned despatch. On that date I marched out of Ladysmith at dawn with the 5th Lancers, 19th Hussars, Imperial Light Horse, Natal Mounted Volunteers, 42nd and 53rd Batteries, Royal Field

Artillery; No. 10 Mountain Battery, Royal Garrison Artillery; 1st Bn. Liverpool Regiment, 1st Bn. Devonshire Regiment, 1st Bn. Gloucestershire Regiment, and 2nd Bn. King's Royal Rifle Corps. The mounted troops were sent on in advance, and, after going about 6 miles along the Newcastle Road, came under rifle fire from the hills on their left on Rietfontein Farm. The 19th Hussars pushed on over the Modder Spruit and seized and held a ridge about 2 miles beyond that stream by dismounted fire, while watching the country to the front and flanks with patrols. The 5th Lancers similarly seized and held ridges south of the Modder Spruit, as also did the Imperial Light Horse. By this disposition of the mounted troops my right flank was entirely protected during the subsequent action.

2. At 8 a.m. I arrived at Rietfontein at the head of the main body. At this moment the enemy opened artillery fire on my advanced Cavalry from a point high up on the Intintanyone Mountain, and about 5,000 yards to the west of the main road, at which he had apparently posted four guns. My artillery was at once ordered to wheel off the road and come into action against these guns, which opened fire on them, but were quickly silenced. Leaving the 2nd Bn. King's Royal Rifle Corps with the baggage waggons, I moved the remainder of the Infantry under the shelter of a high ridge, parallel to the road, and facing the Intintanyone Mountain. The 1st Bn. Gloucestershire Regiment on the left, and the 1st Bn. Liverpool Regiment on the right were then advanced to the crest of this ridge, the Artillery also advancing and coming into action on the crest line between these two regiments. The position thus attained was one most suitable to my purpose, which was to prevent the enemy moving to the east, across the Newcastle Road, and attacking Brigadier-General Yule's force during its retirement from Dundee.

3. Our Artillery was entirely successful in preventing the enemy from making any further use of his guns, but a severe fire fight gradually developed between my troops and the enemy's infantry, and it became necessary to push the 1st Bn. Devonshire Regiment also to the crest of the ridge, half the 2nd Bn. King's Royal Rifle Corps being brought up from the wagons to take their place in reserve. In this Infantry fight our Artillery rendered great assistance, searching out the crest line and reverse slopes of the opposing ridges most effectively, and thus keeping down the enemy's rifle fire. Meanwhile the Natal Mounted Volunteers, who had been with the Cavalry, had been recalled, and, as the enemy showed some disposition to work round my left flank, as if to cut me from Ladysmith, I sent this force, under Colonel Royston, to work round the Boer right and cover my left flank, a movement which was most success-fully performed. It was no part of my plan to deliver an attack on the enemy,

posted as he was in ground exceptionally well suited to his tactics, and especially difficult for our troops; I contented myself, therefore, with maintaining the position I had gained. The Boers, on the other hand, were unwilling to attack us except by fire at long ranges, and, as they could not approach Brigadier-General Yule's force without doing so, they gradually withdrew to the westward. By 2 p.m. firing had ceased, and as time had now been afforded for the Dundee column to pass the point of danger I returned with my troops to Ladysmith. Our casualties consisted of one Officer and 11 non-commissioned officers and men killed, six Officers and 97 non-commissioned officers and men wounded, and two non-commissioned officers and men missing. The enemy's loss was heavy, particularly from artillery fire.

4. On 25th October I sent out a force, under Lieut.-Colonel Coxhead, R.A., to meet and, if necessary, to assist Brigadier-General Yule. This force got touch with the Dundee column that afternoon, and, as already reported, both columns reached Ladysmith next morning (26th October) without any interference from the enemy.

5. On 27th, 28th and 29th October the enemy gradually approached Ladysmith from the west, north, and north-east. These days were spent by us in reconnaissances with a view to finding a favourable opportunity to strike a blow at him. On 29th October our Cavalry located a considerable Boer force, with artillery on Long Hill, north-east of Ladysmith, and well within striking distance. I accordingly issued orders for an attack next day, which resulted in the action of Lombard's Kop.

6. My object was, in the first instance, to carry Long Hill, and, in the event of success, to similarly carry Pepworth's Hill, sending, at the same time, a considerable mounted force round over Nicholson's Nek to cut the enemy's line of retreat and endeavour to capture his laagers. To gain these objects I employed the entire force assembled at Ladysmith. 200 Natal Mounted Volunteers were sent out the evening before to hold Lombard's Kop and Bulwana Mountain. The 5th Lancers, 19th Hussars, and the remainder of the Natal Mounted Volunteers were ordered to move out, under Major-General French, at 3 a.m. on 30th October, cross Lombard's Nek and the Modder Spruit and cover my right flank during the operations. A Brigade Division of Royal Field Artillery, the Natal Field Battery, 1st and 2nd Bns. King's Royal Rifle Corps, 1st Bn. Leicestershire Regiment, 1st Bn. Liverpool Regiment, and 2nd Bn. Royal Dublin Fusiliers, the whole under Colonel Grimwood, King's Royal Rifle Corps, were detailed for the attack on Long Hill (moving at night so as to be ready to commence the attack at dawn. An Infantry Brigade, under Colonel Ian Hamilton, C.B., D.S.O., consisting of 2nd Bn.

Gordon Highlanders, 1st Bn. Manchester Regiment, 1st Bn. Devonshire Regiment, and 2nd Bn. Rifle Brigade, together with the Divisional Troops, consisting of a Brigade Division, Royal Artillery, 5th Dragoon Guards, 18th Hussars, Imperial Light Horse, and two companies, Mounted Infantry, were directed to rendezvous at the railway crossing on the Newcastle Road, and proceed to take up a position under cover of Limit Hill. This latter Brigade Division was directed, in the first instance, to assist in shelling Long Hill, the Infantry being intended for the attack on Pepworth's Hill. To cover my left flank and open a way for the action of the Cavalry after the position had been carried, No. 10 Mountain Battery, the 1st Bn. Royal Irish Fusiliers, and the 1st Bn. Gloucestershire Regiment, the whole under Lieut.-Colonel F. Carleton, Royal Irish Fusiliers, with Major W. Adye, D.A.A.G., for Intelligence, as Staff Officer and Guide, were directed to fall in at 11 p.m., on 29th October, and make a night march up Bell's Spruit to seize as strong a position as could be obtained towards Nicholson's Nek; if possible, the Nek itself.

7. The troops moved out in accordance with these instructions. The mounted troops, under General French, passed between Lombard's Kop and Bulwana Mountain, but failed to penetrate further than the line of kopjes north-east of the Nek, where at daybreak they came under the fire of the enemy's guns and rifles. They held the enemy in check here but could not advance further. The Infantry Brigade, under Colonel Grimwood, reached their appointed position, and the Artillery opened on Long Hill, which, however, was found to have been evacuated by the enemy during the night. At this moment Colonel Grimwood's force was attacked by guns and mounted infantry in large numbers from beyond the Modder Spruit, and had to change front to the right to meet this development, as the Cavalry, having been unable to get beyond the kopjes north-east of Lombard's Nek, were not in a position to cover that flank. Gradually the enemy's numbers increased, and made continual efforts to turn both flanks of the position occupied by Colonel Grimwood's force, necessitating a constant prolongation of his fighting line, and thus using up his supports and reserves, which, by 10 a.m., had all been absorbed in the firing line. Meanwhile artillery fire had been opened by the enemy from Pepworth Hill, one of the guns employed being a 15-cm. gun, throwing a shell of about 100lbs. weight, which commenced firing on the town of Ladysmith at a range of 8,000 yards. These guns were silenced by our Field Artillery, which also drove the enemy from the crest of Pepworth Hill. It was now about 8 a.m. At this period Major-General French reported that he was holding his position with difficulty against superior forces of the enemy, and I detached the 5th Dragoon Guards and 18th Hussars, under

Brigadier-General Brocklehurst, to his assistance; the 69th and 21st Field Batteries being also moved to his support, and with this assistance he easily held his own till the end of the action. Of the remaining batteries, the 13th and 53rd were engaged in supporting Colonel Grimwood's force, while the 42nd and 67th were still firing on Pepworth Hill, from which the enemy had reopened fire, while he had also brought fresh guns on to Long Hill.

8. About 10 a.m. I withdrew the Manchester Regiment from Colonel Hamilton's force, and placed it in a position to support Colonel Grimwood. The fight now became stationary, our troops holding their positions without any great difficulty, but being unable to advance. The Boers on the other hand, were unable to make any headway. This condition of affairs continued until 11.30 a.m., when, finding that there was little prospect of bringing the engagement to a decisive issue, I determined to withdraw my troops. I accordingly moved the 2nd Bn. Gordon Highlanders from my left to a strong position on Flag Hill, and sent Major-General Sir A. Hunter, K.C.B., my Chief of Staff, to arrange a retirement in echelon from the left, covered by the fire of our Artillery. This was most successfully carried out, the Artillery advancing in the most gallant manner, and covering the Infantry movement with the greatest skill and coolness.

9. Meanwhile the Naval Brigade landed from H.M.S. "Powerful," which had reached Ladysmith that morning, under Captain Hon. H. Lambton, R.N., had moved out with their long 12-pr. guns on improvised field mountings, drawn by oxen, and had engaged the enemy's artillery on Pepworth Hill, directing their special attention to the heavy gun mounted there, which they temporarily silenced. The enemy did not follow up our retirement, and the whole force employed on this side returned to camp at 1.30 p.m.

10. Turning now to this force, consisting of No. 10 Mountain Battery, Royal Irish Fusiliers, and the Gloucestershire Regiment, under Lieut.-Colonel F. Carleton, Royal Irish Fusiliers, which proceeded by a night march up Bell's Spruit towards Nicholson's Nek to cover my left flank, I regret that, owing to the circumstances about to be related, I have no official report of their movements. My information has been obtained from subordinate Officers, who, being severely wounded, were sent into my camp here by General Joubert. From this information it appears that the force moved off, as ordered, at 11 p.m. on 29th October, and proceeded for some distance without seeing signs of the enemy. When passing along the foot of a steep hill, known as Cainguba, stones were suddenly rolled down on them and some shots were fired. The Infantry at once fixed bayonets and carried the hill without difficulty, but unfortunately both the Mountain Battery mules and those carrying

the Infantry ammunition took fright and stampeded. Mules carrying two guns eventually returned to camp, one was retained with the force, but no trace has been found of the other three, which presumably fell into the enemy's hands.

The force took up a position on Cainguba, which they strengthened with breastworks to some slight extent, and remained unmolested till daybreak. It was then found that the position was too large for them to adequately occupy, and that only the most pronounced salients could be held. The Boers appear to have gradually surrounded the hill, and after a fight extending over several hours, our men's ammunition began to fail owing to the ammunition mules having stampeded, as already described. The advanced parties holding the salients were driven back on the main body in the centre of the plateau, and the Boers gained the crest line of the hill, whence they brought a converging fire to bear from all sides on our men crowded together in the centre, causing much loss. Eventually it was seen that this position was hopelessly untenable, and our force hoisted a white flag and surrendered about 12.30 p.m.

11. Including under the head of "missing" those thus taken prisoners, our losses this day amounted to six Officers and 63 non-commissioned officers and men killed, 10 Officers and 239 non-commissioned officers and men wounded, and 37 Officers and 917 non-commissioned officers and men missing.

12. Next day, 31st October, General Sir Redvers Buller, V.C., G.C.B., &c., arrived at Cape Town, and assumed the command in the whole of South Africa. My independent command in Natal consequently came to an end, and I therefore close this Despatch with the events of 30th October. Subsequent events will be reported to the General Officer Commanding in South Africa in the ordinary course.

13. I desire to place on record my gratitude to the Government of Natal and to all departments under the Government, for the most willing and hearty assistance which they have afforded me in every matter in which their co-operation was required.

14. I desire to bring the following Officers very specially to your notice as eminently deserving of reward for the services rendered by them:-

The late Lieut.-General Sir W. Penn Symons, K.C.B. – I cannot too strongly record my opinion of the energy and courage shown by this distinguished General Officer in the exercise of his command, until he was mortally wounded in the action on the Talana Hill, near Dundee, on the 20th October last. In him the country has lost an Officer of high ability and a leader of exceptional valour.

Major-General Sir A. Hunter, K.C.B., D.S.O., Chief of the Staff. – The services of this Officer have been of the very highest value to the State. His zeal is indefatigable, and he has carried out the business of the force under my command so as to relieve me of all anxiety. He is equally good in the field, and has the gift of carrying with him all with whom he is brought in contact. I have every confidence in recommending this Officer for advancement as one fitted for the highest commands.

Major-General J.D.P. French, commanding the Cavalry, rendered me most valuable assistance. He commanded the troops engaged at Elandslaagte, where his dispositions resulted in the most decisive victory. I consider his services have merited very special recognition.

Brigadier-General J.H. Yule succeeded to the command of the Dundee force when Major-General Sir W. Penn Symons was wounded, and had a difficult duty to carry out. He conducted the retirement of the force from Dundee to Ladysmith with marked success.

Brigadier-General J. Wolfe Murray, commanding Lines of Communication, is an Officer of great administrative ability, and has done his work excellently well. He has been specially selected for this most important post from the confidence felt in him, and, as it is one that entails hard work and is not as popular as employment in the front, I think the value of the service should be exceptionally recognised.

Colonel Ian Hamilton, C.B., D.S.O., has acted as Brigadier-General in command of a brigade since my head-quarters have been established at Ladysmith. I have made a special recommendation in favour of this Officer for the manner in which he led the Infantry at the action of Elandslaagte on the 21st October, and consider him an Officer of special ability who is well fitted for higher rank and command.

Colonel B. Duff, C.I.E., Indian Staff Corps, has been my Assistant Military Secretary, and has discharged the duties of the office with marked ability and success. His advancement will be a benefit to the Service, and he is well fitted for the highest staff appointments.

Brevet-Colonel E.W.D. Ward, C.B., A.S.C., A.A.G. (B). – I cannot speak too highly of this Officer. His forethought in collecting supplies in Ladysmith while railway communication was open with the sea at Durban has enabled me to occupy the position here with perfect confidence that the garrison could not be starved out. When the force originally at Dundee was thrown back on Ladysmith, having had to abandon the supply provided for it, Colonel Ward's provision was ample, even for the extra strain thus thrown upon the supply, as well as to meet the necessity of finding rations for the civil population. His power of work and resources are most marked, and he has won the confidence of all. I consider him an Officer of the highest administrative ability, and recommend him most strongly for recognition of his exceptionally valuable service with this force.

Colonel C.M. Downing, R.A., Commanding Royal Artillery, has been my adviser on all artillery matters in my command, and I count myself fortunate in having had the assistance of such an experienced and highly-educated Artillery Officer. I cannot speak in too high terms of the behaviour of the Royal Artillery on all occasions on which I have had to call upon them, or of the value of their services to the State.

Colonel W.G. Knox, C.B., Colonel on the Staff, Ladysmith, has, from the appointment he holds, been left in command of Ladysmith on all occasions when the Field Army has gone out. His services have been very valuable.

Colonel W. Royston, Commanding Natal Volunteer Force. – The services which Colonel Royston and the forces under his command have rendered to the State and Colony have been of the very highest value. In him I have found a bold and successful leader, and an adviser whose experience of the Colony and of the enemy has been of great value to me. Employed on arduous duty, from the commencement of the campaign in touch with the enemy, I have found him prompt and ready for every emergency. He and his force reflect the highest credit on the Colony of Natal.

Colonel J.G. Dartnell, C.M.G., Chief Commissioner, Natal Police, rendered valuable service to the late Lieut.-General Sir W. Penn Symons and to Brigadier-General Yule when the Dundee column fell back on Ladysmith. His advice and experience were of the highest value, and I found him always ready and willing to help me in any way in his power.

Brevet-Colonel Sir H. Rawlinson, Bart., Coldstream Guards, D.A.A.G., has acted as A.A.G. since this force was formed, and has proved himself a Staff Officer of very high ability. He has great power of work, and carries out his duties pleasantly and thoroughly. He is also a most valuable Staff Officer in action, and possessed of a quick eye and great dash. I recommend him for advancement.

Lieut.-Colonel R. Exham, R.A.M.C., Principal Medical Officer, has had an anxious time in the charge of the sick and wounded of this force, and has done everything in his power to meet the medical requirements of the various phases of the present campaign. His zeal and assiduity are worthy of recognition.

The services of the Royal Artillery have been so valuable that I have special pleasure in recommending Lieut.-Colonels J.A. Coxhead and E.H. Pickwood, Commanding Brigade Divisions with this force, and the conduct of the individual batteries has been so good, and the services of each so valuable, that I consider the following Majors have well earned special mention:-

Royal Field Artillery.

Major J.W.G. Dawkins, 13th Battery.

Major W.E. Blewitt, 21st Battery.

Major C.E. Goulburn, 42nd Battery.

Major A.J. Abdy, 53rd Battery.

Major J.F. Manifold, 67th Battery.

Major F.D.V. Wing, 69th Battery.

Major S.R. Rice, R.E., acting as Commanding Royal Engineer, has been indefatigable in the discharge of his duties, and his services have been most valuable in preparing the entrenched positions occupied by the garrison of Ladysmith, and in other matters connected with this particular branch.

Major E.A. Altham, Royal Scots Regiment, A.A.G., Field Intelligence, has had a very difficult office to fill. I consider he has done all that was possible. He has kept me informed of the enemy's movements, as well as changes in his strength and dispositions. I have a very high opinion of his ability and aptitude for the particular branch in which he is employed.

Major D. Henderson, Argyll and Sutherland Highlanders, D.A.A.G., Field Intelligence, is a most painstaking and reliable Intelligence Officer. He possesses boldness, discretion, and reticence, and is an Officer of high promise.

Major W. Adye, Royal Irish Rifles, D.A.A.G., Field Intelligence, has proved himself an Officer of a most adventurous spirit in reconnoitring and reporting upon the enemy's positions, and his services have been valuable to me.

Major H.G. Morgan, D.S.O., A.S.C., Assistant Director of Supplies, rendered most valuable service in disembarking and entraining the first reinforcements that arrived in Natal, and hurrying them on to the front.

The following Officers have also carried put the duties of their departments with advantage to the State and credit to themselves:-

Veterinary Lieut.-Colonel I. Mathews, P.V.O.

Major W.C. Savile, R.A., Army Ordnance Department.

Major A.J. Murray, Royal Inniskilling Fusiliers, who acted as Staff Officer to Brigadier-General Yule during the retirement from Dundee.

Brevet Lieut.-Colonel H.M. Lawson, R.E., A.A.G., Lines of Communication and Commanding at Durban.

Major S.C.N. Grant, R.E., Special Service.

Commander Holland. Royal Indian Marine, Disembarkation Officer at Durban.

The railway administration, under David Hunter, Esq., C.M.G., was most excellently carried out, and was worked most harmoniously and successfully in concert with the military and naval Officers.

15. I also desire to bring to your notice the following Officers, &c., who have rendered excellent services:-

Colonel C.E. Beckett, C.B., A.A.G.

Lieut-Colonel R.W. Mapleton, R.A.M.C.

Major C. de C. Hamilton, R.A., who has been acting throughout as D.A.A.G. on my Head-quarter Staff.

Major H. Mullaly, R.E., D.A.A.G.

Brevet-Major A.J. King, Royal Lancaster Regiment, A.D.C. to Major-General Sir A. Hunter, K.C.B., D.S.O.

Captain F. Lyon, R.F.A., A.D.C.

Captain J.R. Young, R.E., Railway Staff Officer.

Captain F.S. Tatham, Natal Mounted Rifles.

Rev. E.J. Macpherson, B.A., Senior Chaplain, Church of England.

Rev. O.S. Watkins, Acting Wesleyan Chaplain.

T.R. Bennett, Esq., Resident Magistrate, Ladysmith.

D.G. Giles, Esq., Resident Magistrate, Upper Tugela Magistracy.

Conductor W.C. Ashmore, Indian Unattached List.

Quarter-Master-Serjeant E.H. Morton, Corps of Military Staff Clerks.

No. S.C./227, Serjeant P. Burke, Staff Clerk Section, A.S.C.

Guide A.B. Allison, Natal Corps of Guides.

   ,,   T. Loxton,   ,,   ,,

   ,,   P. Greathead,   ,,   ,,

16. The following Officers, Warrant and non-commissioned officers, and men, have been brought to my notice by General Officer commanding and Officers Commanding units. (The names are arranged in the order of precedence of corps):-

Officers.

4th Dragoon Guards (attached to 5th Dragoon Guards).

Captain G.F. Mappin.

5th Lancers.

Major A.C. King.

Lieutenant and Adjutant H.H. Hulse.

7th Hussars.

Major D. Haig.

Captain R.G. Brooke. D.S.O.

11th Hussars.

Lieutenant P.D. Fitzgerald.

53rd Battery, Royal Field Artillery.

Captain W. Thwaites.

Royal Engineers.

Captain G.H. Fowke.

1st Bn. Devonshire Regiment.

Major M.C. Curry.
Captain W.B. Lafone.
Captain and Adjutant H.S.L. Ravenshaw.
Lieutenant J.E.I. Masterson.
Lieutenant H.N. Field.

Somersetshire Light Infantry.

Captain J.M. Vallentin.

1st Bn. Leicestershire Regiment.

Lieutenant B. de W. Weldon.

1st Bn. Scottish Rifles –
(attached to 2nd Bn. King's Royal Rifle Corps.)

Lieutenant N.M. Tod.

1st Bn. King's Royal Rifle Corps.

Lieut-Colonel R.H. Gunning (killed in action).
Captain and Adjutant H.R. Blore (killed in action).

2nd Bn. King's Royal Rifle Corps.

Major H.E. Buchanan-Riddell.

1st Bn. Manchester Regiment.

Major J.E. Watson.
Captain A.W. Marden.
Lieutenant H. Fisher.

2nd Bn. Gordon Highlanders.

Major W.A. Scott.
Captain C.F.N. Macready.
Captain and Adjutant E. Stretfeild.

2nd Bn. Royal Dublin Fusiliers.

Major S.G. Bird.
Captain G.A. Weldon (killed in action).
Captain and Adjutant M. Lowndes.

Army Service Corps.

Captain A. Long.

Royal Army Medical Corps.

Lieut-Colonel P.H. Johnston.
Major H. Martin.
Major M.W. Kerin.
Captain G.S. Walker.

Indian Staff Corps.
Major W.J.R. Wickham.

Imperial Light Horse.
Colonel J.J. Scott-Chisholme (killed in action.)
Major A. Wools-Sampson.
Major W. Karri Davis.
Captain J.E. Orr.
Captain C.H. Mullins.
Captain J.C. Knapp (killed in action).

Natal Volunteer Force.
Permanent Staff, Natal Volunteer Force.
Major H.T. Bru-de-Wold (Senior Staff Officer, Natal Volunteer Force).

Volunteer Medical Staff.
Captain H.T. Platt.

Warrant and Non-Commissioned Officers and Men.
Royal Engineers.
No. 21916, Corporal H. Rawlinson.
No. 28457, Sapper S. Hudson.
No. 27735, Sapper C. Spurling.

1st Bn. Devonshire Regiment.
No. 2034, Colour-Serjeant G. Palmer.

1st Bn. King's Royal Rifle Corps.
Bandmaster F. Tyler.

1st Bn. Manchester Regiment.
No. 2699, Serjeant R. Lloyd.

2nd Bn. Gordon Highlanders.
No. 3747, Serjeant H. Shepherd.

Army Service Corps.
No. 4709, 1st Class Staff-Serjeant-Major T. Curtis.

Royal Army Medical Corps.
No. 7598, Serjeant E.J. Cadogan.

Indian Commissariat – Transport Department.
Conductor H. Young.

Sub-Conductor M.W. Tyler.
I have, &c.,
GEORGE S. WHITE, Lieut.-General,
Commanding Natal Field Force.

*Already published.

4

BATTLE OF STORMBERG

War Office, March 16, 1900.
THE following Despatch, with enclosure, has been received from Field-Marshal Lord Roberts, V.C., G.C.B., &c., Commanding-in-Chief, South Africa:-

From Field-Marshal Lord Roberts to the Secretary of State for War.

Army Head-Quarters, South Africa,
MY LORD,   *Cape Town, February,* 1900.
I HAVE the honour to submit for your Lordship's information a duplicate Despatch, dated 19th January, 1900, from Lieutenant-General Sir W.F. Gatacre, K.C.B., D.S.O., describing the action of Stormberg on the 10th December, 1899. General Sir Redvers Buller was in chief command in South Africa on the date of the action, and up to the 10th January, 1900, but the original Despatch, which was forwarded some time ago to the Chief of the Staff in Natal, has not reached him.

2. I am of opinion that the failure of Lieutenant-General Gatacre's attempt to seize the Stormberg railway junction was mainly due to reliance on inaccurate information regarding the ground to be traversed, and the position held by the Boers, to the employment of too small a force, and to the men being tired out by a journey by train, followed by a long night march before they came into contact with the enemy.

3. When it became evident shortly after midnight that the guides were leading the column in a wrong direction, I consider that Lieutenant-General Gatacre should have halted and endeavoured to find the proper road, or should have fallen back on Molteno, rather than have risked the safety of the entire force by following a route which brought the troops into difficult ground commanded on both sides by the enemy.

4. The failure of the mounted detachment from Penhoek, with four 2.5-inch guns and one Maxim, to join the column doubtless contributed to the reverse which Lieutenant-General Gatacre experienced. This failure is ascribed in the report to the remissness of a telegraph clerk; but if, when the order was handed in for despatch, the precaution had been taken to request a telegraphic acknowledgment of its receipt, the General Officer Commanding would have

known whether his instructions had been duly received by the Officer Commanding at Penhoek.

5. It is stated that, when directed to retire, a large portion of the 2nd Battalion Northumberland Fusiliers and of the 2nd Battalion Royal Irish Rifles remained behind, and were eventually made prisoners. No explanation of this incident is furnished by Lieutenant-General Gatacre, but, presumably, it must be ascribed to the men being exhausted by their long march, and, consequently, unable to fall back with sufficient rapidity under a hostile fire.

6. The conduct of the Officers, non-commissioned officers, and men, brought to notice by the General Officer Commanding, seems deserving of acknowledgment, especially that of Band-Sergeant J. Stone, 2nd Battalion Northumberland Fusiliers, whose services are detailed in the accompanying memorandum, dated 26th January, 1900.

I have, &c.

ROBERTS, Field-Marshal,

Commanding-in-Chief, South Africa.

P.S. – Since writing the above, I have heard by telegraph from Sir Redvers Buller that the original Despatch has at last reached him. To advoid delay, I forward the duplicate.

Sterkstroom,

January 19, 1900.

SIR,

IN continuation of my telegram, No. 1578c, I have the honour to submit a duplicate Despatch on the action of Stormberg on the 10th December, 1899.

The original despatch was posted to the Chief of Staff, Natal, with appendices in original. No copy was retained, but the accompanying report is, in substance, identical with that sent to General Buller.

I have, &c.,

W. GATACRE, Lieutenant-General,

Commanding 3rd Division.

The Chief of the Staff, Cape Town.

DESPATCH.

The Engagement at Stormberg on 10th December, 1899.

On the 9th December, 1899, the following moved from Putters Kraal to Molteno:-

BY TRAIN. – Divisional Staff; Royal Artillery Staff with 74th and 77th Batteries, Royal Field Artillery; Staff, Royal Engineers, and 12th Company,

Royal Engineers; 2nd Battalion Northumberland Fusiliers; head-quarters and four companies, 2nd Battalion Royal Irish Rifles; three companies, 1st Battalion Royal Scots (of which one company was left at Bushman's Hoek, and two companies remained at Molteno); Royal Army Medical Corps field hospital and bearer company. At Bushman's Hoek the remaining four companies of the Royal Irish Rifles were picked up.

BY ROAD. – Two companies Mounted Infantry and 42 Cape Mounted Police, also from Bushman's Hoek one company Royal Berkshire Mounted Infantry.

160 Brabant's Horse and 235 Cape Mounted Rifles with four 2.5-inch guns and one Maxim should have marched from Penhoek, but did not arrive at Molteno owing to the failure of the telegraph clerk to transmit the message handed to him at midnight on the 8th.

On detraining at Molteno the following force marched on Stormberg at about 9 P.M.:- Staff – Lieutenant-General Gatacre; Captain Hare, Aide-de-Camp; Captain Little, Aide-de-Camp; Lieutenant McNeill, Aide-de-Camp; Colonel Allen, Assistant Adjutant-General; Major Sladen, Assistant Provost-Marshal; Captain Cox, Signalling Officer; Lieutenant-Colonel Edge, Principal Medical Officer; Major Twiss, Royal Army Medical Corps. Infantry in front, Royal Irish Rifles leading, followed by 74th Field Battery, Cape Mounted Police, Dewar's Mounted Infantry, 77th Field Battery, Royal Berkshire Mounted Infantry, vehicles and field hospital, escorted by 12th Company, Royal Engineers. Guides were provided by the Cape Mounted Police.

The force marched with the usual halts for about 8 miles by moonlight, and halted near Roberts' farm at about 12.30 A.M. on the morning of 10th December.

The chief guide now reported that we were within 1½ miles of the enemy's position, and after a rest of about ¾ hour we marched off again in the dark.

It was soon found that the guide had gone wrong, and instead of a march of 1½ miles to the position, the force marched till 3.45 A.M., and found itself, after a long detour, not at the point which I wished to reach.

The place to which the column was led was a strong position occupied by the enemy, who opened fire on the head of the column. Three companies of the Royal Irish Rifles formed to the left and occupied a kopje; the remainder of this battalion and the Northumberland Fusiliers advanced up a steep hill against the enemy's position.

The Artillery was ordered forward to the kopje occupied by the three companies, Royal Irish Rifles, and in crossing a nullah one of the guns unfortunately stuck, and was temporarily abandoned. The team was subsequently shot down, and it was impossible to get the gun away. The two batteries took up positions, one on, and the other immediately west of the kopje.

The mounted infantry endeavoured to turn the Boer right, but fell back on the kopje occupied by the three companies, Royal Irish Rifles. After about half an hour the Officer Commanding 2nd Battalion Northumberland Fusiliers, finding his position untenable, gave the order to retire across the open to a ridge beyond, but a large proportion of his men, and also of the Royal Irish Rifles, remained behind and were eventually taken prisoners. The Officer Commanding Royal Irish Rifles and his second in command were severely wounded early in action.

The Artillery, who experienced great difficulty in coming into action owing to the difficulties of the ground, covered his retirement. The two batteries again retired to the south-east to a position on the neck of a ridge where they remained in action for a considerable time (over an hour), and covered the retirement of the Royal Irish Rifles and the Mounted Infantry. The enemy now brought a big gun into action, which made excellent practice, and was never silenced. Fortunately, the large majority of the shells only burst on impact or not at all. At about 6 A.M. mounted bodies of the enemy were observed trying to get round both our flanks, and the batteries, facing east and west, drove them back with a few well-placed shells.

A retirement on Molteno was now commenced; the Royal Artillery, Mounted Infantry, and Cape Mounted Police covering the Infantry. During the retirement across a ravine a gun got stuck in a quicksand and had to be abandoned. The retirement continued to Molteno, a distance of some nine or ten miles along the direct road, the Artillery and Mounted Infantry keeping the enemy at a distance.

At one portion of the line of retirement the enemy had evidently trained a position gun, which made good practice at 6,000 yards range.

Molteno was reached about 11 A.M.

At 5 P.M. Infantry entrained: the two companies 1st Battalion Royal Scots and Royal Engineers for Bushman's Hoek, the Northumberland Fusiliers and Royal Irish Rifles for Sterkstroom, the Divisional Staff, Royal Artillery, and Mounted Infantry for Cyphergat. Brabant's Horse (160) arrived in afternoon and scouted towards Stormberg; they saw a party of about 50 Boers patrolling, and counted about 1,100 mounted men on the position.

They bivouacked at Molteno, falling back the next morning on Ciphergat.

With regard to the foregoing, I have the honour to report that, from information received from the most reliable sources at my disposal, it appeared there were about 1,700 Boers only at Stormberg, that there were two or three guns there, and that, if the position was approached from the west, Artillery could be brought into action on the kopjes which lie to the west of the Stormberg basin, and from which the whole of the Boer positions could be commanded. It appeared to me that the moment afforded an excellent opportunity for seizing the junction with all its attendant advantages, so I decided to move from Putter's Kraal with as many troops as I could spare and attempt a surprise. To give such movement any chance of success, it had to be carried through in one night, as a halt at Molteno would have given the enemy information of our intended attack.

I thought the plan out and discussed it with Commanding Officers, and after considering the details of ground with the police who belong to Molteno and its neighbourhood, and who are supposed to know every yard of the ground, I decided to carry out the project.

I was aware that the column, when it moved off from Roberts' farm about 12.30 A.M., 10th December, was moving too much to the west, and I questioned the guide and Sergeant Morgan, Cape Mounted Police, who were leading us, but both declared they knew the way perfectly, and that they were taking us by a road which, although slightly longer, would enable us to avoid wire and a bad piece of track which the guns would find a difficulty in getting over at night. This difficult piece of road had not been mentioned by them before, the whole way had been reported fit and easy for wheeled transport. The police guides said that the road, though longer than the originally named road, was not much longer, and that it would bring us out at the spot I wished to arrive at.

The column therefore proceeded, but half an hour after moving off the Officer Commanding 2nd Battalion Royal Irish Rifles (whose regiment was leading) reported to me that he thought the guide had lost his way. I immediately questioned Sergeant Morgan again, but he assured me that the guides (two Europeans and two natives – police) knew the road accurately, and that he also was positive about it. I made Sergeant Morgan himself go to the head of the column and lead it.

I moved myself with the leading battalion and constantly questioned the guide, but was as constantly assured by Sergeant Morgan that we were moving on the right road, though it was further than he had estimated.

Just before dawn he pointed out to me the kopje, which he said was our objective, but it was then I should say about two miles off. I considered that as he reported the remainder of the road to be very good going, it was better, notwithstanding the fatigue of the men, to push on and seize the position. It became a question of doing this, or of retracing our steps to Molteno. The dawn was just breaking when the column was suddenly fired into, before the Mounted Infantry, who were kept behind the Infantry during the night march, had pushed out to cover the front.

Owing to the precipitous nature of the ground, the Artillery was unable for some time to find a suitable position, but one battery managed to come into action on the south end, while the second battery opened fire from the west of this kopje.

The retirement of the guns was steadily and carefully carried out by alternate batteries, covered by the Mounted Infantry, and Lieutenant-Colonel Jeffreys showed great judgment in the selection of positions.

It was not reported to me that the men of the Infantry regiments (who were subsequently taken prisoners) had not rejoined their regiments when I gave the order to fall back, and I was under the impression that they had reached the ridge, as I was with the Mounted Infantry the whole time, and had seen numbers of men of both regiments crossing the plain, falling back to where the regiments were assembling. It appears many of these men remained in the nullah under shelter of the banks instead of retiring to the second ridge to their regiments. When I saw no more men coming back I gave the order to the remaining battery of Artillery to move back, covered by the Mounted Infantry.

The retirement, though under Artillery fire, was steadily conducted.

I much regret the serious loss in Officers and men entailed by the non-success of the operation.

An eye sketch of the country and a nominal roll of Officers wounded and missing are attached.* I bring the names of-

Second Lieutenant Duncombe-Shafto;

No. N.F. 2270, Band Sergeant J. Stone;

No. N.F. 1989, Colour-Sergeant A. Landen;

No. N.F. 3923, Private G. Benson,

2nd Battalion Northumberland Fusiliers, to the notice of the Commander-in-Chief.

Major E.M. Perceval, 77th Battery, Royal Field Artillery, though severely wounded, continued to command his battery till the end of the day, and I would wish to bring his name prominently to notice in this connection.

W. GATACRE, Lieutenant-General,
Commanding 3rd Division.

19th January 1900.

*Not printed.

5

THE BATTLE OF MAGERSFONTEIN

FRIDAY, MARCH 16, 1900.

War Office, March 16, 1900.

THE following Despatch has been received from Field-Marshal Lord Roberts, V.C., G.C.B., &c., Commanding-in-Chief, South Africa:-

From Field-Marshal Lord Roberts to the Secretary of State for War.

Army Head-Quarters, South Africa,
Camp, Jacobsdal,
MY LORD,   *February* 17, 1900.

1. I HAVE the honour to forward a Despatch, which Lieutenant-General Lord Methuen has prepared on the action at Magersfontein, on the 10th and 11th December, 1899.

2. Lord Methuen has been requested to expedite the submission of the complete list of the Officers and men belonging to the Black Watch, whom he considers worthy of special mention.

I have, &c.,
ROBERTS, Field-Marshal,
Commanding-in-chief, South Africa.

Modder River Camp,
SIR,   *February* 15, 1900.

1. I HAVE the honour to inform you that any further advance by the railway was out of the question, owing to the large kopjes on either side which had been strongly entrenched. Besides, there was not sufficient water by that route to Kimberley.

2. Anticipating my possible advance along the Modder River, the enemy had entrenched a very strong position running north-west.

3. The northern portion of the position consists of a kopje about 3 miles long, the southern end terminating in a high hill which is the key of the position. From the south end of this kopje, an underfeature, covered with low bush, extends about 5 miles to the Modder River. This portion of the position was also entrenched.

4. So long as this kopje, named Majesfontein, remained in possession of the enemy, I did not feel justified with my small force in marching up the Modder River, for my line of communication would have been in danger, and my transport could only carry five days' provisions. Had I marched round by Jacobsdal to Brown's Drift, I should have had to fight my way across the river in the face of a mobile force consisting of 16,000 men.

5. Had I elected to fight my way through the bushy ground with small slope between Majesfontein and the Modder River, I should have incurred very heavy loss, and in addition to the guns not being able to render me very great assistance, they would run a good chance of being captured.

6. In any case I had to be prepared for a second heavy action at Spytfontein, and a blow dealt to the enemy's centre at Majesfontein would render any future fight at Spytfontein easier than any success on their left flank could have done.

7. The reconnaissance work had been extremely difficult on account of the large amount of wire between the two rivers, whilst on the north side of the Modder, owing to the enemy's entrenchments, the Cavalry had not been able to advance any great distance.

8. My orders were to relieve Kimberley, and the longer I remained inactive the stronger the enemy would become in my front. Therefore, on the day my last reinforcement arrived I decided to continue my advance to Kimberley, and attack the Majesfontein Kopje.

9. With this purpose I gave orders for the kopje to be bombarded from 4.50 P.M. to 6.40 P.M. on the 10th December with all my guns, including the naval 4.7-inch.

10. At daybreak on 11th December the southern end of the kopje was to be assaulted by the Highland Brigade, supported by all the guns, their right and rear being protected by the Guards Brigade.

11. Judging from the moral effect produced by the guns in my three previous actions, and the additional anticipated effect of lyddite, I expected great destruction of life in the trenches, and a considerable demoralizing effect on the enemy's nerves, thereby indirectly assisting the attack at daybreak.

12. In accordance with the orders issued, of which I attach a copy, the Artillery on the 10th fired with accuracy and effect on the kopje, and the trenches at the foot from 4.30 P.M. to 6.45 P.M.

13. The night march was ordered for 12.30 A.M., the bearings and distance having been ascertained at great personal risk by Major Benson, Royal

Artillery, my Deputy-Assistant Adjutant-General (A). The distance is 2½ miles, and daybreak was due at 3.25 A.M.

14. About half an hour after the Highland Brigade marched off it came on to pour, a heavy thunderstorm accompanying the rain. The downpour lasted until daybreak.

15. The Brigade was led with perfect accuracy to the point of assault by Major Benson. The advance was slow, even for a night march. Major Benson, with a compass in each hand, had frequently to halt on account of the lightning and rifles affecting the compasses.

16. I may remark that two rifles went off by accident before the march commenced, and it is pretty clear flashes from a lantern gave the enemy timely notice of the march.

17. Before moving off, Major-General Wauchope explained all he intended to do and the particular part each battalion of his brigade was to play in the scheme. Namely, that he intended to march direct on the south-west spur of the kopje, and on arrival near the objective before daybreak the Black Watch were to move to the east of the kopje, where he believed the enemy to be posted under shelter, whilst the Seaforth Highlanders were to march straight to the south-east point of the kopje, with the Argyll and Sutherland Highlanders prolonging the line to the left; the Highland Light Infantry to be in reserve until the action was developed.

The Brigade was to march in mass of quarter columns, the four battalions keeping touch, and if necessary ropes were to be used for the left guides; these ropes were taken, but I believe used by only two battalions.

The three battalions were to extend just before daybreak, two companies in firing line, two companies in support, and four companies in reserve, all at five paces interval between them.

18. What happened was as follows:- Not finding any signs of the enemy on the right flank just before daybreak, which took place at 4 A.M., as the Brigade was approaching the foot of the kopje, Major-General Wauchope gave the order for the Black Watch to extend, but to direct its advance on the spur in front, the Seaforth Highlanders to prolong to the left, the Argyll and Sutherland Highlanders to prolong to the right, the Highland Light Infantry in reserve. Five minutes earlier (the kopje looming in the distance), Major Benson had asked Major-General Wauchope if he did not consider it to be time to deploy. Lieutenant Colonel Hughes-Hallett states that the extension could have taken place 200 yards sooner, but the leading battalion got thrown into confusion in the dark by a very thick bit of bush about 20 to

30 yards long. The Seaforth Highlanders went round this bush to the right, and had just got into its original position behind the Black Watch when the order to extend was given by Major-General Wauchope to the Black Watch. The Seaforth Highlanders and two companies of the Argyll and Sutherland Highlanders were also moving out, and were in the act of extending when suddenly a heavy fire was poured in by the enemy, most of the bullets going over the men.

Lieutenant-Colonel Hughes-Hallett at once ordered the Seaforths to fix bayonets and charge the position.

The Officers commanding the other battalions acted in a similar manner. At this moment someone gave the word "Retire." Part of the Black Watch then rushed back through the ranks of the Seaforths. Lieutenant-Colonel Hughes-Hallett ordered his men to halt and lie down, and not to retire. It was now becoming quite light, and some of the Black Watch were a little in front, to the left of the Seaforths.

19. The Artillery, advancing to the support of the attack, had opened fire from the time it was light enough to see.

20. No orders having been received by the Seaforths, the Commanding Officer advanced the leading units to try and reach the trenches, which were about 400 yards off; but the Officers and half the men fell before a very heavy fire, which opened as soon as the men moved. About ten minutes later the Seaforths tried another rush,

with the same result. Colonel Hughes-Hallett then considered it best to remain where he was till orders came.

21. Meanwhile the 9th Lancers, the 12th Lancers, "G" Battery, Royal Horse Artillery, and Mounted Infantry were working on the right flank.

22. At 12 midnight on the 10th the 12th Lancers and Guards marched from camp, the former to join the Cavalry Brigade, the latter to protect the rear and right of the Highland Brigade. Considering the night, it does Major-General Sir Henry Colvile immense credit that he carried out his orders to the letter, as did Major-General Babington.

23. A heavy fire was maintained the whole morning. The Guards Brigade held a front of about 1¾ miles. The Yorkshire Light Infantry protected my right flank with five companies, three companies being left at a drift.

24. Captain Jones, Royal Engineers, and Lieutenant Grubb were with the Balloon section, and gave me valuable information during the day. I learnt from this source, at about 12 noon, that the enemy were receiving large reinforcements from Abutsdam and from Spytfontein.

25. The enemy held their own on this part of the field, for the underfeature was strongly entrenched, concealed by small bushes, and on slight undulations.

26. At 12 noon, I ordered the battalion of "Gordons," which was with the supply column, to support the Highland Brigade. The trenches, even after the bombardment by lyddite and shrapnel since daybreak, were too strongly held to be cleared.

27. The "Gordons" advanced in separate half battalions, and though the attack could not be carried home, the battalion did splendid work throughout the day.

28. At 1 P.M., the Seaforth Highlanders found themselves exposed to a heavy crossfire, the enemy trying to get round to the right. The Commanding Officer brought his left forward. An order to "Retire" was given, and it was at this time that the greater part of the casualties occurred. The retirement continued for 500 yards, and the "Highlanders" remained there till dusk. Lieutenant-Colonel Downman, Commanding Gordons, gave the order to retire, because he found his position untenable, so soon as the Seaforth Highlanders made the turning movement to the right.

29. This was an unfortunate retirement, for Lieutenant-Colonel Hughes-Hallett had received instructions from me to remain in position until dusk, and the enemy were at this time quitting the trenches by tens and twenties.

30. I have made use of Lieutenant-Colonel Hughes-Hallett's report (the acting Brigadier) for the description of the part the Highland Brigade took in this action.

31. Major-General Wauchope told me, when I asked him the question, on the evening of the 10th, that he quite understood his orders, and made no further remark. He died at the head of the Brigade, in which his name will always remain honoured and respected. His high military reputation and attainments disarm all criticism. Every soldier in my Division deplores the loss of a fine soldier, and a true comrade.

32. The attack failed: the inclement weather was against success; the men in the Highland Brigade were ready enough to rally, but the paucity of Officers and non-commissioned officers rendered this no easy matter. I attach no blame to this splendid brigade. From noon until dark I held my own opposite to the enemy's entrenchments.

33. "G" Battery, Royal Horse Artillery, fired hard till dark, expending nearly 200 rounds per gun.

34. Nothing could exceed the conduct of the troops from the time of the failure of the attack at daybreak. There was not the slightest confusion, though the fight was carried on under as hard conditions as one can imagine, for the men had been on the move from midnight, and were suffering terribly from thirst. At 7.15 P.M. fighting ceased, the Highland Brigade formed up under cover, the Guards Brigade held my front, the Yorkshire Light Infantry secured my right flank, the Cavalry and guns were drawn in to behind the Infantry.

35. The men carried half ration, they had half ration given them from the Supply Column, and they had a lot of rum served out, as well as a good supply of water.

36. I decided that if I found the trenches vacated in the morning I would advance to Brown's Drift, occupying Magersfontein kopje; if, on the contrary, the entrenchments were still occupied, I would retire slowly to this place. The wounded I sent during the night to the rear, and also the Supply Column.

37. In the morning I found the trenches still occupied, and although Major-General Sir H. Colvile expressed his opinion that it would be advisable to hold on, I found, after going over the position with the senior Officers of my force, there was a concurrence of opinion that my judgment was sound and a retirement advisable.

38. I retired in excellent order at 12 noon, Sir H. Colvile, with the Guards, Cavalry, and Artillery, covering the retirement. About 300 of the "Gordons" volunteered to act as stretcher bearers to carry back the wounded to camp. There were only two casualties during the retirement.

39. I have to express my appreciation of the clear orders given out, and the careful arrangements made by Colonel Douglas, A.D.C., my Chief Staff Officer, for the attack.

 Major-General Sir Henry Colvile showed coolness and judgment throughout two trying days.

 The same remark applies to Major-General Babington.

 I again recognize the business-like manner in which Lieutenant-Colonel Hall, Commanding Royal Artillery, carries out his duties in the field.

 Major Bannatine Allason performed splendid work, and assisted greatly in checking the enemy on the right of our attack.

 Lieutenant Cuthbert, Scots Guards, my extra Aide-de- Camp, showed considerable coolness in taking a message from me to the Gordon Highlanders. A volley was fired at him, killing his horse; he took off wallets and saddle and returned, letting me learn from others how he had behaved.

Major Milton, Commanding Mounted Infantry, behaved gallantly, and was shot three times before he died; he was making a successful effort to rally some men of the Highland Brigade.

Lieutenant-Colonel the Earl of Airlie did excellent work with two dismounted squadrons, when good service was much needed.

Major Little, in the firing line, did good work all day.

Lieutenant Allhusen, 9th Lancers, and Lieutenant Macnaghten, 12th Lancers, did good work with their Maxims.

Major Maberly, Royal Horse Artillery, acting galloper to Major-General Babington, after rallying 30 or 40 men of different regiments, was severely wounded.

Major O'Donnell, Royal Army Medical Corps, and Lieutenant Delap, Royal Army Medical Corps, were indefatigable in attending wounded under fire. Lieutenant-Colonel Codrington, Officer Commanding Coldstream Guards, though wounded, insisted on remaining in command of his battalion till nightfall.

Major the Honourable W. Lambton, Coldstream Guards, refused to be carried because the bearers were exposed to fire. He remained on the ground 37 hours without food or water.

Captain the Master of Ruthven, Scots Guards, performed, as on several other occasions, valuable services.

Major the Marquis of Winchester was killed whilst displaying almost reckless courage.

Sergeant Wilkinson, 2nd Battalion Coldstream Guards, showed great courage in collecting ammunition. Corporal Bartlet, 2nd Battalion Coldstream Guards, under a very heavy fire, went 1,000 yards to get a stretcher for Major Milton.

Corporal Webb, 2nd Battalion Coldstream Guards, showed great courage in taking messages.

Corporal Munro, of the Black Watch, and Lieutenant Hore-Ruthven, of the Black Watch, carried the Marquis of Winchester out of action after he was hit.

The Brigade Major, Captain Ruggles-Brise, and the Aide-de-Camp of Sir H. Colvile's Staff, again earn honourable mention, not only in delivering orders, but also for their clear and accurate description of the position.

Captain A. Campbell, Argyll and Sutherland Highlanders, displayed great coolness throughout the day, and helped to dress the wounds of Captain Gordon under a hot fire.

Lance-Corporal Ray, No. 6766, and Private Phipps, No. 3724, specially mentioned by Major-General Babington as having helped him to rally men and taking them into the firing line.

Highland Light Infantry.

Major Garland performed good service throughout the day.

Major the Honourable H. Anson performed good service throughout the day.

Captain Richardson and Captain Wolfe Murray were wounded, but remained in the front with their companies.

Captain and Adjutant Cowan, D.S.O., gallantly led and rallied his men, and was killed at close quarters.

Sergeant-Major Stevens rallied men.

No. 4050 Sergeant McDonald, gallant behaviour specially brought to notice for carrying messages to guns, and to Medical Officer under heavy fire.

No. 4896 Lance-Corporal Fraser, No. 4653 Sergeant Piper Ross, and No. 4741 Piper McLellan specially brought to notice for their cheery conduct under fire and helping to rally men.

No. 3113 Corporal Shaul brought to notice for several specific cases of bravery when in charge of the stretcher bearers of the battalion.

No. 3269 Private Peat, No. 3426 Private Richmond, and No. 1674 Private Stewart, excellent service and setting a good example to their comrades.

Gordon Highlanders.

Captain E.B. Towse recommended for special reward by his Commanding Officer for his gallantry and devotion in assisting the late Colonel Downman when mortally wounded in the retirement, and when close up to the front of the firing line. He endeavoured to carry Colonel Downman on his back, but finding this not possible supported him till joined by Colour-Sergeant Nelson and Lance-Corporal Hodgson. The conduct of these non-commissioned officers is described as admirable.

Seaforth Highlanders.

Captain the Honourable Forbes Sempill, conspicuous and gallant manner in which he rallied and led his men straight up to the front.

Lieutenant Grant did good service taking messages to the front from Colonel Hughes-Hallett under a heavy fire.

Lieutenant Lindsay, very gallant and conspicuous behaviour when in charge of the Maxim gun.

Band Sergeant Hoare, conspicuous for his coolness and gallantry during the day in helping Dr. Ensor to succour wounded. Personally carried Captain Fetherstonhaugh (wounded) on his back some 800 yards to the dressing station.

Black Watch.

Lieutenant Douglas, Royal Army Medical Corps, showed great gallantry and devotion, under a very severe fire, in advancing in the open and attending to Captain Gordon (Gordon Highlanders), who was wounded; also attending to Major Robinson and other wounded men under a fearful fire.

Corporal Gayner, Black Watch, rallying men, and by his example encouraging his comrades.

Private A. Bettington, Cape Mounted Rifles, attached to Cape Medical Corps, and Private Johnson, Argyll and Sutherland Highlanders, were instrumental in removing a wounded Highlander from the front under a heavy fire.

The complete list of the men and Officers considered worthy of special mention in the Black Watch I have not yet been able to obtain. I would add that I left Major-General Pole-Carew, C.B., at Modder River Camp with the 9th Brigade, minus the battalion of Yorkshire Light Infantry; he has also Rimington's Guides, and the Naval 4.7-inch. He carried out his orders quite correctly, making a diversion against Majersfontein Ridge along the railway.

I am, Sir,
Your obedient Servant,
METHUEN, Lieutenant-General,
Commanding 1st Division.

6

THE BATTLE OF SPION KOP

War Office, April 17, 1900.
THE following Despatch, with its enclosures, has been received from Field-Marshal Lord Roberts, V.C., G.C.B., &c., Commanding-in-Chief, South Africa:-

To the Secretary of State for War.

Army Head-quarters, South Africa,
Camp, Dekiel Drift, Riet Kiver,
MY LORD,   13th February, 1900.

I HAVE the honour to submit, for your Lordship's information, despatches from General Sir Redvers Buller, describing the advance across the Tugela River on the 17th and 18th January, 1900, and the capture and evacuation of the Spion Kop position on the 23rd and 24th January, as well as certain minor operations between the 19th and 24th January on the right or eastern line of advance.

2. The plan of operations is not very clearly described in the despatches themselves, but it may be gathered from them, and the accompanying documents themselves that the original intention was to cross the Tugela at or near Trichardt's Drift, and thence by following the road past "Fair View" and "Acton Homes," to gain the open plain north of Spion Kop, the Boer position in front of Potgieter's Drift being too strong to be taken by direct attack. The whole force, less one brigade, was placed under the orders of Sir Charles Warren, who, the day after he had crossed the Tugela, seems to have consulted his General, and principal Staff Officers, and to have come to the conclusion that the flanking movement which Sir Redvers Buller had mentioned in his secret instructions was impracticable on account of the insufficiency of supplies. He accordingly decided to advance by the more direct road leading north-east and branching off from a point east of "Three Tree Hill." The selection of this road necessitated the capture and retention of Spion Kop, but whether it would have been equally necessary to occupy Spion Kop, had the line of advance indicated by Sir Redvers Buller been followed, is not stated in the correspondence. As Sir Charles Warren considered it impossible to make the wide flanking movement which was recommended, if not actually prescribed, in his secret instructions, he should at once have

acquainted Sir Redvers Buller with the course of action which he proposed to adopt. There is nothing to show whether he did so or not, but it seems only fair to Sir Charles Warren to point out that Sir Redvers Buller appears throughout to have been aware of what was happening. On several occasions he was present during the operations. He repeatedly gave advice to his subordinate Commander, and on the day after the withdrawal from Spion Kop he resumed the chief command.

3. As regards the withdrawal of the troops from the Spion Kop position, which, though occupied almost without opposition in the early morning of the 24th January, had to be held throughout the day under an extremely heavy fire, and the retention of which had become essential to the relief of Ladysmith, I regret that I am unable to concur with Sir Redvers Buller in thinking that Lieut.-Colonel Thorneycroft exercised a wise discretion in ordering the troops to retire. Even admitting that due preparations may not have been made for strengthening the position during the night, reorganizing the defence, and bringing up artillery – in regard to which Sir Charles Warren's report does not altogether bear out Sir Redvers Buller's contention – admitting also that the senior Officers on the summit of the hill might have been more promptly informed of the measures taken by Sir Charles Warren to support and reinforce them, I am of opinion that Lieut.-Colonel Thorneycroft's assumption of responsibility and authority was wholly inexcusable. During the night the enemy's fire, if it did not cease altogether, could not have been formidable, and, though lamp signalling was not possible at the time, owing to the supply of oil having failed, it would not have taken more than two or three hours at most for Lieut.-Colonel Thorneycroft to communicate by messenger with Major-General Coke or Sir Charles Warren, and to receive a reply. Major-General Coke appears to have left Spion Kop, at 9.30 p.m., for the purpose of consulting with Sir Charles Warren, and up to that hour the idea of a withdrawal had not been entertained. Yet almost immediately after Major-General Coke's departure Lieut.-Colonel Thorneycroft issued an order, without reference to superior authority, which upset the whole plan of operations, and rendered unavailing the sacrifices which had already been made to carry it into effect.

On the other hand, it is only right to state that Lieut.-Colonel Thorneycroft appears to have behaved in a very gallant manner throughout the day, and it was doubtless due, in a great measure, to his exertions and example that the troops continued to hold the summit of the hill until directed to retire.

4. The conduct of Captain Phillips, Brigade-Major of the 10th Brigade, on the occasion in question, is deserving of high commendation. He did his best to rectify the mistake which was being made, but it was too late. Signalling

communication was not re-established until 2.30 a.m. on the 25th January, and by that time the Naval guns could not have reached the summit of the hill before daybreak. Major-General Coke did not return and Lieut.-Colonel Thorneycroft had gone away. Moreover, most of the troops had begun to leave the hill, and the working parties, with the half company of Royal Engineers, had also withdrawn.

5. It is to be regretted that Sir Charles Warren did not himself visit Spion Kop during the afternoon or evening, knowing as he did that the state of affairs there was very critical, and that the loss of the position would involve the failure of the operations. He was, consequently, obliged to summon Major-General Coke to his head-quarters in the evening in order that he might ascertain how matters were going on, and the command on Spion Kop thus devolved on Lieut.-Colonel Thorneycroft; but Major-General Coke was not aware of this. About midday, under instructions from Sir Redvers Buller, Sir Charles Warren had directed Lieut.-Colonel Thorneycroft to assume command on the summit of the hill, with the temporary rank of Brigadier-General, but this order was not communicated to Major-General Coke, who, until he left the position at 9.30 p.m. was under the impression that the command had devolved on Colonel Hill, as senior officer, after Colonel Crofton had been wounded. Omissions or mistakes of this nature may be trivial in themselves, yet may exercise an important influence on the course of events; and I think that Sir Redvers Buller is justified in remarking that "there was a want of organization and system which acted most unfavourably on the defence."

6. The attempt to relieve Ladysmith, described in these despatches, was well devised, and I agree with Sir Redvers Buller in thinking that it ought to have succeeded. That it failed may, in some measure, be due to the difficulties of the ground and the commanding positions held by the enemy – probably also to errors of judgment and want of administrative capacity on the part of Sir Charles Warren. But whatever faults Sir Charles Warren may have committed, the failure must also be ascribed to the disinclination of the Officer in supreme command to assert his authority and see that what he thought best was done, and also to the unwarrantable and needless assumption of responsibility by a subordinate Officer.

7. The gratifying feature in these despatches is the admirable behaviour of the troops throughout the operations.

I have, &c.,
ROBERTS, Field-Marshal,
Commander-in-Chief, South Africa.

From General Sir Redvers Buller to the Secretary of State for War.
(Through Field-Marshal Lord Roberts, G.C.B.,
Commander-in-Chief, Cape Town.)

Spearman's Hill,
SIR,   30th January, 1900.
I HAVE the honour to report that General Sir Charles Warren's Division
having arrived at Estcourt, less two battalions, 10th Brigade, which were left
at the Cape, by the 7th January, it moved to Frere on the 9th.

The column moved as ordered, but torrents of rain fell on the 9th, which
filled all the spruits, and, indeed, rendered many of them impassable for many
hours. To forward supply alone took 650 ox wagons, and as in the 16 miles
from Frere to Springfield there were three places at which all the wagons had
to be double spanned, and some required three spans, some idea may be
formed of the difficulties, but these were all successfully overcome by the
willing labours of the troops.

The 4th Brigade reached Springfield on the 12th in support of the mounted
troops who had surprised and seized the important position of Spearman's
Hill, commanding Potgieter's Drift, on the 11th.

By the 13th all troops were at Springfield and Spearman's Hill, and supply
was well forward.

On the 16th a reserve of 17 days' supply having been collected, General
Sir C. Warren, in command of the 2nd Division, the 11th Brigade of the
5th Division, the Brigade Division Royal Field Artillery, 5th Division, and
certain corps troops, including the Mounted Brigade, moved from Springfield
to Trichardt's Drift, which is about 6 miles west of Potgieter's.

I attach Sir C. Warren's report of his operations.

On the night of the 23rd, General Warren attacked Spion Kop, which
operation he has made the subject of a special report. On the morning of the
25th, finding that Spion Kop had been abandoned in the night, I decided to
withdraw General Warren's force; the troops had been continuously engaged
for a week, in circumstances entailing considerable hardships, there had been
very heavy losses on Spion Kop. I consequently assumed the command, commenced the withdrawal of the ox and heavy mule transports on the 25th; this
was completed by midday the 26th; by double spanning the loaded ox wagons
got over the drift at the rate of about eight per hour. The mule wagons went
over the pontoon bridge, but all the mules had to be taken out and the
vehicles passed over by hand. For about 7 hours of the night the drift could
not be used as it was dangerous in the dark, but the use of the pontoon went
on day and night. In addition to machine guns, six batteries of Royal Field
Artillery, and four howitzers, the following vehicles were passed:- ox wagons,

232, 10-span mule wagons, 98, 6-span, 107, 4-span, 52; total, 489 vehicles. In addition to these, the ambulances were working backwards and forwards evacuating the sick and wounded.

By 2 p.m. the 26th, all the ox wagons were over, and by 11.30 p.m. all the mule transports were across and the bridge clear for the troops. By 4 a.m. the 27th, all the troops were over, and by 8 a.m. the pontoons were gone and all was clear. The troops had all reached their new camps by 10 a.m. The marches averaged for the mounted troops, about 7 miles, and for the Infantry and Artillery an average of 5 miles. Everything worked without a hitch, and the arrangements reflected great credit on the Staff of all degrees; but I must especially mention Major Irwin, R.E., and his men of the Pontoon Troop, who were untiring. When all men were over, the chesses of the pontoon bridge were so worn by the traffic, that I do not think they would have lasted another half hour.

Thus ended an expedition which I think ought to have succeeded. We have suffered very heavy losses, and lost many whom we can ill spare; but, on the other hand, we have inflicted as great or greater losses upon the enemy than they have upon us, and they are, by all accounts, thoroughly disheartened; while our troops are, I am glad and proud to say, in excellent fettle.

I have, &c.,
REDVERS BULLER,
General Officer Commanding.

From Lieutenant-General Sir C, Warren, to the Chief of the Staff.

Hatting's Farm,
29th January, 1900.

SIR,
I HAVE the honour to make the following report on the operations on the north side of Tugela, west of Spion Kop, from the 17th to the 27th of January, 1900:-

1. On the 8th January field orders were published constituting the 10th Brigade of the 5th Division a Corps Brigade, and placing the 4th Brigade in the 5th Division. The 5th Division thus constituted marched from Frere on the 10th instant, arriving at Springfield on the 12th instant.

2. On the 15th January I received your secret instructions to command a force to proceed across the Tugela, near Trichardt's Drift to the west of Spion Kop, recommending me to proceed forward, refusing my right (namely Spion Kop) and bringing my left forward to gain the open plain north of Spion Kop. This move was to commence as soon as supplies were all in, and the

10th Brigade (except two companies) removed from Springfield Bridge to Spearman's Hill.

3. I was provided with 4 days' rations with which I was to cross the Tugela, fight my way round to north of Spion Kop, and join your column opposite Potgieter's.

4. On the 15th January I made the arrangements for getting supplies, and moved the 10th Brigade on the following day; and on the evening of the 16th January I left Springfield with a force under my command, which amounted to an Army-Corps (less one brigade), and by a night march arrived at Trichardt's Drift, and took possession of the hills on the south side of the Tugela.

5. On the 17th January I threw pontoon bridges across the Tugela, passed the Infantry across by ponts, and captured the hills immediately commanding the drift on the north side with two brigades commanded by Generals Woodgate and Hart. The Commander-in-Chief was present during part of the day and gave some verbal directions to General Woodgate.

The Mounted Brigade passed over principally by the drift, and went over the country as far as Acton Homes, and on the following day (18th) had a successful action with a small party of Boers, bringing in 31 prisoners.

During the night of the 17th, and day of the 18th, the whole of the wagons belonging to the force were brought across the Tugela, and the artillery were in position outside of Wright's Farm.

6. On the 19th, two brigades advanced, occupying the slopes of the adjoining hills on the right, and the wagons were successfully brought to Venter's Spruit.

In the evening, after having examined the possible roads by which we could proceed, I assembled the General Officers and the Staff, and the Officer Commanding Royal Artillery, and Commanding Royal Engineer, and pointed out to them that of the two roads by which we could advance, the eastern one by Acton Homes must be rejected, because time would not allow of it, and with this all concurred. I then pointed out that the only possible way of all getting through by the road north of Fair View would be by taking 3 or 4 days' food in our haversacks, and sending all our wagons back across the Tugela; but before we could do this we must capture the position in front of us.

7. On the following day, 20th January, I placed two brigades and six batteries of Artillery at the disposal of General Sir C.F. Clery, with instructions to attack the Boer positions by a series of outflanking movements, and by the

end of the day, after fighting for 12 hours, we were in possession of the whole part of the hills, but found a strongly entrenched line on the comparatively flat country beyond us.

8. On the 21st, the Boers displayed considerable activity on our left, and the Commander-in-Chief desired me to move two batteries from right to left. At a subsequent date, during the day, I found it impossible to proceed without howitzers, and telegraphed for four from Potgieter's. These arrived early on the morning of the 22nd, and the Commander-in-Chief, arriving about the same time, directed me to place two of these howitzers on the left, two having already been placed on the right flank. I pointed out to the Commander-in-Chief that it would be impossible to get wagons through by the road leading past Fair View, unless we first took Spion Kop, which lies within about 2,000 yards of the road. The Commander-in-Chief agreed that Spion Kop would have to be taken. Accordingly that evening orders were drawn up giving the necessary instructions to General Talbot Coke to take Spion Kop that night, but, owing to an absence of sufficient reconnaissance, he requested that the attack might be put off for a day.

9. On the 23rd January the Commander-in-Chief came into camp, the attack on Spion Kop was decided upon, and Lieut.-Colonel àCourt, of the Head-quarter Staff, was directed by the Commander-in-Chief to accompany General Woodgate, who was detailed to command the attacking column. The account of the capture of Spion Kop is given in another report.

10. On the morning of the 25th January the Commander-in-Chief arrived, decided to retire the force, and assumed direct command. The whole of the wagons of the 5th Division were got down to the drift during the day, and were crossed over before 2 p.m. on the 26th January.

11. The arrangements for the retirement of the 5th Division were exceedingly well got out, and the retirement was made in good order during the night of the 26th, the whole of the troops crossing to the south side of the Tugela before daylight, and the wagons were packed, and the troops bivouacked near the spruit about 2 miles to the east of the pontoon bridges. About 10 p.m., previous to the retirement, heavy musketry was heard to the north of our position, which has been attributed to a Boer commando thinking we were going to make a night attack.

12. I propose to forward as soon as possible a more detailed report of the movements of brigades and units, and acts of individuals.

C. WARREN, Lieut.-General,
Commanding 5th Division.

From the General Officer Commanding, Natal, to the
Secretary of State for War.
(By the Field-Marshal Commanding-in-Chief, Cape Town.)

Spearman's Hill,
SIR,   30th January, 1900.

IN forwarding Lieut.-General Sir C. Warren's report on the capture and evacuation of Spion Kop, I have the honour to offer the following observations:-

Sir C. Warren is hardly correct in saying that he was only allowed 3½ days'
provisions. I had told him that transport for 3½ days would be sufficient
burden to him, but that I would keep him filled up as he wanted it. That he
was aware of this is shown by the following telegram which he sent on the day
in question. It is the only report I had from Sir C. Warren:-

(Sent 7.54 p.m. Received 8.15 p.m.)

"To Chief of the Staff,   "Left Flank, 19th January,
"I find there are only two roads by which we could possibly get from
Trichardt's Drift to Potgeiter's, on the north of the Tugela, one by Acton
Homes, the other by Fair View and Rosalie; the first I reject as too long, the
second is a very difficult road for a large number of wagons, unless the enemy
is thoroughly cleared out. I am, therefore, going to adopt some special
arrangements which will involve my stay at Venter's Laager for 2 or 3 days.
I will send in for further supplies and report progress. – WARREN."

The reply to this was that 3 days' supply was being sent.

I went over to Sir C. Warren on the 23rd. I pointed out to him that I had no
further report and no intimation of the special arrangements foreshadowed by
this telegram of the 19th, that for 4 days he had kept his men continuously
exposed to shell and rifle fire, perched on the edge of an almost precipitous
hill, that the position admitted of no second line, and the supports were
massed close behind the firing line in indefensible formations and that a panic
or sudden charge might send the whole lot in disorder down the hill at any
moment. I said it was too dangerous a situation to be prolonged, and that he
must either attack or I should withdraw his force. I advocated, as I had
previously done, an advance from his left. He said that he had the night before
ordered General Coke to assault Spion Kop, but the latter had objected to
undertaking a night attack on a position the road to which he had not
reconnoitred, and added that he intended to assault Spion Kop that night. I
suggested that as General Coke was still lame from the effects of a lately
broken leg, General Woodgate, who had two sound legs, was better adapted
for mountain climbing.

As no heliograph could, on account of the fire, be kept on the east side of Spion Kop, messages for Sir C. Warren were received by our signallers at Spearman and telegraphed to Sir C. Warren; thus I saw them before he did, as I was at the signal station. The telegram Sir C. Warren quotes did not give me confidence in its sender, and, at the moment, I could see that our men on the top had given way and that efforts were being made to rally them. I telegraphed to Sir C. Warren: "Unless you put some really good hard fighting man in command on the top you will lose the hill. I suggest Thorneycroft."

The statement that a staff officer reported direct to me during the day is a mistake. Colonel àCourt was sent down by General Woodgate almost as soon as he gained the summit.

I have not thought it necessary to order any investigation. If at sundown the defence of the summit had been taken regularly in hand, entrenchments laid out, gun emplacements prepared, the dead removed, the wounded collected, and, in fact the whole place brought under regular military command, and careful arrangements made for the supply of water and food to the scattered fighting line, the hills would have been held, I am sure. But no arrangements were made. General Coke appears to have been ordered away just as he would have been useful, and no one succeeded him; those on the top were ignorant of the fact that guns were coming up, and generally there was a want of organization and system that acted most unfavourably on the defence. It is admitted by all that Colonel Thorneycroft acted with the greatest gallantry throughout the day, and really saved the situation. Preparations for the second day's defence should have been organized during the day, and have been commenced at nightfall.

As this was not done, I think Colonel Thorneycroft exercised a wise discretion.

Our losses I regret to say were very heavy, but the enemy admitted to our doctors that theirs were equally severe, and though we were not successful in retaining the position, the losses inflicted on the enemy and the attack generally have had a marked effect upon them. I cannot close these remarks without bearing testimony to the gallant and admirable behaviour of the troops, the endurance shown by the Lancashire Fusiliers, the Middlesex Regiment, and Thorneycroft's Mounted Infantry was admirable, while the efforts of the 2nd Bn. Scottish Rifles and 3rd Bn. King's Royal Rifles were equally good, and the Royal Lancasters fought gallantly.

I am writing to catch the mail, and have not any particulars yet to enable me to report more fully on details.

I have, &c.,
REDVERS BULLER.

Report by Lieutenant-General Sir Charles Warren, K.C.B., upon the
Capture and subsequent Evacuation of Spion Kop.

CHIEF OF THE STAFF,
I MAKE the operations against Spion Kop in a separate report, because they
did not enter into my original plans.

Under the original instructions of the General Officer Commanding-
in-Chief, of 15th January, 1900, I was to act as circumstances required, but
according to instructions was generally to continue throughout refusing my
right and throwing my left forward until I gained the open plain north of
Spion Kop.

Upon the 19th of January, on arrival at Venter's Laager, I assembled all the
General Officers, Officers Commanding Royal Artillery, and Royal Engineers
of Divisions, and Staff Officers, together. I pointed out to them that, with the
three and a-half (3½) days' provisions allowed, it was impossible to advance by
the left road through Acton Homes. In this they unanimously concurred. I
showed them that the only possible road was that going over Fair View
through Rosalie, but I expressed my conviction that this could not be done
unless we sent the whole of our transport back across the Tugela, and
attempted to march through with our rations in our haversacks – without
impedimenta.

The hills were cleared on the following day, and very strong entrenchments
found behind them. The Commander-in-Chief was present on the 21st and
22nd January, and I pointed out the difficulties of marching along the road,
accompanied by wagons, without first taking Spion Kop.

Accordingly, on the night of the 22nd, I ordered General Coke to occupy
Spion Kop.

He, however, desired that the occupation might be deferred for a day in
order that he might make a reconnaissance with the Officers Commanding
battalions to be sent there.

On 23rd January, the Commander-in-Chief came into camp, and told me
that there were two courses open, (1) to attack, (2) to retire. I replied that I
should prefer to attack Spion Kop to retiring, and showed the Commander-
in-Chief my orders of the previous day.

The Commander-in-Chief then desired that I should put General Woodgate in command of the expedition, and detailed Lieut.-Colonel àCourt to
accompany him as Staff Officer.

The same evening General Woodgate proceeded with the Lancashire
Fusiliers, the Royal Lancaster Regiment, a portion of Thorneycroft's Horse,
and half company Royal Engineers, supported by two companies of the
Connaught Rangers and by the Imperial Light Infantry, the latter having just
arrived by Trichardt's Drift.

The attack and capture of Spion Kop was entirely successful. General Woodgate, having secured the summit on the 24th, reported that he had entrenched a position and hoped he was secure, but that the fog was too thick to permit him to see. The position was rushed without casualties, other than three men wounded.

Lieut.-Colonel àCourt came down in the morning and stated that everything was satisfactory and secure, and telegraphed to the Commander-in-Chief to that effect. Scarcely had he started on his return to head-quarters when a heliogram arrived from Colonel Crofton (Royal Lancaster). The message was: "Reinforce at once or all lost. General dead."

He also sent a similar message to Head-quarters. I immediately ordered General Coke to proceed to his assistance, and to take command of the troops. He started at once and was accompanied by the Middlesex and Dorsetshire Regiments.

I replied to Colonel Crofton: "I am sending two battalions, and the Imperial Light Infantry are on their way up. You must hold on to the last. No surrender."

This occurred about 10 a.m.

Shortly afterwards, I received a telegram from the Commander-in-Chief, ordering me to appoint Lieut.-Colonel Thorneycroft to the command of the summit. I accordingly had heliographed: "With the approval of the Commander-in-Chief, I place Lieut.-Colonel Thorneycroft in command of the summit, with the local rank of Brigadier-General."

For some hours after this message I could get no information from the summit. It appears that the signallers and their apparatus were destroyed by the heavy fire.

I repeatedly asked for Colonel Thorneycroft to state his view of the situation. At 1.20 p.m. I heliographed to ascertain whether Colonel Thorneycroft had assumed command, and at the same time asked General Coke to give me his views on the situation on Spion Kop. Still getting no reply, I asked whether General Coke was there, and subsequently received his view of the situation. He stated that, unless the Artillery could silence the enemy's guns, the men on the summit could not stand another complete day's shelling, and that the situation was extremely critical.

At 6.30 p.m. I asked if he could keep two battalions on the summit, removing the remainder out of reach of shells, also whether two battalions would suffice to hold the summit; this was in accordance with a telegram on the subject sent me by the Commander-in-Chief. Later in the evening I made arrangements to send two (Naval) 12-prs. and the Mountain Battery, Royal Artillery, to the summit, together with half company Royal Engineers (and working parties, two reliefs of 600 men each), to strengthen the entrenchments and provide shell covers for the men. I may here mention that the 17th Company, Royal Engineers, proceeded at the same time as General Woodgate's force, and were employed until daylight upon the entrenchments, then upon road making and water supply.

Sandbags were sent up early on the 24th instant.

While Colonel Sim was, with this party, ascending the hill, he met Colonel Thorneycroft descending, having evacuated the position.

I wish to bring to notice that I heard from all but one expression of the admirable conduct and bravery shown by Officers and men suffering under a withering Artillery fire on the summit of the slopes, and also of those who, with so much endurance, persisted in carrying up water and food and ammunition to the troops during this day.

During the day a Staff Officer of the Head-quarter Staff was present on the summit, and reported direct to the Commander-in-Chief.

At sunset I considered that the position could be held next day, provided that guns could be mounted and effective shelter provided. Both of these conditions were about to be fulfilled, as already mentioned.

In the absence of General Coke, whom I ordered to come to report in person as to the situation, the evacuation took place under orders, given upon his own responsibility, by Lieut.-Colonel Thorneycroft. This occurred in the face of the vigorous protests of General Coke's Brigade-Major, the Officer Commanding the Middlesex Regiment, and others.

It is a matter for the Commander-in-Chief to decide whether there should be an investigation into the question of the unauthorized evacuation of Spion Kop.

CHARLES WARREN,
Lieut.-General.

7

BATTLE OF PAARDEBERG

From Field-Marshal Lord Roberts to the Secretary of State for War.

Army Head-Quarters, South Africa,
Camp Paardeberg,

MY LORD,   28th February, 1900.

IN my letter No. 2, dated the 16th February, 1900, the narrative of the operations in the Orange Free State was carried up to the occupation of Jacobsdal, and the pursuit of the enemy in an easterly direction to Klip Drift, on the Modder River. On the above date 78 ox wagons loaded with stores, and two wagons containing Mauser rifles, explosives, and ammunition, were captured at Klip Drift, by the 6th Division. On the evening of that day I ordered the 9th Division, consisting of the 3rd and 19th Brigades under Lieutenant-General Sir Henry Colvile, to Klip Kraal Drift. Early the next morning Lieutenant-General Tucker, commanding the 7th Division, with the 14th Brigade, marched from Wegdraai Drift to Jacobsdal which the other brigade of the division, the 15th, under Major-General Wavell, had occupied since the 15th February.

On the 17th February arrangements were made for the military administration of Kimberley, and the protection of the railway line between that place and the Orange River. The command was entrusted to Lieutenant-General Lord Methuen, who was directed to move his head-quarters to Kimberley as soon as the railway had been repaired. The following troops were placed at his disposal:-

1,000 Imperial Yeomanry.
20th and 38th Batteries, Royal Field Artillery.
2 Canadian Field Batteries.
1 New South Wales Field Battery.
The 9th Infantry Brigade, consisting of-
   1st Battalion Northumberland Fusiliers.
   1st Battalion Loyal North Lancashire Regiment.
   2nd Battalion Northamptonshire Regiment.
   2nd Battalion Yorkshire Light Infantry.
A second Infantry Brigade consisting of-
   1st Battalion Highland Light Infantry.

3 Militia Battalions, leaving England on the 15th February, and due at
Cape Town about the 10th March.

On the arrival of the Militia Battalions, the 2nd Battalion Royal Warwickshire
Regiment is to join the 18th Brigade, and the 1st Battalion Munster Fusiliers
the 19th Brigade.

The 1st or Guards Brigade was thus set free to join the force operating in
the Orange Free State.

While leaving it to Lord Methuen to employ the troops under his command as he might think best, I impressed on him the desirability of holding
the Modder Railway Bridge with a battalion of Infantry in an entrenched
position, and of guarding other important points along the line. I also desired
him gradually to break up the Field Hospital at Modder River by the transfer
of the sick and wounded to Cape Town.

On the 17th and 18th February my head-quarters remained at Jacobsdal
with the 7th Division. On the former date the pursuing troops came into
contact with the enemy under Cronje below Paardeberg Drift. Throughout
the day a series of rear-guard actions took place, the enemy skilfully seizing
one defensible position after another and delaying our advance. The Boers
continued their retreat, and on the morning of the 18th were found to be
holding a position in the bed and on the north bank of the Modder, 3 miles
above Paardeberg Drift, where the river makes a curve to the north. In this
position they had begun to entrench themselves during the previous night.
As soon as our troops came up, the 6th Division occupied the ground to the
south of the stream opposite the Boer laager, with Mounted Infantry in its
front to the east. The Highland Brigade was also on the south side of the
Modder, while the19th Brigade of the same Division, under Major-General
Smith-Dorrien, advanced along the north side, on which also two Brigades of
Cavalry under Lieutenant-General French were converging from the direction of Kimberley. Early in the afternoon it seemed likely that the laager
would be captured, but the Boers held their ground so obstinately, and it was
so difficult to force a passage through the trees and undergrowth fringing
the river on both banks, that the troops had to be drawn off. Heavy loss was
inflicted on the enemy, while our own loss was hardly less serious, the
casualties being as follows:-

Officers (Duke of Cornwall's Light Infantry. – Lieutenant-Colonel W.
Aldworth, D.S.O.; Captain E.B. Wardlaw; Captain B.A. Newbury. Sea-
forth Highlanders. – 2nd Lieutenant R.H. McClure. Argyll and Sutherland
Highlanders. – Lieutenant G.E. Courtenay. West Riding Regiment. –
Lieutenant F.J. Siordet. 1st Battalion Yorkshire Regiment. – 2nd Lieu-
tenant A.C. Neave. Oxfordshire Light Infantry. – Lieutenant A.R. Bright;

2nd Lieutenant Y.A. Ball-Acton. King's Royal Rifles. – Captain J. Dewar; Lieutenant E. Percival. Norfolk Regiment. – Lieutenant J.C. Hylton-Joliffe. Seaforth Highlanders. – 2nd Lieutenant D.P. Monypenny. Mounted Infantry Staff. – Colonel O.C. Hannay. Welsh Regiment. – Lieutenant Angell) killed, 15; wounded, 54; missing, 8; prisoners, 3.

Men – killed, 183; wounded, 851; missing, 88; prisoners, 9.

The Officers and men shown as missing must, I am afraid, have been killed, as the enemy could not have sent prisoners to the rear, while only the numbers shown above as prisoners have been released by the eventual capture of the laager.

A kopje to the south-east of the position, commanding the Boer entrenchments, and the whole course of the stream from the Paardeberg Drift upwards, was captured during the afternoon of the 18th, but retaken by the enemy after nightfall, owing to the Mounted Infantry who held it having gone down to the river to water their horses.

On the evening of this day I directed the Brigade of Guards to march from their camp at Modder along the north bank of the river to Klip Drift. I also ordered the 14th Brigade of the 7th Division, under Major-General Sir Herbert Chermside, to proceed from Jacobsdal to the Paardeberg camp, distant about 30 miles, which was reached on the evening of the 19th.

Leaving Jacobsdal at 4 A.M. on the 19th, I reached Paardeberg at 10 A.M. When I arrived on the scene I learnt that an armistice of 24 hours had been granted to General Cronje, who had asked for it on the plea that he desired to bury his dead. This armistice I immediately revoked, and ordered a vigorous bombardment of the enemy's position. General Cronje knew, as we knew, that considerable reinforcements were hastening to his assistance from Natal and from the south, and his request was obviously only an expedient to gain time.

I found the troops in camp were much exhausted by their previous marching and fighting, and I therefore decided not to make a second assault on the laager, the capture of which by a "coup-de-main" would have entailed a further loss of life, which did not appear to me to be warranted by the military exigencies of the situation. During the morning of the 20th February the kopje on the south-east, which I have already mentioned, was recaptured, the enemy abandoning their defences on being threatened in rear by the Cavalry and Mounted Infantry. In the afternoon the Boer laager and the entrenchments surrounding it were bombarded for several hours with Naval guns, 5-inch howitzers and field guns, much damage being done to the enemy's wagons, trek oxen, and horses. On the 21st and 22nd the bombardment was continued, and trenches were gradually pushed forward on both flanks of the river, but chiefly on the north, in view of an eventual assault, should such an alternative be forced upon me.

After his force had been surrounded, Cronje contrived to open heliographic communication with Bloemfontein, and doubtless asked for assistance, as reinforcements began to come up in scattered parties of varying strength from the east and south-east. Each commando was composed of men belonging to different districts, some of them having been withdrawn from Ladysmith and others from the northern frontier of the Cape Colony. On the morning of the 23rd February the 1st Battalion Yorkshire Regiment engaged one of these parties, about 2,000 strong, at the eastern end of the position south of the river, and drove off the enemy with heavy loss, losing themselves 3 Officers and 17 men wounded. Later in the day the 2nd Battalion of the Buffs, which had come up in support of the Yorkshire Regiment, captured 80 Boer prisoners. Similar parties of the enemy appeared in other directions, but were beaten back without difficulty by our troops. After being repulsed the Boers seem in most cases to have dispersed, whether to their homes or to join other commandoes it is impossible to say.

On this day a balloon reconnaissance was made of the Boer laager and entrenchments, which showed that much injury had been done to the enemy's wagons and stores by shell fire. On the 24th February 40 more prisoners were taken and a considerable number of Natives came in from the enemy's camp both on this day and on the previous days, having managed to escape during the night time. The services of these Kaffir refugees are being utilised to look after trek oxen and slaughter cattle, about 800 of which were captured in the vicinity of the Boer laager. Our casualties from the 19th to the 24th February inclusive, were as follows:-

Officers – wounded, 12.
Men – killed, 9; wounded, 102; missing, 8.

Nothing calling for special notice occurred on the 25th February, except that heavy rain caused the Modder River to rise over 3 feet, and thus delayed the movement of convoys from and to the advanced base at the Modder Station as well as from and to Kimberley, where a supplementary Commissariat Depôt had been established. I may here mention that the railway to Kimberley was re-opened on the 18th, and that Lord Methuen established his headquarters there on the same day.

Early on the 26th four 6-inch howitzers arrived at this camp from Modder, and the Boer laager was again shelled during the afternoon.

At 3 A.M. on the 27th the Royal Canadian Regiment, and No. 7 Company, Royal Engineers, commanded respectively by Lieutenant-Colonel W.D. Otter and Lieutenant-Colonel W.F. Kincaid, supported by the 1st Battalion

Gordon Highlanders, advanced under a heavy rifle fire to within 80 yards of the enemy's defences, and succeeded in entrenching themselves, with the loss of 2 Officers wounded, 7 men killed, and 27 wounded. A gallant deed, creditable to all who took part in it.

At 6 A.M. I received a letter from General P.A. Cronje, making an unconditional surrender, and throwing himself and his troops on Her Majesty's clemency. The following is a translation:-

> "Head-quarter Laager,
> "Modder River,
> "27th February, 1900.

"Honoured Sir.

"Herewith I have the honour to inform you that the Council of War, which was held here last evening, resolved to surrender unconditionally with the forces here, being compelled to do so under existing circumstances. They therefore throw themselves on the clemency of Her Britannic Majesty.

"As a sign of surrender a white flag will be hoisted from 6 A.M. to-day. The Council of War requests that you will give immediate orders for all further hostilities to be stopped, in order that more loss of life may be prevented.

> "I have, &c.,
> "(Signed) P.A. CRONJE,
> "General.

"To Field Marshal Lord Roberts.

"P.S. – Messrs. G.R. Keizer, my secretary, and H.C. Penzhorn, are authorized to arrange all details with your Lordship."

Cronje was received by me in camp at 8 A.M., and he with the other prisoners, numbering 3,919 men, exclusive of 150 wounded, were despatched in the afternoon to Cape Town.

In addition to the prisoners' rifles and a large quantity of Mauser ammunition, three 7.5 centimetre Krupp field guns, one old pattern 12-pr. quick-firing gun, and one Vickers-Maxim automatic 3.7 centimetre quick-firing gun have been taken, as well as many ox and mule wagons.

A very large area has to be occupied in a country like this, consisting of flat plains with isolated hills or kopjes, to prevent the enemy from seizing one or more of the latter, and thence by long-range gun and rifle fire rendering the interior of the position untenable. The perimeter of the Paardeberg encampment surrounding the Boer laager was about 24 miles, and the distances from one point to another added greatly to the labours of the troops.

I enclose a list of prisoners taken on 27th February.

I am sanguine enough to hope that the complete defeat and surrender of Cronje will materially improve the prospects of the campaign. For over two months he held us in check at Magersfontein, and his following included many influential men both from the Orange Free State and from the South African Republic. The despatch of these men, with nearly 4,000 other prisoners, to Cape Town, cannot fail to encourage the loyal inhabitants of the Cape Colony and Natal, and to dishearten the disaffected, while the capture of one of their ablest and most determined commanders must inflict a severe blow on the Boer cause.

It is my present intention to halt here for about a week longer, in order to get the Cavalry and Artillery horses into better condition, replenish my supplies of food and ammunition, and prepare my transport train for a further advance. On reaching Bloemfontein I propose to reopen railway communication between that place and the Midland railway line, and to transfer my advanced base from the Modder River Station and Kimberley to Colesberg or Naauwpoort. In anticipation of this transfer, and to relieve the congested state of the docks at Cape Town, I have directed a number of vessels carrying stores and supplies to proceed to East London.

Since I last addressed your Lordship the situation on the frontier north of Naauwpoort has remained virtually unchanged. On the enemy at Colesberg being reinforced, Major-General Clements found it necessary to withdraw from Rensburg to Arundel, where he experienced no difficulty in maintaining his position. A portion of the Boer force has now retired for the purpose of covering Bloemfontein, and on the 27th February Rensburg was re-occupied by our troops.

On the eastern frontier Brigadier-General Brabant moved forward on the evening of the 16th February, and, after continuous fighting on the 17th, stormed the Boer position near Dordrecht.

On the 23rd February Lieutenant-General Gatacre made a reconnaissance in the direction of Stormberg, which showed that the hostile garrison had been reduced in men and guns. Our casualties on this occasion amounted to 2 killed, 2 wounded, and 6 missing, among the last being included Captain the Hon. R. de Montmorency, V.C., 21st Lancers, and Major P.R. Hockin, 2nd Devonshire Volunteer Artillery, two very promising Officers.

On the 24th February Lieutenant-General Sir W. Gatacre provided a garrison for Dordrecht by moving to that place from Bird River 2 guns, 2 companies of infantry, 50 signallers, and 50 mounted police. The garrison was directed to entrench and occupy a commanding position to the south of the town.

As regards Natal, the reports received from General Sir Redvers Buller are to the following effect. On the 14th February he attacked strong positions held by the enemy on the right bank of the Tugela immediately to the east of Colenso. These positions on the Cingolo and Monte Cristo heights covered the left flank of the Boers. Cingolo was gradually occupied by our troops, and on the 18th February the 4th and 6th Brigades assaulted the entrenchments on Monte Cristo, the enemy falling back after having offered but slight resistance, and being driven across the Tugela with the loss of their camps and supplies. Sir Redvers Buller has brought to special notice the work done by the 2nd Battalion The Queen's, 2nd Battalion Royal Scots Fusiliers, Rifle Brigade, and Irregular Cavalry; but all the troops are reported to have behaved admirably, and the Royal Artillery and Naval gun detachments to have rendered great assistance.

On the 21st February Sir Redvers Buller telegraphed that commandoes from the Bethlehem, Heilbron, and Senekal Districts had returned by train the previous week from Spion Kop to the Orange Free State. On the same date he reported that the 5th Division had that day crossed the Tugela by a pontoon bridge, driving back the enemy's rear guard.

Subsequent telegrams show that on the 22nd the 11th Brigade forced the passage of the Onderbrook Spruit and seized the Landrat heights which command it, while on the 23rd the 5th Brigade crossed the Langawachti Spruit and similarly occupied the adjacent heights. On the 25th the force had not advanced far enough to the north to keep down the enemy's long-range Artillery and Infantry fire, and the country is stated to be extremely difficult, but Sir Redvers Buller is endeavouring to turn the Boer position to the east, and hopes to succeed in outflanking the enemy and reaching Ladysmith.

Apart from the progress of the war, there are two matters affecting the force under my command, to which a brief reference seems desirable. On the 25th February, I telegraphed to your Lordship requesting that 100,000 khaki warm coats of the Indian pattern might be sent to the Cape Colony and Natal from India. These coats proved very serviceable during the expeditions on the North-west frontier in 1897–98, and will greatly conduce to the health and comfort of the troops in South Africa as soon as the cold season sets in. On the 26th February, in reply to a telegram from your Lordship, I asked for the 8th Infantry Division to be despatched to South Africa as quickly as possible, more troops being needed in my opinion to enable me to operate in sufficient strength in the Orange Free State and Transvaal.

I have, &c.,
ROBERTS, Field-Marshal,
Commanding-in-Chief,
South Africa.

8

THE RELIEF OF KIMBERLEY

SOUTH AFRICAN DESPATCHES.

War Office, February 8, 1901.
THE following Despatches and Enclosures have been received from Lord
Roberts, K.G., V.C., Commander-in-Chief, South Africa:-,

No. 1.
From Field-Marshal Lord Roberts to the Secretary of State for War.
Army Head-Quarters, South Africa.

Cape Town,
MY LORD,   6th February, 1900.
NOW that I have been nearly a month in South Africa, and will shortly be
leaving Cape Town for the operations which I propose to carry out for the
relief of Kimberley and in the Orange Free State, it seems desirable that I
should submit for the information of Her Majesty's Government a concise
account of the state of affairs in this country as I found them on my arrival on
the 10th January.

The force which was despatched from England between the 20th October
and the early part of December had been greatly scattered. The Army Corps
organization had been broken up, and even the formation of the Divisions and
Brigades materially differed from what had been originally contemplated. On
assuming the chief command, the first step which Sir Redvers Buller undertook was to despatch Lord Methuen with the Brigade of Guards, the 3rd, or
Highland Brigade, and a third Brigade, improvised from three and a half
battalions on the Lines of Communication which were immediately available,
for the relief of Kimberley. As your Lordship is aware, this force succeeded in
crossing the Modder River; but the subsequent attack on the Boer position at
Magersfontein having been repulsed, Lord Methuen fell back on the river,
where he has formed an entrenchment facing that thrown up by the enemy.

The original intention was that, simultaneously with Lord Methuen's
advance, Lieutenant-General Clery, with the Second Division, should operate
from Port Elizabeth by the Midland line of railway through Naauwpoort on
Colesberg, and that Lieutenant-General Gatacre should similarly move from
East London by the Eastern line of railway on Stormberg and Burghersdorp.

This plan for occupying the Northern frontier of the Colony had to be abandoned owing to the urgent demands for assistance from Natal. In the middle of November, Lieutenant-General Clery was sent to Durban with the 2nd, 4th, and 6th Brigades, being followed shortly afterwards by Sir Redvers Buller himself. On the 1st December, the 5th Brigade was ordered from Cape Town to Natal. With these reinforcements, and the force previously available, an attempt was made on the 15th December to effect the passage of the Tugela River in the vicinity of Colenso, but this having failed, Sir Redvers Buller was obliged to withdraw his troops to Chieveley. Meanwhile, the 5th Division had arrived at Cape Town, and after the action of the Tugela, Sir Redvers Buller directed its commander, Sir Charles Warren, with half of the 10th Brigade and the whole of the 11th Brigade, to proceed to Natal. Towards the end of November, the 1st Royal Dragoons and the 13th Hussars were also transferred to Natal, followed shortly afterwards by two squadrons of the 14th Hussars.

On arrival here on the 10th January, I found the state of affairs to be as follows:- On the west of the Cape Colony, Lieutenant-General Lord Methuen was occupying the position already described. Lieutenant-General French, with three Cavalry regiments and one and a half battalions of Infantry, was holding the line from Naauwpoort to Rensburg. Lieutenant-General Sir W.F. Gatacre, who had two batteries of Artillery and four and a half battalions under his orders, having been defeated in his attack on Stormberg, was occupying Sterkstroom and the country in its vicinity. In Natal, Sir Redvers Buller, having found himself unable to advance by the direct route to the relief of Ladysmith, had fallen back on Chieveley to await reinforcement by the 5th Division under Lieutenant-General Sir Charles Warren.

In view of the distance of my head-quarters from Natal, and of the fact that on the date of my arrival Sir Redvers Buller had made his dispositions for the second attempt to relieve Ladysmith, I thought it best to leave him a perfectly free hand, and not to interfere with his operations.

In the Cape Colony a serious feeling of unrest prevailed. The withdrawal of so large a portion of the Army Corps had encouraged the disloyal among the inhabitants, and I found that His Excellency the High Commissioner was extremely anxious as to whether it would be possible to preserve peace and order through-out the province. After consulting Sir Alfred Milner, I decided that it would be best to remain on the defensive until a sufficient force was available to enable an advance to be made into the Orange Free State. I hoped that the effect of such an advance, if adequately supported, would be to relieve the hostile pressure at Ladysmith, and between Ladysmith and the Tugela, and also between the Modder River and Kimberley. In pursuance of this policy, and with a view to facilitating offensive action as soon as the strength and organization of the troops at my disposal would admit of it, I directed Lieutenant-Generals Lord Methuen and Gatacre to remain strictly on the defensive. Lieutenant-General French, with his headquarters at Rensburg, was instructed to patrol the country round Colesberg, and to keep the enemy, into whose hands that place had fallen, from moving farther to the south. Shortly after my arrival, the troops of the 6th Division, under Lieutenant-General Kelly-Kenny, reached Cape Town, and were despatched to Naauwpoort, one of the brigades being temporarily detached for employment under Lieutenant-General French. The duty assigned to Lieutenant-General Kelly-Kenny was to allay unrest and check disaffection among the Colonial population, and to open up the railway line as far as possible from Middleburg in the direction of Stormberg.

A subject which from the first attracted my special attention was the development and organization of the Colonial forces, of which I was inclined to think that sufficient use had not been made. I therefore arranged for one mounted corps to be raised by Colonel Brabant, to whom, with the approval of the High Commissioner, the rank of Brigadier-General has been given. Inclusive of this corps, it is intended to place a body of Colonial mounted troops, about 3,000 strong, under Brigadier-General Brabant's command, on Lieutenant-General Gatacre's right flank, for the purpose of guarding the eastern portion of the Colony and pushing back the enemy from the neighbourhood of Stormberg. The head-quarters of this Colonial force will be at Dordrecht, where it will be in readiness to operate northward towards Jamestown. Two other regiments, designated at the particular request of the members "Roberts's" and "Kitchener's Horse," have also been formed, chiefly from men who have found their way to South Africa from various parts of the world. Additional corps are being raised by influential gentlemen in the Colony, and every encouragement and assistance are being given to the men who desire to enlist.

Shortly after my arrival the question of reinforcements had to be dealt with. I was reluctant to indent on the home Army for an 8th Infantry Division and an additional Cavalry Brigade, and I expressed the opinion that it would suffice to order out two more Line battalions (one from Malta and the other from Egypt), two companies of Mounted Infantry from Burma, and 13 Militia battalions from England for duty on the Lines of Communication. The failure of the second attempt to relieve Ladysmith may possibly necessitate the despatch of the larger reinforcement, which I was at first prepared to dispense with.

Since I have been here I have taken no steps to render active assistance to General Sir Redvers Buller, as he had a force at his disposal which seemed sufficient for the relief of Ladysmith, and, after being reinforced by the 5th Division, he had informed me that his task would not be rendered easier by a further addition to the number of his troops. Moreover, I had no troops to spare. The frontier of the Cape Colony was weakly held, and the attitude of a portion of the Colonists bordering the Orange Free State was in some cases doubtful, and in others disloyal. The conclusion I arrived at was that no sensible improvement in the military situation could be hoped for until we were prepared to carry the war into the enemy's country, and all my efforts have accordingly been exerted in that direction.

This plan was, however, attended with considerable difficulties. The two main roads leading from Cape Colony to the Orange Free State were held in force by the Boers at the points where those roads crossed the Orange River, and it seemed certain that the bridges over that river would be destroyed, if the enemy could be forced to retire to the northern bank. Moreover, I could not overlook the fact that, even if either of these routes could be utilized, the movement of an army solely by means of a line of railway is most tedious, if not practically impossible. The advantage is all on the side of the enemy, who can destroy the line and occupy defensible positions when and where they please. In a hilly, enclosed country, or where any large river has to be crossed, they can block the line altogether, as was proved in the case of Lieutenant-General Lord Methuen on the Modder River, of Lieutenant-General French on the Orange River, and of General Sir Redvers Buller on the Tugela.

A railway is of the greatest assistance, it is indeed essential to an army for the conveyance of stores and supplies from the base, and it is a most valuable adjunct if it runs in the direction of the objective, but, even then, a certain proportion of the troops must be equipped with wheel or pack transport to enable supplies to be collected, and to render the force sufficiently mobile to deal with many tactical difficulties which have to be surmounted owing to the greatly increased range and power of modern projectiles.

No organized transport corps existed when I arrived in South Africa. Some thousands of mules have been collected and a number of ox and mule wagons had been purchased, but what is known as the regimental system had been adopted, which consists in providing each unit with sufficient transport for its ammunition, baggage, and two or three days' supplies. Such a system may answer well enough for peace manoeuvres where the troops march short distances daily for a week or ten days, and where depôts are established in advance from which the regimental supplies can be replenished. But this system is quite unsuitable, for extensive operations in a district where no food, and scarcely any forage can be procured, where advance depôts cannot be formed, and where all the necessaries required by an army in the field have to be carried for a considerable distance. It is, moreover, a very extravagant system, for during a campaign every corps is not required to be continually on the move. A certain number have to garrison important points and guard lines of communication, and for these transport is not needed. On the regimental system, the transport attached to such corps would remain with them, and would therefore not be available for general purposes, or, in the event of its being taken away from them, no one would be specially responsible for its supervision.

Major-General Lord Kitchener's experience in this important matter co-incided with my own, and we decided that the first thing to be done was to form a properly organized Transport Department.

On the 26th January I received intelligence of Sir Redvers Buller's with-drawal from Spion Kop to Potgieter's Drift. The second attempt to relieve Ladysmith having failed, it has become imperatively necessary to give early effect to the policy indicated above. With this object I am collecting as large a force as possible to the north of the Orange River Railway Station, with a view of joining the troops under Lord Methuen's command, and proceeding, in the first instance, to relieve Kimberley. The Column, including Cavalry and Mounted Infantry, will number 35,000 men, with about 100 guns. On the relief of Kimberley being accomplished, I propose to leave a moderate garrison at that place, and with the remainder of the force, to move eastward for the purpose of threatening Bloemfontein and seizing some point on the railway between that place and Springfontein. This operation will, I trust, cause the Boers to reduce the force which they have concentrated round Ladysmith, and enable our garrison there to be relieved before the end of February.

In order to carry out the concentration north of the Orange River, I shall have to make use of the whole of the 6th and 7th Divisions, and am obliged to postpone the reinforcement of Lieutenant-General Gatacre's force, although it is barely sufficient effectively to control a civil population which contains many disturbing elements, or to regain possession of the territory which the enemy has invaded. I am compelled also to withdraw the greater part of the force under Lieutenant-General Kelly-Kenny from Naauwpoort and its neighbourhood, in spite of the importance of restoring railway communica-tion between Middleburg and Stormberg. The arrival of 15 additional battalions[*] of the Line and Militia will place matters on a better footing, but in view of the possibility that the third attempt to relieve Ladysmith may fail, the deadlock in Natal which will follow, and its probable effect on the South African population, I have reluctantly arrived at the conclusion that more troops are needed for the active prosecution of the war.

On the 28th January I applied for another Infantry Division and Cavalry Brigade from home. The Cavalry Brigade has been placed under orders for field service, but the despatch of the Infantry Division has I am informed been suspended for the present. If, as I hope, the relief of Ladysmith can be effected, at any rate as soon as the enemy's attention has been distracted by offensive operations on our part in the Orange Free State, the transfer of an Infantry Division from Natal to Cape Colony may perhaps become feasible. On this point, however, I shall be better able to offer an opinion when the result of the further operations in Natal is known.

It might appear at first sight that the force in this country is equal to the military requirements of the situation, but the difficulties of carrying on war in South Africa do not appear to be sufficiently appreciated by the British public. In an enemy's country, we should know exactly how we stood; but out here, we have not only to defeat the enemy on the northern frontier, but to maintain law and order within the Colonial limits. Ostensibly, the Dependency is loyal, and no doubt a large number of its inhabitants are sincerely attached to the British rule and strongly opposed to Boer domination. On the other hand, a considerable section would prefer a Republican form of government, and influenced by ties of blood and association, side with the Orange Free State and Transvaal. Even the public service at the Cape is not free from men whose sympathies with the enemy may lead them to divulge secrets and give valuable assistance to the Boer leaders in other ways.

I append tabular statements showing the strength of the troops in the Cape Colony and Natal respectively on the 31st January, 1900. The numbers as regards Natal are only approximate, as no recent returns are available.

I have, &c.,
ROBERTS, Field-Marshal,
Commanding-in- Chief,
South Africa.

*The Line battalions will not arrive until the middle of March.

Enclosure 1.
Effective Fighting Strength of Force in Natal on 31st January, 1900.
(Approximate only.)

At Ladysmith.

Cavalry – 4 regiments; total 1,200.
Artillery – 6 batteries Royal Field Artillery, 36 guns; total 36 guns and 1,080 men.
Infantry – 11 battalions, total 7,500*.

Between the Tugela River and Durban.

Cavalry – 2⅔ regiments, total 1,100.

Artillery –
  1 battery, Royal Horse Artillery, 6 guns,
  7⅓ batteries, Royal Field Artillery, 44 guns,
  1 mounted battery, 6 guns,
  1 howitzer battery, 6 guns; total 62 guns,
  1,800 men.

Infantry –
  5½ brigades, 16,500,
  Other than above, 800; total 17,300.

Colonial troops –
  Field Artillery, 22 guns; total 22 guns, 550 men.
  Mounted, 1,500,
  Dismounted, 800; total 2,300.
  Infantry Volunteers, 2,000.

Grand total, 34,830 men and 120 guns.

To above may be added –
  Royal Engineers, 1,100.
  Army Service and other departmental corps, 1,472.
  Sick – Number unknown.
  Men at depots, and otherwise employed – Number unknown.

Effective Fighting Strength of Force in Cape Colony on 31st January, 1900.

Cavalry – 8⅓ regiments; total 4,196.

Artillery –
  8 batteries, Royal Horse Artillery, 48 guns.
  12 batteries, Royal Field Artillery, 72 guns.
  2 howitzer batteries, 12 guns.
  2 siege companies, 12 guns.[†]
  1 siege company, 6 guns.[‡]
    Total 150 guns and 4,500 men.

Mounted Infantry; total 3,050.

Infantry—
  1st Brigade, 3,754.
  3rd   „   3,121.
  9th   „   2,754.
  13th   „   2,885.
  14th   „   3,322.
  15th   „   3,601.

Other than above, 14,372.§
  Total 33,809
Colonial troops –
  Cape Colony, mounted, 2,000.
  Over sea, mounted, 1,385.
    Total 3,385.
  Cape Colony, Infantry Volunteers, 2,960.
Grand total 51,900 men and 150 guns.
To above may be added –
  Royal Engineers, 2,000.
  Army Service and other departmental corps, 4,278.
  Sick, 2,118.
Grand total, including above, 60,296 men and 150 guns.

* Including 7th and 8th Brigades.
† 8 – 6 inch howitzers; 4 – 4.7 inch guns.
‡ 5 inch B.L. guns.
§ Including Royal Canadian Regiment, 925 strong.

From Field-Marshal Lord Roberts to the Secretary of State for War.
Army Head-Quarters, South Africa,

Camp Jacobsdal,
MY LORD,   16th February, 1900.
IN continuation of my letter No. 1, dated 6th February, 1900, I have the honour to report, for your Lordship's information, that I left Cape Town for the Modder River on the evening of that date, arriving at Lord Methuen's camp on the morning of the 8th. Before quitting the seat of Government I received a memorandum from the High Commissioner, in which Sir Alfred Milner reviewed the political and military situation, and laid stress on the possibility of a general rising among the disaffected Dutch population, should the Cape Colony be denuded of troops for the purpose of carrying on offensive operations in the Orange Free State. In reply I expressed the opinion that the military requirements of the case demanded an early advance into the enemy's country; that such an advance, if successful, would lessen the hostile pressure both on the northern frontier of the Colony and in Natal, that the relief of Kimberley had to be effected before the end of February,* and would set free most of the troops encamped on the Modder River, and that the arrival of considerable reinforcements from home, especially of Field Artillery, by the 19th February, would enable those points along the frontier which were weakly held to be materially strengthened. I trusted, therefore, that his Excellency's apprehensions would prove groundless. No doubt a

certain amount of risk had to be run, but protracted inaction seemed to me to involve more serious dangers than the bolder course which I have decided to adopt.

Since the date of my former letter important events have occurred in Natal. As your Lordship is aware, Sir Redvers Buller telegraphed on the 29th January to the effect that he had discovered a new drift to the east of the Spion Kop, and that in view of the objections to further delay in relieving Ladysmith he proposed to make a fresh attempt by that route as soon as a battery of Horse Artillery had reached him from India, without waiting to see what effect my intended operations in the Orange Free State might produce on the force opposed to him.

On the 6th February I received a telegram from Sir Redvers Buller reporting that he had pierced the enemy' line, and could hold the hill which divided their position, but that to drive back the enemy on either flank, and thus give his own artillery access to the Ladysmith plain 10 miles from Sir George White's position would cost him from 2,000 to 3,000 men, and success was doubtful. General Buller enquired if I thought that the chance of relieving Ladysmith was worth such a risk. On the same day I replied that Ladysmith must be relieved even at the cost anticipated. I urged Sir Redvers Buller to persevere, and desired him to point out to his troops that the honour of the Empire was in their hands, and to assure them that I had no doubt whatever of their being successful.

On the 9th February General Buller reported that he found himself not strong enough to relieve Ladysmith without reinforcements, and that, with the force at his disposal, he regarded the operation upon which he was engaged as impracticable.

As Sir Charles Warren confirms the views of Sir Redvers Buller, I have informed the latter that, though I have no wish to interfere with his dispositions, or to stop his harassing the Boers as much as possible, my original instructions must hold good.

I received reports on the 2nd February that parties of the enemy had been observed some 8 miles to the west of the railway between the Orange and Modder Rivers, their object apparently being either to injure the line or to get grazing for their horses and oxen. I therefore gave orders on the 3rd February for Major-General MacDonald with the Highland Brigade, two squadrons of the 9th Lancers, the 62nd Field Battery and No 7 Field Company, Royal Engineers, to move from the Modder camp down the left bank of the Modder River and make a show of constructing a small field redoubt commanding the Koodoosberg Drift, distant about 17 miles from the camp. The object I had in view was to threaten the enemy's line of communication from the west of the railway to their position at Magersfontein, and also to lead the Boers to believe that I intended to turn their entrenchments from the left of the Modder River camp.

The troops marched early on the 4th, bivouacked for the night at Fraser's Drift, and reached Koodoosberg Drift at 2 P.M. on the 5th, the enemy's scouts being met with as soon as the cavalry approached the drift. The position was reconnoitred that afternoon, and on the morning of the 6th February work was begun on the redoubt, a site for which was chosen on the north or right bank of the stream in close proximity to the drift. The enemy, however, had now occupied in some strength a kopje to the north of the drift, whence the site of the redoubt was within artillery range, and it became necessary to dislodge them. After some desultory fighting the southern portion of the kopje was occupied by the Highland Brigade, and fighting continued throughout the day, both on the summit of the hill and between it and the river. As the number of the enemy was manifestly increasing, Major-General MacDonald thought it desirable to ask for the reinforcement which had been held in readiness to support him. This, consisting of two batteries of Horse Artillery and a Brigade of Cavalry, under Major-General Babington, marched from the camp at Modder to Koodoosberg along the northern bank of the river, and arrived at about 3 P.M. on the 7th. The fight which had recommenced at daybreak continued until nightfall, the enemy gradually falling back, and being followed up by the Horse Artillery and Cavalry.

It being evident that permanently to hold the Koodoosberg Drift would require a larger force than could be spared, and the troops employed there being by this time required elsewhere, the Cavalry and Infantry Brigades were ordered to return to the Modder River camp, which they did on the 8th without molestation, the Boers having previously fallen back from the position.

I will now briefly describe the operations for the relief of Kimberley, the troops selected for this purpose being detailed in the annexed return.

On the 11th February the Cavalry Division, under Lieutenant-General French, with seven batteries of Horse Artillery and three Field batteries, proceeded from Modder River camp direct to Ramdam, the 7th Infantry Division, under Lieutenant-General Tucker, proceeding to the same point from the railway stations of Enslin and Graspan. On the 12th February I moved to Ramdam; the Cavalry Division marched to the Riet River, occupied with slight opposition the Dekiel and Waterval Drifts, and reconnoitred across the river; the 7th Division proceeded to the Dekiel Drift; and the 6th Division, under Lieutenant-General Kelly-Kenny, which had moved by rail to Enslin and Graspan, replaced the 7th at Ramdam. On the 13th February the Cavalry Division advanced to the Modder River, seizing the Ronddavel and Klip Drifts, while the 6th Division moved from Ramdam to the Waterval Drift on the Riet River. The 9th Division, under Lieutenant-General Sir

Henry Colvile, proceeded on this day to Ramdam, while the 7th Division was occupied in getting supply wagons across the Dekiel Drift, where I established my head-quarters. On the 14th February the Cavalry Division reconnoitred to the north of the Modder River; the 6th Division moved down the Riet River from the Waterval to the Wegdraai Drift; the 7th Division from the Dekiel Drift to the Waterval Drift, and the 9th Division from Ramdam to the Waterval Drift. My head-quarters were at the Waterval Drift.

For some time previous to this, I had been moving troops to the east of the Orange River station, in order to attract the enemy's attention to that quarter, and, if possible to give rise to the idea that my intention was to make for Bloemfontein, viâ Fauresmith.

A considerable force of Cavalry and Mounted Infantry was collected at Zoutpan's Drift, under the command of Colonel Hannay, and that Officer was ordered to proceed on the 11th February towards the Riet River, to act in conjunction with the Cavalry Division. Near Wolve Kraal Colonel Hannay came in contact with the Boers, who held the hills on his right flank. He handled his troops with ability, and while he contained the enemy with a portion of his force, he pushed his baggage and main body through to Ramdam.

Late in the evening of the 14th February, the 6th Division marched to Ronddavel Drift, on the Modder, and the 7th Division to the Wegdraai Drift, on the Riet. On this date troops from the 6th Division entered Jacobsdal, and found it deserted by the enemy, though the houses were still occupied by their women and children. The troops were fired on when returning to camp, and a further encounter took place on a stronger detachment being sent out to drive off the Boers. This detachment fell back before nightfall with the loss of eight killed and wounded. On the 15th February I proceeded from the Waterval Drift to Wegdraai, accompanied by the 9th Division.

During the day of the 14th I informed Lieutenant-General Kelly-Kenny how essential it was that he should join hands with Lieutenant-General French, in order to free the Cavalry for a further advance, and notwithstanding the long and fatiguing march of the previous day, the 6th Division pushed on that night across the veldt, and reached Klip Drift before day break on the 15th February.

Being thus free to act, Lieutenant-General French at 9.30 A.M. proceeded on his journey towards Kimberley. The enemy's suspicions had by this time been aroused, and they had been able to occupy two lines of kopjes, a few miles north of the Modder River, and through which the road to Kimberley viâ Abons Dam and Olifantsfontein runs. Bringing a fire to bear upon these kopjes by the Brigade Divisions of Horse Artillery, under command of Lieutenant-Colonels Eustace and Rochfort, and escorted by the 1st Cavalry

Brigade under Colonel Porter, Lieutenant-General French, with the 2nd and 3rd Brigades under Brigadier-Generals Broadwood and Gordon, and the Brigade Division Horse Artillery under Colonel Davidson, galloped through the defile in extended order until he reached some low hills from which he was able to cover the advance of the rear troops. Casualties – 1 Officer (Lieutenant A.E. Hesketh, 16th Lancers) killed, and 20 of all ranks wounded.

At Kimberley, the inhabitants were found to be in good health and spirits. On the 16th the 6th Division marched to Klip Drift and was opposed by the enemy, who were driven off with loss. The 9th Division joined the 7th at Wegdraai, 200 Mounted Infantry under Colonel Ridley being left behind at Waterval to escort a supply column of ox wagons thence to Wegdraai. Shortly after the departure of the 9th Division from Waterval, a Boer force with several guns, which must have come up during the night, attacked Colonel Ridley's detachment, and did a good deal of injury to the oxen and wagons of the supply column. On hearing of this, I sent back a reinforcement, consisting of one Field battery, one battalion, and 300 Mounted Infantry at 10 A.M., and subsequently despatched a second battery and battalion, on the arrival of which the enemy disappeared.

The native ox drivers had, however, taken to flight, so that it was impossible to inspan the ox teams. The wagons contained a quantity of supplies of groceries for the troops and of grain for animals, and I felt that to abandon them meant a considerable loss to the stores on which we had to depend. In view, however, of the absolute necessity of pushing on the advance, and realising, as I did, that to leave troops at Waterval Drift until such time as the convoy could again be set in motion would weaken my force and probably cause it to be delayed, I decided to abandon the supplies, wagons, and oxen, and to order the troops to withdraw to Wegdraai Drift during the night, which operation was carried out unmolested by the enemy.

At 11 A.M. on this day, I directed Major-General Wavell's Brigade, of the 7th Division, to occupy Jacobsdal, which was done with very slight opposition. The officers and men who had been wounded and taken prisoners the previous day were found in the hospital at this place, as well as several other wounded men, both British and Boer. All had been taken the greatest care of by the German Ambulance.

On the 16th February I moved my head-quarters to Jacobsdal, replenished my supplies from Honey Nest Kloof and the Modder camp, and established telegraphic communication between the latter place and Jacobsdal. The Cavalry Division has been following up the enemy to the north of Kimberley, and the 6th Division, which has marched to the east of Klip Drift, has been similarly occupied. By midday I received information from Lord Methuen that the Magersfontein entrenchments had been abandoned, and the latest reports point to a general retreat of the Boers in the direction of Bloem-fontein. It is my intention to follow them up as rapidly as possible, and by taking full advantage of the shock which they have sustained, to break up their organization as a fighting force. Lord Methuen has been ordered to proceed to Kimberley, after restoring the railway line, for the purpose of putting affairs into order, arranging for the military control of the town and district, and taking steps to re-open communication with Mafeking.

In conclusion I may mention a few matters of minor importance which have been dealt with during the last 10 days.

On my way from Cape Town to the Modder River I inspected the field hospitals at De Aar and Orange River, and finding the accommodation in-adequate gave orders for its being enlarged, and for more nurses' quarters being provided. I also arranged that additional nurses should be posted to these hospitals.

To meet medical requirements I have applied to your Lordship for the personnel needed to establish another general hospital in the vicinity of Cape Town.

One of the most pressing needs in South African warfare is the supply of a sufficient quantity of drinking water to the troops when marching, especially in the daytime, the climate being an extremely dry one and the sun's heat very trying. The number of water-carts at present available is inadequate. Moreover, these carts cannot follow the troops over stony or broken ground, and I have, therefore, asked for 2,000 bheesties, with a due proportion of mussacks and pakhals to be sent here from India.

I have, &c.,
ROBERTS, Field-Marshal,
Commanding-in-Chief,
South Africa.

*I had enquired by heliograph and been informed by Lieutenant-Colonel Kekewich that Kimberley could not hold out longer than the end of February.

9

THE SIEGE OF MAFEKING

Mafeking,
18th May, 1900.

MY LORD,

I HAVE the honour to forward herewith my report on the siege of Mafeking by the Boers, from 13th October, 1899, to 17th May, 1900, for the information of his Excellency the Field-Marshal Commanding in South Africa.

I have, &c.
R.S.S. BADEN-POWELL,
Major-General.

Table of Contents.

I. – Résumé of Report on the Siege of Mafeking.

I arrived in the beginning of August in Rhodesia, with orders-

1. To raise two regiments of Mounted Infantry.
2. In the event of war, to organize the defence of the Rhodesia and Bechuanaland frontiers.
3. As far as possible, to keep forces of the enemy occupied in this direction away from their own main forces.

I had the two regiments raised, equipped, supplied, and ready for service by the end of September.

As war became imminent, I saw that my force would be too weak to effect much if scattered along the whole border (500 miles), unless it were reinforced with some men and good guns. I reported this, but as none were available I decided to concentrate my two columns at Tuli and Mafeking respectively, as being the desirable points to hold.

Of the two, Mafeking seemed the more important for many reasons, strategical and Political-

1. Because it is the outpost for Kimberley and Cape Colony.
2. Also, equally, for the Protectorate and Rhodesia.

3. It threatens the weak flank of the Transvaal.
4. It is the head-centre of the large native districts of the north-west, with their 200,000 inhabitants.
5. It contains important railway stocks and shops.
6. Also large food and forage supplies.

Therefore I left the northern column in charge of Colonel Plumer, and went myself to Mafeking, and organized its defence.

Mafeking.
Mafeking is an open town, 1,000 yards square in open undulating country, on the north bank of the Molopo stream. Eight miles from the Transvaal border. White population about 1,000.

The native Stadt lies ½ mile south-west, and contains 6,000 inhabitants.

Defence Force.
700 whites, of whom 20 were Imperial Army, remainder Protectorate Regiment, British South Africa Police, Cape Police, and Bechuanaland Rifles (Volunteers). These were used to man the forts and outworks.

300 able-bodied townsmen, enrolled as town guard. Employed to garrison the town itself.

300 natives enrolled as cattle guards, watch-men, police, &c.

Half the defenders were armed with L.M., half with M.H. rifles, with 600 rounds per rifle.

Total Numbers.
White men, 1,074; white women, 229; white children, 405; natives, 7,500. Our armament consisted of-

Four 7-pounder M.L. guns, one 1-pounder Hotchkiss, one 2-inch Nordenfelt – all old.
Seven 303 Maxims.

To this armament we afterwards added-

One 6-pounder M.L. old ship's gun, one 16-pounder M.L. howitzer (made in our own shops).

I had two armoured engines promised from Kimberley. I had armoured trucks made at Bulawayo and Mafeking. One engine arrived, the other was cut off en route by the enemy and captured at Kraaipan.

The Siege.
On the 13th October the siege began.

General Cronje with an army of 8,000 Boers and 10 guns, most of them of modern pattern and power, surrounded the place.

On the approach of the enemy we sallied out and, in a sharp little engagement, dealt them a severe blow, by which they lost 53 killed and many more wounded, and which had a lasting moral effect.

During the first phase of the siege, October and November, General Cronje made various attempts to take the place. These attacks we beat off without difficulty in every case, and responded by sorties, varying their nature every time as far as possible, and making them so sudden and so quickly withdrawn as not to give the enemy's supports time to come up and overpower us. Of these "kicks" we delivered half-a-dozen, on 14th, 17th, 20th, 25th, 27th, 31st October, and 7th November (the Boers quote 14, but they include demonstrations and shelling of dummy forts, guns, and armoured trucks, &c., which we put up to draw their fire).

The enemy's losses in this period were very heavy as compared with ours-

Boers' losses – 287 killed, 800 wounded.*

Our losses – 35 killed, 101 wounded, 27 missing.

Cronje having lost a month of valuable time at Mafeking, now gave up the idea of taking the place by storm, and moved off south for Kimberley with 4,000 men and 6 guns (leaving General Snyman with the remainder, viz., 3,000 to 4,000 men and six guns, including a 94-pounder siege gun) to invest us.

Seeing then that we could not be relieved for many weeks, if not months, I took over into our own management all details such as hospital, municipality, police, treasury, post and telegraph, railway, native affairs, water supply, ordnance shops, &c.

I also took over all food, forage, liquor stores, and native supplies, &c., and put everybody on rations.

I had disposed my garrison over what some of my Officers considered a rather extended perimeter (about 5 or 6 miles), but everything was arranged for drawing in our horns if necessary. However, in the event we were able to maintain our original position, and even farther to extend it as became necessary.

The next phase lasted 3 months, November to January, during which Snyman pushed his works and trenches nearer to the place.

He also drew a cordon of natives around the whole.

His artillery kept up a continual bombardment on the town.

On our part, during January, February, and March, we pushed out counterworks, and gradually gained point after point of ground till we obtained grazing for our live stock, and finally (after a hard tussel in the "Brickfields," in trenching and counter-trenching up to within 70 yards of the enemy's works), we drove them back at all points out of range for rifle fire of the town.

During this period, owing to the careful and systematic sharp-shooting of our men, the enemy's losses continued to be largely in excess of ours. 40 per month killed was admitted by the Boer medical officer.

In April the enemy withdrew the siege gun, and contented themselves with investing us at a distance, and shelling our cattle in the hope of starving us into submission.

On the 12th May the enemy made a bold night attack on the place, and succeeded in getting into the Stadt with their storming party, but we beat back their supports and surrounded the remainder, inflicting on them a loss of 70 killed and wounded, and 108 prisoners, including Eloff their commandant (grandson of President Kruger).

In the meantime, Colonel Plumer had near Tuli prevented a force of Boers from invading Matabeleland from the south. After their retreat the rising of the river made the border comparatively safe, and I called him down to defend the railway and the Protectorate border (which were already being held by a small force organized from Bulawayo by Colonel Nicholson).

Colonel Plumer accordingly pushed down the line, repairing it to within 40 miles of Mafeking, and pushing back the enemy who had been holding it. He then established himself in a good position 35 miles north-west of us, where he was in touch by means of runners and pigeons, was able to afford refuge to our natives escaping out, and he was also able to put a stop to enemy's depredations and to give security to the natives throughout the Protectorate, his force being too small to effect more till reinforced. His presence enabled us to get rid of nearly 2,000 native women and children, which materially relieved the strain on our food supply.

Early in May, he was reinforced by Canadian Artillery and Queensland Infantry, &c., and on 15th he joined hands with a relief column from the south under Colonel Mahon.

And, on the 17th May, the relief of Mafeking was successfully effected by the combined columns, after a siege of 218 days.

One of the most noticeable features of the long and trying siege has been the loyalty, patience, and good feeling which have prevailed throughout the community, civil, military, and native. The steadiness and gallantry of the troops in action, and their cheerful acceptance of hardships, are beyond praise.

The ladies, and especially those who acted as nurses in the hospitals, displayed the greatest patience and fortitude.

Résumé of Points gained by the Rhodesian Frontier Force.
(October, 1899, to May, 1900).
I. – At Mafeking.

1. A force of 8,000 Boers and 10 guns was contained at the first outbreak of war, and prevented from either combining with the Tuli column, and

invading Rhodesia, or joining the forces against Kimberley. Cronje's commando was thus held here for a month.

2. From 2,000 to 3,000 Boers and eight guns (including a 94-pounder) were kept employed here for over 6 months.

3. The enemy expended considerably over 100 tons of ammunition, and lost over 1,000 men killed and wounded, and had four guns disabled and one captured.

4. Large stores of food and forage, and general stocks, were prevented from falling into the enemy's hands.

5. Valuable railway plant, including 18 locomotives, rolling stock, shops, coal, &c., were saved.

6. Refuge was given to a large number of British from the Transvaal.

7. Most of the local neighbouring tribes, and all those of the protectorate and South Matebeleland, remained loyal, which they could not have continued to do had Mafeking fallen and they been at the mercy of the Boers.

8. Loss of prestige to Cronje's force, who had apparently expected to take possession at once on first arrival, and had had proclamation printed annexing the district to the South African Republic.

9. Eloff and 108 Boers and foreigners made prisoners of war.

II. – The Rhodesian Column.

During the same period the northern portion of my force under Colonel Plumer (in spite of its small numbers and the exceptionally difficult country and trying climate in which it was operating) succeeded-

1. In holding and sending back the enemy in their attempt to invade Rhodesia, viâ Tuli.

2. In holding the Bulawayo railway for some 200 miles south of the Rhodesian border.

3. In giving direct support and protection to the natives in Khama's and Linchwe's domains, and Bathoen's and the Protectorate generally when threatened by the enemy.

4. In pushing down and repairing the railway in the face of the enemy to within 40 miles of Mafeking, and there establishing a place of security for our natives escaping from Mafeking, and collecting supplies ready to effect our relief of Mafeking on arrival of reinforcements.

III. – The Palapye Column.

A small column organized by Colonel Nicholson, from Bulawayo, with armoured trains, &c., held Mangwe, Palapye, Mochudi, &c., on the railway until Plumer's column was available for the duty.

The whole of the frontier force, north and south columns combined, numbered under 1,700, while the Boers during the early part of the campaign had between 9,000 and 10,000 out on their northern and north-western border.

Country operated over, between Mafeking and Tuli, 450 miles in length.

II. – Minor Points connected with the Siege.

(Alphabetically arranged.)

Ammunition.
Artillery.
Casualties.
Communications.
Civil administration.
Compensation.
Correspondents.
Defence accounts.
Defence works.
Enemy's artillery – fighting, treachery, field work.
Finance.
Food supply.
Fuel.
Garrison.
Hospital.
Natives.
Railway.
Relief Committee.
Specialities.
Staff.
Spies.
Transport.
Women's laager.

Artillery.

Our so-called artillery should of course have been entirely outclassed by the modern high velocity guns of the enemy, but in practice they managed to hold their own in spite of their using powder, shells, and fuzes all made in our own shops.

The artillery and also the ordnance shops were under Major Panzera, assisted by Lieutenant Daniell, British South Africa Police.

Casualties.

I. – Combatants.

Whites-

    Officers. – 6 killed and died of wounds; 15 wounded; 1 missing; total 22.

    Non-commissioned officers and men. – 61 killed and died of wounds; 103 wounded; 26 missing; 16 died; 5 accidents; total 211.

Total-

    Whites. – 67 killed and died of wounds: 118 wounded; 27 missing; 16 died; 5 accidents; total 233.

    Coloured. – 25 killed and died of wounds; 68 wounded; total 83. [*sic*]

Total combatants, 316.

II. – Non-combatants.

    Whites. – 4 killed and died of wounds; 5 wounded; 32 died; total 41.

    Natives. – 65 killed and died of wounds; 117 wounded; total 182.

    Baralongs. – 264 killed and died of wounds; total 264.

Total non-combatants, 487.

Total all casualties during siege, 803.

Out of 44 officers, 21 were killed, wounded, or missing.

Out of 975 men, 190 were killed, wounded, or missing.

Communications.
Local.

Telephone. – All outlying forts and look-out posts were connected up with head-quarters, under management of Mr. Howat, postmaster, and his staff. I was thus able to receive reports and issue orders for all parts of the defence instantaneously.

Postal. – To cover the heavy expenses of runners, and for the convenience of the public, postage was established at: 1*d.* for town, 3*d.* for outlying forts, 1*s.* for up country.

Signalling. – Heliograph, lamp, and flag signalling was established for defence purposes by brigade signallers, under Major Panzera and Serjeant-Major Moffat.

Megaphones were also made and used in outlying trenches and posts.

Phonophores were also used on the armoured train, attached to ordinary telegraph lines.

Distant.

Runners. – Native runners were employed twice weekly, or oftener when necessary, to take despatches, letters, &c., to our northern column. They had to be highly paid, as the risk of capture and death was very great.

I was thus practically in touch with my force on the railway, and through them with Colonel Nicholson at the base, and Colonel Plumer's column at Tuli.

Civil Administration.

I established, for the trial of all cases not directly amenable to military law, a Court of Summary Jurisdiction–

Members:

Resident Commissioner.
Resident Magistrate.
Town Commandant.
Officer Commanding Protectorate Regiment.
Chief Staff Officer.

At first it was a little difficult to make the civilians appreciate the restrictions of martial law, and, as times grew more critical, there came a tendency to spread rumours and to grumble, this had to be stopped.

I also published some explanatory remarks and advice on the working of martial law, &c., and these steps had a most marked effect, obedience to orders and a good spirit thenceforward prevailed in the garrison.

Compensation.

From the commencement of the siege careful record was kept of all shell-fire damage to property, and claims of owners considered and assessed. Total assessed, 16,462*l.* 10*s.* 2*d.* No promise was held out that Government would grant compensation, the proceedings were merely intended to assist the commission should one afterwards be assembled, and to protect Government against exorbitant claims.

A record was also made of losses suffered by refugees, in property, live-stock, &c.

All livestock killed or wounded by shell fire was bought at a fair price and utilized for food, so that the owners have no claims on this head, at the same time the value of the animals is in many cases not represented by cash, and it would be far more satisfactory to the owners if they could be repaid in kind. This is a point which I venture to suggest be taken into consideration when dealing with the Boers after the war; a substantial fine in cattle would touch them heavily without leaving them destitute, and the bestowal of such cattle on deserving and looted loyalists would give great satisfaction and be far more acceptable to them, and less expensive to Government, than grants of money.

Correspondents.

(Under Lieutenant to Hon. A. Hanbury-Tracy as Press Censor).
These gentlemen gave a certain amount of trouble at first, as for the most part they were more reporters than correspondents. Further reforms in the matter

of correspondents in the field are very desirable. The enemy derived a great deal of information as to our circumstances from the newspapers, not only the local ones, but also from the Colonial and English papers, in spite of a strict censorship on our part.

Defence Accounts.
(Under Captain Greener, British South Africa Police).
Expenditure during the siege.

To labour, 13,024*l*.
To pay, local corps and trench allowance 20,777*l*.
To pay, clerical and civil staff, 3,543*l*.
To foodstuffs, grain, rations, &c., 36,076*l*.
To material, clothing, equipment, &c., 10,801*l*.
To hospital staff, comforts, &c,, 5,411*l*.
To local transport, 890*l*.
Total, 90,522*l*.
To payments other than defence, viz., frontier forces, special pay, &c., 32,729*l*.
Total, 123,251*l*.

Receipts.

By foodstuffs, and grain sales, 5,184*l*.
By soup kitchens, 3,242*l*.
By sales of Government property, 442*l*.
By local post office, 238*l*.
By dog tax, 67*l*.
By fines, 127*l*.
Total, 9,300*l*.
Weekly average expenditure in pay, 1,550*l*.
Average receipts for rations, 625*l*.
Soup, 600*l*.
Total, 1,225*l*. [*sic*]

Defence Works.
(Under direction of Major Vyvyan, for town and East Front;
Major Godley, West Front.)

Scheme. – General scheme at first was to secure the town and Stadt by clearing front, laying mines, fortifying outskirts, &c.

Then to push out advanced trenches to drive back those of the enemy, and finally to establish a girdle of outlying forts.

The scheme included the provision of bombproofs and extensive covered ways, gun emplacements, drainage, &c.

In all some 60 works were made, and about 6½ miles of trenches.

The perimeter of the works at first was approximately 7 miles, latterly it extended to a little over 10 miles.

Nature. – Generally semicircular redans, but no two works were similar in trace, they varied according to position, ground, &c. At first dug out and kept very low, latterly, owing to difficulties of drainage, long grass, inaccuracy of enemy's shell fire, &c., they were made more upstanding. Head cover was found to be essential. When trenches were near, steel loopholes had to be used, the ordinary sandbag and wooden ones being too good a target to the enemy.

Huts. – A good form of portable iron and wood hut was devised, and used for housing the garrisons of the forts.

Enemy's Artillery – Fighting, Treachery, Field Works.

Artillery. – Guns employed-

    1 – 94-pr. Creusot, 15-cm., 20-lb. charge.

    2 – 7-pr. (Jameson's).

    2 – 5-pr. Armstrong's B.L.

    1 – 12-pr. B.L.

    1 – 9-pr. Krupp, B.L.

    2 Q.F. 14-prs., high velocity.

    2 – 1-pr. Maxims.

  Total, 11 guns.

The 94-pr. fired 1,497 rounds, and the artillery altogether fired 2,000 rounds during the siege.

The damage done was very small, partly owing to the open nature of the town and lowness of our forts, but more especially on account of the want of intelligent directing of the fire.

Fighting. – The enemy's attacks invariably failed from want of discipline and pluck on the part of the men.

In the attack on Cannon Kopje they got within 400 yards, and even started digging shelter trenches, but when the men began to fall the rest retreated promptly.

The night attack on the Stadt, on 12th May, was boldly led by Eloff and a number of foreigners, and had their supports come on with equal pluck, we should have had a hard task to drive them out, but as it was the supports were easily beaten off and the storming party surrounded.

Treachery. – The enemy fired on numerous occasions on our hospital, convent, and women's laager, although these were conspicuously marked with Red Cross flags, stood in isolated positions, and had been fully pointed out by me to the Boer Generals.

The women's laager was deliberately shelled in particular on 24th and 30th October, 27th January, and 11th April.

The Red Cross flag was used to cover artillery taking up position on 24th, 30th, and 31st October.

Convent deliberately shelled, 16th October, 3rd and 8th November.

Our white flag, returning from a conference with the enemy, was deliberately volleyed, 17th January.

Field works. – The enemy's trenches were of a very good design, and made in well selected positions. The typical trench or fort consisted of a chain of small chambers 10 feet square, partly excavated, partly built up with sandbags, having stout walls, loopholed to front and rear, the whole roofed in with corrugated iron and railway rails. Command, about 3 feet.

Finance.
(Under Captain Greener, as Chief Paymaster.)

I ordered all Government accounts to be kept settled up to date, so as to leave as little as possible for subsequent settlement; much work and confusion has thereby been saved.

The accounts were well kept by Captain Greener and his staff. An examiner of accounts was appointed to check accounts before payment, and also an auditor for the larger amounts.

Cash in bank amounted to 12,000*l*., of which only 650*l*. was in silver. Cash soon became scarce, because the public, especially the natives and Indian traders, concealed all the cash they could get, in anticipation of the place being taken by the enemy.

Paper money thus became necessary, and I issued coupons for 1*s*., 2*s*., and 3*s*. Ultimately gold also became scarce, and 1*l*. notes were printed in cyanotype and issued; but they never got into real circulation, as people kept them as curios to the extent of 700*l*. 10*s*. coupons were issued with satisfactory result.

For the convenience of the men, and to get cash from the public, a "Garrison Savings Bank" was opened. Deposits amounted to 8,800*l*.

Total Government expenditure to end of May, 142,660*l*.

Total Government receipts to end of May, 11,828*l*.

Food Supply.
(Under Captain Ryan.)

Early in the siege, I took over all merchant stocks and put everybody on rations.

Beginning on the usual scale, I gradually reduced it to the lowest that would allow of the men being fit for duty. During the latter part of the siege no extras of any kind were obtainable. All lived strictly on the following scale:-

Meat, at first, 1 lb.; latterly, ¾ to 1 lb.
Bread, at first, 1 lb.; latterly, 5 oz.
Vegetables, at first, 1 lb.; latterley, 6 oz.
Coffee, at first, 1/3 oz.; latterly, 1/3 oz.
Salt, at first, ½ oz.; latterly, ½ oz.
Sugar, at first, 2 oz.
Tea, at first, ½ oz.
Sowens, latterly, 1 quart.

We had a large stock of meat, both live and tinned.

For livestock, we had to open up wide extent of grazing ground. We ate the fresh meat first in order to avoid loss from enemy's fire, failure of grass and water, lung sickness, &c.

The tinned meat we stored in bombproof chambers, and kept as reserve.

During the last two months we were on horseflesh three days a week.

Our stocks of meal were comparatively small, but we had a large supply of forage oats. These we ground into flour, and fermented the residue into sowens (a form of porridge) and the remaining husks went as forage to the horses.

Fresh vegetables were largely grown within the defences, and for a greater part of the siege formed a regular portion of the ration.

The cost of feeding the troops was 1s. 3d. per ration, or, with fresh vegetables, 1s. 6d.; about 3d. below the contract price in peace. Civilians paid 2s., and women in the laager 1s. 2d.

All liquor was taken over and issued in "tots" to the troops on wet nights, and I think saved much sickness.

Natives. – For the natives, we established four soup kitchens at which horse stew was sold daily, and five sowen kitchens, Natives were all registered, to prevent fraud, and bought rations at 1 quart per adult, and 1 pint per child, at 3d. per pint.

Defence watchmen, workmen, police, &c., and certified destitute persons were given free rations. The kitchens so managed paid their own expenses.

They were under Captain Wilson, A.D.C., with Mr. Myers as cash taken and inspector.

Fuel.

Coal. – 300 tons available at railway store, was used for armoured train, ordnance foundry, pumping station, flour mills, forage factory, forges, &c.

Wood. – 25,000 lb. weekly for bakery, soup, and oat-sowen kitchens, cooking, &c. Procured from roofs of huts in the Stadt, old wagons, lopped trees, fencing, &c.

Petroleum. – Asbestos stove made, but was not a success.

ord Kitchener (mounted on the white horse) and other senior officers, believed to include Lord oberts, reviewing British troops entering Kroonstadt. (*US Library of Congress*)

ritish infantry crossing the Sand River (also known as the Zand River) whilst an observation alloon is used to observe the approach of Boer soldiers. (*US Library of Congress*)

The Battle of Belmont, 23 November 1899, during which British troops, under the command of Lord Methuen, attacked a Boer position on a kopje (hill) near that town. British losses were seventy-five dead and twenty-two wounded; among the latter were Lieutenant Colonel Eyre Crabbe, the commanding officer of the 3rd Battalion, Grenadier Guards, who was soon back in action, and a war correspondent, Edward Knight of the *Morning Post*, who lost his arm. (*US Library of Congress*)

A pair of naval guns, mounted on carriages for land service, are pictured on the march to Bloemfontein. It is known that such guns were sourced from HMS *Monarch* and HMS *Doris*, and were served by members of the ships' crews. HMS *Monarch* was the first seagoing warship to carry her guns in turrets, and the first Royal Navy warship to carry guns of 12-inch calibre. She served as a guard ship in Simon's Town, on the Cape Peninsula, between 1897 and 1902. (*US Library of Congress*)

4.7-inch gun, known as 'Joe Chamberlain' firing during the artillery barrage unleashed upon Boer positions at Magersfontein. The barrage was one of the biggest since Sevastopol but only served to arn the Boers of the imminence of the British attack.

An artist's depiction of the Battle of Magersfontein on 11 December 1899. During the fighting, the British lost twenty-two officers and 188 other ranks killed, forty-six officers and 629 other ranks wounded, and one officer and sixty-two other ranks missing. Of this, the Highland Brigade suffered losses of 747 men being killed, wounded, and missing. Among the battalions, the Black Watch suffered the most severely, losing 303 officers and other ranks. (*US Library of Congress*)

A view of the hill at Magersfontein depicting the plain where the battle was fought on 11 December 1899. Remnants of the trenches can still be seen in the veld. (*Courtesy of Renier Maritz*)

British dead after the battle at Spion Kop, 24 January 1900. The British suffered 243 fatalities during the battle; approximately 1,250 British were either wounded or captured. Among those involved in the battle was Winston Churchill, who acted as a courier between Spion Kop and General Buller's HQ. Churchill made this statement about the scene: 'Corpses lay here and there. Many of the wounds were of a horrible nature. The splinters and fragments of the shells had torn and mutilated them. The shallow trenches were choked with dead and wounded.' (*Courtesy of the Transvaal Archive*)

This image shows a section of the British graves at the site of the Battle of Spion Kop. Many of the dead were buried in the trenches where they died. These graves therefore give a general indication of where the trenches were located at the time of the battle. Another of those present during the battle was Mahatma Gandhi, who was serving as a stretcher-bearer in the Indian Ambulance Corps. (*Courtesy of Renier Maritz*)

Spion Kop today. Although the common English name for the battle is *Spion Kop*, by which it is known throughout the Commonwealth and in historical literature, the official South African Englis and Afrikaans name for the battle is Spioenkop – *spioen* means 'spy' or 'look-out', and *kop* means 'hill' or 'outcropping'. (*Courtesy of Tim Giddings*)

British troops pictured in trenches, reportedly near the Orange River, during the Second Boer War. (*US Library of Congress*)

surviving British Boer War blockhouse near the town of Wolseley in South Africa's Western Cape ovince. An information panel near the structure states that these blockhouses could house twenty n with water, ammunition and supplies stored on the lower floor. The 'living' area was the ddle floor and was accessible by a retractable ladder, whilst the top floor was the 'look-out' deck. ough around 1,000 of these blockhouses were built few have survived.

urtesy of Danie van der Merwe)

Boer women and children in a British concentration camp during the Second Boer War. The camps had originally been set up by the British Army as refugee camps to provide shelter for civilian families who had been forced to abandon their homes due to the fighting. However, when Kitchen succeeded Roberts as Commander-in-Chief in South Africa on 29 November 1900, new tactics were introduced in an attempt to break the guerrilla campaign and the influx of civilians grew dramatically as a result. The conditions in the camps were often poor, mainly due to lack of food, medicines and poor sanitation, with escalating death rates.

Celebrations in Yonge Street, Toronto, as the men of one Canadian unit return home at the end of the Second Boer War on 5 June 1901 – scenes that were witnessed across the British Empire at the time. In all, the war had cost around 75,000 lives; 22,000 British and Allied soldiers (7,792 killed in battle, the rest through disease), between 6,000 and 7,000 Boer fighters, and, mainly in the concentration camps, between 20,000 to 28,000 Boer civilians (predominantly women and children) and perhaps 20,000 black Africans (both on the battlefield and in the concentration camps).
(*US Library of Congress*)

Patent fuel. – Cow dung and coal dust, mixed in equal parts and baked, produced 20 tons good fuel.

Hospital.
(Victoria Hospital – 70 beds. Base hospital.)

Major Anderson, Royal Army Medical Corps, Principal Medical Officer.

Dr. W. Hayes (acted as Principal Medical Officer during first part of the siege).

Surgeon-Major Holmden, British South Africa Police.

Dr. T. Hayes, District Surgeon.

Dr. Elmes.

Garrison.
Protectorate Regiment.
Lieutenant-Colonel Hore, Commander. – 21 Officers, 448 men.

British South Africa Police.
Lieutenant-Colonel Walford, Commander. – 10 Officers, 81 men.

Cape Police, Division 1.
Inspector Marsh, Commander. – 2 Officers, 45 men.

Cape Police, Division 2.
Inspector Browne, Commander. – 2 Officers, 54 men.

Bechuanaland Rifles.
Captain Cowan, Commander. – 4 Officers, 77 men.

Deduct missing at Lobatsi. – 1 Officer, 26 men.

Total drilled men. – 38 Officers, 679 men.

Town Guard, 296 men (untrained).

Total garrison – 44 Officers, 975 men.

From the above Town Guard was formed the Railway Division, 2 Officers, 20 men, under (local) Captain More.

The following commanded sections of the defence:-

Western defences, Major Godley.

Stadt and south-western forts, Captain Marsh.

Cannon Kopje and south front, Colonel Walford.

South-eastern works (brickfields), Inspector Marsh, at first, Inspector Browne, latterly.

North-east works, Captain Cowan.

Town, Colonel Vyvyan, at first, Major Goold-Adams, latterly.

Head-quarters Staff-

Chief Staff Officer – Lord E. Cecil

Deputy-Assistant Adjutant-General (B) – Captain Ryan.
Intelligence Officer – Lieutenant Hon. Hanbury-Tracy.
Aide-de-Camp – Captain Wilson.
Commanding Royal Artillery – Major Panzera.
Commanding Royal Engineer – Colonel Vyvyan.

Hospital.
(Under Major Anderson, Royal Army Medical Corps,
as Principal Medical Officer.)

Staff-

Dr. W. Hayes (acted as Principal Medical Officer during the first part of
the siege).

Surgeon-Major Holmden, British South Africa Police.

Dr. T. Hayes, District Surgeon.

Dr. Elmes.

Victoria Hospital (base hospital). – Nursing Staff: Miss Hill (Matron) and
three nurses, assisted by four volunteer nurses; also by Mother Teresa
and six sisters.

Convalescent hospital. – At convent, Lady Sarah Wilson.

Women and children's hospital. – Miss Craufurd.

On outbreak of war I took over the town hospital, but at first the administration was not satisfactory, on account of want of supervision over expenses
of stores, and sanitation. I therefore appointed an issuer and storekeeper, and
a sanitary inspector. To existing accommodation I added a native ward,
nurses' quarters, a ward for Colonial Contingent, and a boarded marquee for
shell wounds, &c.

Both doctors and nurses did excellent work, always shorthanded, and
frequently under fire. (All the hospital buildings were struck by shells and
bullets, and the first convalescent hospital was wrecked, and the second
damaged by 94-pounder shells).

Natives.
(Under Mr. Bell, Resident Magistrate and Civil Commissioner.)

Natives in Mafeking, during the siege, were-

Baralongs, 5,000.

Fingoes, Shangans, and district Baralongs, 2,000.

Total, between 7,000 and 8,000.

The Shangans were refugees from the Johannesburg mines, and were sent
into Mafeking by the Boers on the outbreak of war. Being accustomed to
digging, they proved useful for working gangs on the defences.

The district Baralongs, Fingoes, and Cape Boys, came into Mafeking when their villages were burnt and their cattle looted by the Boers. From among them we got about 300 men to act as armed cattle guards, watchmen, police, &c.

The local Baralongs living in the Stadt displayed their loyalty, and did some good service (especially after I had deposed their Chief Wessels for want of energy), and supplied good despatch runners, spies, cattle runners, &c.

Of the natives living in the district, Saani remained particularly loyal, and although a prisoner in the hands of the Boers, he managed to send us information from time to time. Bathoen was loyal, but too timid to be of use. Copane, a subject of the Boers, although forced to supply them with men, offered us his allegiance. Hatsiokomo and Matuba (British subjects), joined the enemy, and the latter and his men fought with them.

Railway.
(Under Captain More.)

132 men, 46 women, 86 children.

Eighteen locomotives, only one of which was damaged by shell fire, as they were moved round to the "lee" side of the railway buildings with every move of the enemy's big gun.

Also a large amount of rolling stock.

Value of railway plant, 120,000*l*.

A defence railway, 1½ miles long, was laid round the north-east front.

We made three armoured trucks, walls of steel rails, iron lookout tower, acetyline search light, speaking tubes, electric bells, water, medicine chests, stretchers, &c.

200 tons of rails were used in construction of bombproofs.

The armoured trains did much good service.

Specialities.

Ammunition. – Mr. Fodisch, our gunsmith, reloaded Martini Henry cartridges, using ordinary gun caps fixed with plaster of Paris for detonators. Powder and bullets were home made.

Armoured train. – We armoured ordinary long-bogey trucks with steel rails (iron ones not being bullet-proof) to a height of 5 feet, with loopholes and gun ports. I had three prepared at Mafeking under the able direction of Mr. More, Resident Engineer, Bechuanaland Railway, also three at Bulawayo by Mr. Wallis, Resident Engineer.

Brawn was made from ox and horse hides and feet, and was much appreciated as meat.

Bombs. – Dynamite bombs were made up in small potted meat and milk tins for use as hand grenades, with slow match fuzes, with complete success, by Lieutenant Feltham. Sergeant Page, champion bait thrower of Port Elizabeth, by using a whip stick and short line, was able to throw these with accuracy over a distance of 100 yards.

Fuel. – When coal and wood began to run low, a very satisfactory fuel was made up of coal dust and cowdung mixed.

Fuzes. – A simple and useful percussion fuze was invented by Lieutenant Daniell, British South Africa Police, in which the butt end of a Lee-Metford cartridge was used as detonator. This fuze was in regular use with our locally-made shells.

Howitzer. – A 6-inch howitzer was made in our workshops, under the orders of Major Panzera, by Mr. Conolly. The bore was a tube of steel, with iron rings shrunk on in two tiers. The breech was a block of cast bronze. The trunnions and ring were a similar solid casting. The gun threw a 18-lb. ball (shell), and reached a distance of 4,000 yards.

Lookout poles. – Telescopic look-out poles were made of lengths of iron piping, and set up with steel wire stays, with a pulley and slung seat to hoist the man to the masthead. Height, about 18 feet.

Oat bread. – Mr. Ellitson, our master baker, made up our forage oats into a good form of bread. The oats were winnowed, cleaned, kiln-dried, ground, steam sieved (twice), and made into bread in the usual way, with a small admixture of Boer meal.

Search light. – Mr. Walker, agent for the Acetyline Gas Company, under Captain More's direction, made a very effective and portable acetyline search light with an engine head-light and a theodolite stand. These we had stationed in the principal forts and on the armoured train.

Signalling lamp. – Sergeant-Major Moffat and Mr. Walker devised a very effective and portable acetyline signalling lamp, which is reckoned to be readable at 15 miles. We had two in work.

Sowens. – This is a form of porridge, made from the fermented bran of oats after the flour had been extracted for making bread. 100 lb. of bran in 37 gallons of water give 33 gallons of sowens. On this food we fed both natives and whites. We had five sowen kitchens, each capable of producing 800 gallons daily. It was sold at 6*d.* per quart to those not entitled to it as a ration.

Sausages. – The horses which we used for meat were, as a rule, so poor in condition that we found it best to cut off the flesh from the bones and mince it for issue as ration. The remainder of the carcase then went to the soup kitchen. The mince was then mixed with spice and saltpetre, and made up into sausages, the intestines of the same animal being used for sausage skins. The meat thus treated lasted longer, and was more palatable.

Steel loopholes. – Finding that the enemy shot through ordinary loopholes at short distances, especially in trench work, I devised a form of steel loophole with two plates of ½-inch steel bolted together at an angle of 45 degrees, with a hole 2 inches square in the middle of the joint, the shield being 2 foot high and 2 feet wide.

Steel sap roller. – I also had a sapping shield made of two sheets of 3/8-inch steel, each 4 feet square, bolted together at an angle and mounted on wheels, to be pushed in front of a party pushing a sap under fire.

Relief Committee.

Numbers of the refugees and some of the townspeople, being without means during the siege, I formed a relief committee, consisting of the Mayor, the Base Commandant, the Chaplain, and other representative men, with myself as president, for disbursing funds for purchase of clothing and necessaries, &c., and for the issue of rations to deserving cases.

Sums received from England, from the various relief funds, were thus carefully and advantageously administered and accounted for, and there was no real suffering among the white population.

Staff.

Head-quarters-

Colonel Commanding – Colonel Baden-Powell.

Chief Staff Officer – Major Lord E. Cecil, D.S.O.

Deputy-Assistant Adjutant-General (B) – Captain Ryan, Army Service Corps.

Aide-de-Camp – Captain G. Wilson, Royal Horse Guards.

Intelligence Officer – Lieutenant Hon. A. Hanbury-Tracy, Royal Horse Guards.

Local-

Commanding Artillery and Deputy-Assistant Adjutant-General – Major Panzera, British South Africa Police.

Base Commandant and Commanding Engineer – Major C.B. Vyvyan, "Buffs."

Principal Medical Officer – Dr. W. Hayes (at first), Major Anderson, Royal Army Medical Corps.

Chief Paymaster – Captain Greener, British South Africa Police.

Town Commandant and Protectorate, Natives – Major Goold-Adams, C.B., C.M.G.

Local Natives – Mr. C.G.H. Bell, Resident Magistrate and Civil Commissioner.

Women and children – Mr. P. Whiteley, Mayor.

Transport – Lieutenant McKenzie.

Post and Telegraphs – Mr. Howat, Postmaster.

Chaplains – Rev. W.H. Weekes (Church of England), Rev. Father Ogle (Roman Catholic).

Spies.

The enemy were well informed of all that went on in Mafeking during the siege. We had over 30 suspects in the gaol for the greater part of the time, but it was almost impossible to get proofs against them. The stationmaster had undoubtedly been in communication with an ex-Fenian, Whelan, a prominent member of the Irish Land League. This man we arrested on the outbreak of war, and kept in gaol. He had among his papers a code for messages.

The natives acted as spies for the enemy; we caught two and tried them, and shot them.

More than half the families in the women's laager were Dutch, and of pro-Boer sympathies.

Four of our men deserted to the enemy at different times.

Transport.
(Under Lieutenant McKenzie).

This department was very ably managed, and, though at first much hired transport was employed, Lieutenant McKenzie gradually arranged so that the whole of the Army Service Corps, Royal Engineers, sanitary, &c., duties (as well as the regimental work) were carried out by the Government transport available, viz.-

11 wagons.
6 Scotch carts.
2 trollies.
3 ambulances.
188 mules.
12 oxen.

The mules kept their condition wonderfully well, considering the absence of forage and the amount of work.

Water Supply.
(Under Major Vyvyan and Major Hepworth.)

The enemy cut off our water supply from the waterworks during the first few days of the siege. Fortunately the season was unusually wet, and consequently the Molopo stream did not run dry, and house tanks kept fairly filled. But to make sure against contingencies, and to ensure a supply of wholesome water, we cleaned out various wells and dug a new one of great capacity.

The water from these was issued to the town and garrison by means of tank wagons, filled nightly and posted at convenient points during the day.

Women's Laager.
(Under Mr. F. Whiteley, the Mayor.)

Formed at Mr. Rowland's house, where everything was placed at the disposal of the refugees in a most kindly way by Mr. Rowlands.

Number of whites – 10 men, 188 women, 315 children; also about 150 native servant girls.

Health fairly good considering the circumstances. Diphtheria made its appearance, but after four cases was stopped by isolation. Deaths, 24.

A large bombproof, 180 yards by 5 feet, was made for the accommodation of the whole of the inhabitants of the laager, with protected ways, latrines, &c.

The women and children were rationed, the supply and distribution being efficiently carried out by Mr. Whiteley, without any kind of remuneration to himself.

This gentleman carried out the entire management of the laager with conspicuous success, and was very ably assisted by Rev. W.H. Weekes and Mr. Rowlands.

The following were the cases dealt with by the Court of Summary Jurisdiction:-

Charges.

House-breaking, 14.
Treason, 35.
Theft, 197.
Minor offences, 184.
Total, 430.

Punishments.

Death, 5.
Corporal punishment, 115.
Detention in gaol, 23.
Fines, 57.
Imprisonment with hard labour, 91.
Total 291.
Total fines, 140*l*. 3*s*. 6*d*.

III.—Engagements during the Siege.

Action of 14th October.
Six miles north of Mafeking on railway.

Early in the morning of the 14th October our reconnoitring patrols exchanged shots with a strong party of the enemy, who were advancing along the railway 3 miles north of the town.

I ordered out the armoured train, under Captain Williams, British South Africa Police, to endeavour to rush the Boers and pour a heavy fire into them, as I wanted to make the first blow felt by them to be a really hard one. The train carried a 1-pounder Hotchkiss and a .303-inch Maxim, and 15 men, British South Africa Police.

I sent out, in support of the train, a squadron of the Protectorate Regiment, under Captain FitzClarence.

On coming up with the train he found it heavily engaged with the Boers, who had been strongly reinforced from their laager, some 7 miles north; they had also brought up a 7-pounder Krupp and a 1-pounder Maxim.

Captain FitzClarence, dismounting his men, advanced to attack with his left protected by the train.

For a quarter of an hour he was held by the enemy under a very hot fire, and then, pressing forward, well backed up by the train, he drove the enemy back and successfully beat off their several attempts to encircle his flank. Meantime, I sent up an additional troop under Lord Charles Bentinck, and also a 7-pr. These also became hotly engaged and did good work. The fire from the armoured train put the enemy's gun out of action before it had fired a shot, and eventually also drove the 1-pr. Maxim from the field.

The engagement lasted about 4 hours, and the enemy largely outnumbered our men, but Captain FitzClarence made up for this deficiency by the able handling of his men. Moreover, he kept his orders in mind, and when he saw the opportunity he got his wounded on to the train, and after driving the enemy back he withdrew his command quietly on Mafeking, covered by the train, without any attempt on the part of the enemy to follow him up.

In this, their first engagement, the Protectorate Regiment showed a spirit and dash worthy of highly-trained troops, and were most ably led by Captain FitzClarence and Lord C. Bentinck.

This smartly fought little engagement had a great and lasting moral effect on the enemy.

Their losses were afterwards found to amount to 53 killed (including four field cornets) and a large number wounded. They also lost a number of horses.

Our casualties were-

2 killed.

16 wounded (including two Officers).

1 missing (cyclist).

4 horses killed.

12 wounded.

Enemy's Attack on the Stadt,
25th October, 1899.

Enemy commenced shelling at 6.30 A.M. till midday from the east and south with 7 guns. At noon they commenced a general advance against the town from the south-west, east, and north-east; the south-west being the main attack directed against the Stadt. Their number about 3,000. The enemy commenced firing at extreme range, to which we made no reply, reserving our fire for close distances. So soon as our volleys and Maxims commenced the enemy stopped their advance, and soon began to withdraw at all points. Casualties on our side were one man wounded, and two horses and eight mules wounded; the Boers' losses unknown, but probably considerable, as their ambulances were on the field picking up for over an hour after the engagement.

It was afterwards (10th December) ascertained that the attack on the Stadt was intended as a feint, while the main attack should come off to northward, on our western face. The Boers had expected the Baralongs not to fire on them, and so advanced more openly than they would otherwise have done; nor had they expected to find white men defending the Stadt. Their loss was, therefore, pretty heavy, and, surprised at their rebuff, they fell back altogether.

At one period of the action, a small mounted troop of Boers advanced at a gallop towards the western position, and came under fire of the Cape Police Maxim, which dropped five of them; the remainder rapidly dispersed.

During the afternoon some of our scouts near the Brickfields were moving, under fire, when one of them fell with his horse and lay stunned. Two Cape Police troopers in the works ran out and placed the injured man on his horse, and brought him in under heavy fire from the enemy: names, Troopers George Collins and W.F. Green.

Night Attack on Boer Trenches.
27th October, 1899.

During past two days enemy had moved their advanced trenches closer into the east face. I determined to make an attack on their main advanced trench with the bayonet, in order to discourage their advancing further.

A night attack was therefore organized with Captain FitzClarence's squadron, Protectorate Regiment, supported by a party of Cape Police. Guiding lights were hoisted, by which Captain FitzClarence was able to lead his party past the flank of the main trench.

The attacking force moved off 9.30 P.M. in silence, with magazines charged, but no cartridges in the chamber, the order being to use the bayonet only. The men wore white armlets and used "FitzClarence" as their pass word. The night was dark, but still. The squadron attained its position on the left rear of enemy's trench without being challenged or fired at. Captain FitzClarence then wheeled up his men, and with a cheer charged into the main and a subsidiary trench, and cleared both with the bayonet.

The enemy's rearward trenches opened a heavy fire, to which the Cape Police replied from a flank, in order to draw the fire on to themselves, and so to allow Captain Fitz Clarence's squadron to return unmolested.

The whole operation was carried out exactly in accordance with instructions, and was a complete success; the more so as the enemy, being taken by surprise, were in much confusion, and, as we afterwards discovered, fired into each other. Their casualties, we heard on reliable authority, amounted to 40 killed and wounded with the bayonet, 60 killed and wounded by rifle fire. Our casualties were six killed, nine wounded, two missing.

Killed.

4323 Corporal Burt, 17th Lancers.
442 Trooper Josiah Soundy, Protectorate Regiment.
443 Trooper Charles Mayfield Middleditch, Protectorate Regiment.
171 Trooper Thomas Fraser.
202 Robert Ryves MacDonald.
222 Alexander Henry Turner.

Wounded.

Captain FitzClarence, slightly.
Lieutenant Swinburne, slightly.
Corporal Bernard Johnson.
Corporal Clement Adkins.
Trooper Arthur Bodill, severely.
Trooper Charles Donovan.
Trooper A.H. Hodgkinson.
Trooper H.A. Dawson.
Trooper F.W. Hooper.
Missing.
Trooper Thomas Powell.
Trooper Franz Aurel.

The missing men were captured by the enemy.

Action at Cannon Kopje.
31st October, 1899.

The enemy opened a heavy, concentrated shell fire from the south-eastern heights, from the racecourse (east), and from Jackal's Tree (south-west), directed against Cannon Kopje. The fire was well aimed, and the racecourse gun took the work in reverse. For a time little harm was done beyond knocking down parts of the parapet and smashing the iron supports of the lookout tower: most of the garrison were lying in the trenches some 80 yards in rear of the fort. The gun and two Maxims in the work had been previously dismounted and stowed away for safety during shell fire, to which, of course, they were powerless to reply. The telephone wire was cut away early in the proceedings. After half an hour's steady and accurate artillery fire, the enemy, who had been gradually massing on the high ground south and south-east of the fort, began to advance in line of skirmishers from three sides at once; they were backed up by other parties in support. A large force also collected in the Molopo Valley, south-east of the town, and were formed evidently with the idea of storming the town after Cannon Kopje had been captured.

As the enemy began to get within range of the fort, the garrison moved up from their trench and manned the parapets and Maxims. It was then that we suffered some casualties from shell fire. As the enemy continued their advance, I sent to Captain Goodyear's Colonial Contingent to advance a party on to a ridge above them, and so to take enemy's attacking line in flank, but they could not be got to move.

One Maxim at Ellis's Corner now jammed, and I had to replace it by one from the reserve.

Meantime, I had a 7-pounder run out under cover of houses near south corner of the town. This opened, under direction of Lieutenant Marchison, on the flank of the enemy's line as it began to get near the fort. The gun made excellent practice, every shell going in among them, and effectually stopped the further advance of the Boers.

These now hesitated and began to draw off, and as they did so their guns reopened on Cannon Kopje to cover their retirement. The fire then died down, and enemy sent out ambulances under Red Cross flags to recover their dead and wounded. We lost six killed and five wounded.

Killed.

Captain the Hon. Douglas Marsham.
Captain Charles A.K. Pechell.
2391 Troop Sergeant-Major William Henry Connihan.
Troop Sergeant-Major Hugh Bagot Upton.
2566 Trooper Arthur John Martyn.
2517 Frank St. Clair Traill Burroughes.

Wounded.

Quarter-Master-Serjeant E.O. Butler.
Corporal A.J. Cook.
Corporal F.C. Newton.

Trooper C.W. Nicholas.

Trooper F.R. Lloyd.

(The two latter died the following day.)

During this fight the Boers sent out a Red Cross flag on to a commanding point and then brought their guns up into position there. I visited Cannon Kopje after the fight and congratulated Colonel Walford and his men on the gallant and determined stand made by them in the face of a very hot shell fire.

The intention of the enemy had been to storm Cannon Kopje, and thence to bombard the south-eastern portion of the town, and to carry it with the large forces they had collected in the Molopo Valley. Their whole scheme was defeated by the gallant resistance made by the garrison, and by the telling fire it brought to bear on them. We afterwards learnt that the attack was designed and directed by young Cronje. The enemy's loss was not known, but ambulances were seen about the field picking up for a considerable time, and native spies reported there was much mourning in the laagers, and that several cart loads of dead had been brought in and buried.

Surprise on Enemy's Western Laager.

7th November, 1899.

At 2.30 A.M. Major Godley paraded his force, in accordance with a plan I had arranged, to attack the western camp of the enemy with a heavy fire at daylight, and then to retire again before enemy's guns and reinforcements arrived on the scene. The force in enemy's camp was reckoned at 200 to 250. Oar force consisted of-

Two 7-pouuders.

One 1-pounder Hotchkiss, under Major Panzera.

One squadron of 60 men, Protectorate Regiment, dismounted, under Captain Vernon.

One troop of 30 men, Bechuanaland Rifles mounted, under Captain Cowan.

The force moved out along the heights to about 1,500 yards in advance of Major Godley's position; Captain Vernon's squadron leading in attack order, with the guns on his left rear, and Bechuanaland Rifles covering his right rear.

At 4.15 A.M., our guns opened on enemy at 1,800 yards, and the squadron fired volleys by alternate troops into the enemy's camp, over which they had full command from the heights they were on. The surprise was complete, the enemy bolting in all directions to take cover. Their 1-pounder Maxim and 7-pounder Krupp in the Beacons Fort in a short time responded with a heavy and well-directed tire. Large bodies of reinforcements very soon began to come down from the main south-west laager. Major Godley thereupon commenced withdrawing his forces, artillery retiring first; the Bechuanaland Rifles occupying Fort Ayr to cover the retirement, which they did very effectively against a wing of mounted Boers who had worked round to our right flank. The enemy brought a very heavy musketry fire to bear on our force, but the retirement was carried out with the greatest steadiness. Enemy's strength about 800 or 1,000. Our retirement was further covered by 7-pounder at the west end of the Stadt, and the Cape Police Maxim and escort. In the course of the retirement our 1-pounder Hotchkiss upset and broke the limber hook; her crew, Gunners R. Cowan and H. Godson, very pluckily stood up and repaired damage with rope, &c., and got the gun away safely under heavy fire from enemy's 1-pounder Maxim and 7-pounder Krupp and rifle fire.

Three of enemy's ambulances were seen picking up their casualties after the action, and we afterwards learnt that they had lost a considerable number. On our side we had five men wounded, five horses killed, five wounded, and 36 cattle in the refugee laager killed and wounded by bullets.

Names of Wounded.

Major Godley, slightly.
Trooper Hodgkinson, Protectorate Regiment.
Trooper J.G. Thompson, Protectorate Regiment.
Trooper P.J. Westdyk, Bechuanaland Rifles.
Corporal R.B. Christie, Cape Police.

On this day a commando of the Boers made a demonstration against Khama's men on the Limpopo, and opened fire upon them, but shortly after retired across the border.

Action at Game Tree.

26th December, 1899.

The Boers' work at Game Tree, 2,500 yards north of town, had checked our grazing in that direction, and it commanded our line of communication northward. Some shells thrown into it a few days previously had caused enemy temporarily to vacate it, showing it to be a weak open work; this had been confirmed by reconnaissance by our scouts, but as the enemy had been seen strengthening it during the past few days, I determined to attack before they should make it impregnable. Accordingly, two squadrons Protectorate Regiment, supported by armoured train and Bechuanaland Rifles, were ordered to attack from the left flank of the work, under direction of Major Godley, while three guns and Maxim prepared the way from the right front of the work. This scheme was carried out at dawn on the 26th, the guns making good practice, and the two squadrons advancing in attack formation exactly as required. But on pressing home the attack a heavy fire killed or wounded most of the Officers and the loading troops. These succeeded in gaining the parapet, but the work was found to have been strongly roofed in and so closed as to be impregnable.

The attack fell back upon the eastern face, and pushed forward again on the southern face, but eventually had to retire with a loss of-

Captain Vernon,

Captain Sandford,

Lieutenant Paton, and 21 non-commissioned officers and men killed, and,
    Captain FitzClarence and 22 men wounded.

Three missing.

If blame for this reverse falls on anyone it should fall on myself, as everybody concerned did their part of the work thoroughly well, and exactly in accordance with the orders I had issued, Both Officers and men worked with splendid courage and spirit.

Boers' Attack.

12th May, 1900.

At about 4 A.M. on 12th May a very heavy long-range musketry fire was opened on the town from east, north-east, and south-east. I sounded the alarm, and the garrison stood to arms. The fire continued for half-an-hour. I thereupon wired to the south-west outposts to be on the look-out.

At about 4.30, 300 Boers made a rush through the western outposts and got into the Stadt; this they then set fire to. I ordered the western defenders to close in so as to prevent any supports from coming in after the leading body, and sent the reserve squadron there to assist. They succeeded in driving off an attack of about 500 without difficulty and returned to round up their station. In the meantime the Boers in the Stadt had rushed the British South African Police fort and made prisoners the men in it, viz., three Officers and 16 men, staff of the Protectorate Regiment.

In the darkness the attackers had got divided up into three parties, and as it got light we were able to further separate these from each other, and to surround and attack them in detail. The first party surrendered, the second were driven out with loss by three squadrons Protectorate Regiment, under Major Godfrey[†], and the third, in the British South African Police fort, after a vain attempt to break out in the evening, surrendered. During the whole of the day, while the struggle was going on in the Stadt, the enemy outside made demonstrations as if about to attack, and kept up a hot shell fire on the place, but without palpable effect.

We captured this day 108 prisoners, among whom was Commandant Eloff, Kruger's grandson. We also found 10 killed and 19 wounded Boers, and their ambulance picked up 30 more killed and wounded. Our losses were four killed, 10 wounded.

Our men, although weak with want of food and exercise, worked with splendid pluck and energy for the 14 hours of fighting, and instances of gallantry in action were very numerous.

Relief of Mafeking.
16th–17th May, 1900.

When relief became imminent, I formed a small force of 180 men and two guns, under Colonel Walford, capable of taking the field should it be desirable to make a diversion or counter-attack during the probable encounter between the investing force and the relieving column.

On the evening of the 16th May, the enemy contested the advance of the relief column 6 miles west of the place. Colonel Walford's party moved out and demonstrated as if to attack the Boers in rear. This caused them to withdraw a 1-pr. Maxim which had been posted on the probable line of advance of the column, and also a number of men with it. This move left the road open for Colonel Mahon's force to come into Mafeking, which it did during the night without the knowledge of the Boers.

Early next morning, seeing that the enemy were beginning to move wagons from the laager, I pushed forward Colonel Walford's force at once to attack, ordering the relief force to join in as soon as possible. This had a good effect, as our guns opened on their advanced trenches and prevented them from getting their 5-pounder away, and our men from the Brickfields, moving up the river, took the trench in rear and cleared it, killing five Boers and taking their flag and gun. Meanwhile, Colonel Mahon and Colonel Plumer's guns came into action and shelled the enemy's laager with great effect, the Boers going off in full flight, abandoning several wagons, camp equipment, hospital, &c. Colonel Walford's men, who had been working up through the bush, quickly took possession and drove off the enemy's rear guard without difficulty.

The operations connected with the relief of the place have, I assume, been reported on by Colonel Mahon, but I would add that his clever move near Maritzani, when he shifted his line of advance suddenly from one road to another, quite unexpected by the Boers, entirely puzzled them, and disconcerted their plans. And again, after the fight outside Mafeking, when he bivouacked his column at nightfall, the Boers were prepared to renew the attack in the morning only to find that he had slipped into the place during the night, and was through the town and shelling their laager on the other side.

The whole operation of the two relief columns was exceedingly well conceived and carried out.

IV. – Recommendation of Officers and Others.
1. Staff.
2. Regimental.
3. Civil.
4. Warrant and non-commissioned officers and men.

1. Staff – Military.

Major Lord Edward Cecil, D.S.O., as Chief Staff Officer, was of the greatest assistance to me. He stuck pluckily to his work, although much hampered by sickness during the first part of the siege. He did a great amount of hard work in the first organization of the frontier force, and at Mafeking, his tact and unruffled temperament enabled our staff dealings with the Colonial civilians to be carried on with the least possible friction.

Captain Ryan, Army Service Corps, as Deputy-Assistant Adjutant-General (B), proved an exceptionally capable and energetic Supply Officer. On his shoulders fell the whole work of feeding the entire community, garrison, non-combatants, and native, a duty which he carried out with conspicuous success (practically unassisted), as we took the food supply out of the hands of contractors and merchants; and he lost the services of his two chief assistants, Captain Girdwood, killed, and Sergeant-Major Loney, convicted of theft of Government stores. Captain Ryan's work has been invaluable, and has mainly contributed to the successful issue of the siege.

Lieutenant Honourable A. Hanbury-Tracy, Royal Horse Guards, as Intelligence Officer and Press Censor, has worked hard and successfully, and with tact and firmness in his dealings with the Press correspondents.

Captain G. Wilson, Royal Horse Guards, as my Aide-de-Camp, in addition to his other duties, had charge of the soup and sowens kitchens, and did most useful work.

To both the above Officers I am much indebted for their willing work and personal assistance to myself.

Honorary Lieutenant McKenzie as Transport Officer did excellent work in the organisation of his departments, and in the purchase of mules and material, &c. In addition to his other duties, he acted as extra Aide-de-Camp to me, and was an exceptionally energetic and useful Staff Officer.

Major Panzera, British South Africa Police, as Commanding Artillery, showed himself a smart and practical gunner, endowed with the greatest zeal, coupled with personal gallantry in action. The great success gained by our little guns, even when opposed to the modern armament of the enemy, was largely due to Panzera's organization and handling of them.

In addition to these duties, he acted as my Brigade-Major, and proved himself a most reliable and useful Staff Officer.

Major (local Lieutenant-Colonel) C.B. Vyvyan, the Buffs, was Base Commandant, Commanding Engineer, and (for 3 months) Town Commandant during the siege. As such, he organized the Town Guard and defences in the first instance. To his untiring zeal and ability the successful defence of the town is largely due. He carried out a very heavy amount of work, practically single-handed, and with conspicuous success.

Major Anderson, Royal Army Medical Corps, throughout the siege showed untiring zeal, coupled with coolness and gallantry, in attending the wounded under fire in action, in addition to his eminent professional ability. Latterly, as Principal Medical Officer, his unfailing tact and administrative capabilities rendered his services of greatest value. The strain of his devotion to his duty told heavily on his health.

Medical Staff. – Dr. W. Hayes, Surgeon-Major Holmden, British South Africa Police, and Dr. T. Hayes, all worked with conspicuous zeal and skill under a never-ending strain of work; all of them very frequently under fire in carrying out their duties, even in their own hospital.

Nursing Staff. – The work done by the lady nurses was beyond all praise.

Miss Hill, the Matron of the Victoria Hospital, was assisted by a number of lady volunteers, in addition to her regular staff, consisting of Mrs. Parmister and Miss Gamble.

Mother Superior Teresa and eight Sisters of Mercy also worked in the hospital.

Lady Sarah Wilson, assisted by other ladies, managed the Convalescent Hospital.

Miss Craufurd managed the Women and Children's Hospital.

The above ladies worked with the greatest zeal and self devotion throughout the siege.

The protracted strain of heavy work, frequently carried out under fire (Lady Sarah Wilson was wounded), told on most of them, Miss Hill being at one time prostrated by overwork. It was largely due to their unremitting devotion and skill that the wounded, in so many cases, made marvellous recoveries, and the health of the garrison remained so good.

Captain Greener, Paymaster, British South Africa Police, as Chief Paymaster, rendered most efficient and valuable service throughout the siege. He kept account of all Government expenditures and receipts connected with defence, feeding population, &c., in addition to his ordinary police and administrative accounts. By his care and zeal I am convinced that the Government were saved much expense.

2. Regimental.

Lieutenant-Colonel Hore, Staffordshire Regiment, raised, organized, and commanded the Protectorate Regiment, which did invaluable service in the siege.

Major Godley, Royal Dublin Fusiliers, as Adjutant of the Protectorate Regiment, had much to do with the successful organisation of the corps when it was first raised. As commander of the western defences of Mafeking throughout the siege his services were of the highest value. His coolness, readiness of resource, and tactfulness in dealing with the Colonials made him an ideal Officer for such command in action.

He was my right hand in the defence. I cannot speak too highly of his good work.

Colonel Walford, British South Africa Police, commanded the southern defences, with his detachment of British South Africa Police, throughout the siege with conspicuous success. Always cool and quick to see what was wanted, his services were most valuable.

Inspector Browne, Cape Police, commanded the detachment of Division 2, Cape Police. He and the splendid lot of men under his command did excellent work throughout the siege, especially in the occupation of the trenches in the Brickfields, where for over a month they were within close range of the enemy's works, and constantly on the alert and under fire.

Inspector Marsh, Cape Police, Division 1, commanded the detachment of Division 1 throughout the siege, and carried out his duties most efficiently and zealously.

Captain Cowan, commanding the Bechuanaland Rifles (Volunteers), had his corps in such a condition of efficiency as enabled me to employ them in all respects as regular troops. He was at all times ready and zealous in the performance of any duty assigned to him.

(Local) Captain More, Resident Railway Engineer, organized most effectively the railway employés into a paid division for the armoured train, and a division for the Town Guard. He managed their rationing, hospital, defence works, protection for their women and children, &c., in a most practical manner. His energy and resourcefulness were conspicuous throughout the siege. The armoured trains, defence railway, search light, &c., were made under his supervision.

Captain Marsh, Royal West Kent Regiment, commanded a squadron of the Protectorate Regiment, with very good results. He also had charge of the defence of the native Stadt, and displayed great tact and patience in his successful management of the natives.

Captain Vernon, King's Royal Rifle Corps, was a most successful Officer in command of a squadron, and displayed the greatest gallantry in action. He was killed in action on 26th December.

Captain FitzClarence, Royal Fusiliers, commanded a squadron in the Protectorate Regiment. He distinguished himself on numerous occasions during the siege by his personal gallantry and exceptional soldierly qualities. He was twice wounded. I have reported more specially on his good work in a separate letter.

Lieutenant (local Captain) Lord C. Bentinck, 9th Lancers, commanded a squadron of the Protectorate Regiment, with very good results. He did good service by his zeal and readiness in action.

The following Officers also did much good and useful work:-

Captain A. Williams, British South Africa Police.
Captain Scholfield, British South Africa Police.
Lieutenant Daniells, British South Africa Police.
Lieutenant Holden, Protectorate Regiment.
Lieutenant Greenfield, Protectorate Regiment.
Lieutenant Feltham, Protectorate Regiment.

Corporal (local Lieutenant) Currie, City Police, did exceptionally good service in command of the Colonial Contingent, to which he succeeded when Captain Goodyear (who originally raised the corps) was severely wounded while gallantly leading his men.

The following organized and commanded, with most satisfactory results, the native cattle guards, watchmen, &c.:

(Local) Captain McKenzie, Zulus, &c.
Mr. D. Webster, Fingoes.
Corporal (local Serjeant) Abrams, Cape Police Baralongs.

These detachments all did most useful and loyal work at different times during the siege in spite of their privations.

Town Guard.

Major Goold-Adams, C.B., C.M.G., Resident Commissioner of the Protectorate, commanded the Town Guard during the last half of the siege. His extensive knowledge of the country and people (both native and white) was of the greatest value, and his advice was always most willingly at my disposal. I am greatly in-debted for the great assistance he at all times afforded me. The fact that the natives of the Protectorate remained loyal to us at a very critical time is due in a great measure to his advice and great personal influence over them.

3. Civil.

Mr. C.G.H. Bell, Resident Magistrate and Civil Commissioner, had entire charge of native affairs, and he managed the chiefs with great tact, and very successfully, at a critical time, when they were inclined to sit on the fence and see which was going to win, and were being tempted with offers from the Boers. As magistrate he also rendered me great assistance during the siege.

Mr. F. Whiteley, Mayor of Makeing. This gentlemen's services were invaluable during the siege. In a most public-spirited manner he took up, at my request, the difficult task of arranging for the feeding and housing of all the women and children, and carried out their management with marked success throughout the siege, devoting himself to the task without any return whatever.

He was much assisted by Mr. Rowlands, who gave up his house, garden, water supply, &c., to be used by the laager, similarly without drawing any kind of compensation or return.

The Rev. Mr. W.H. Weekes also rendered valuable service in assisting in the management of the women's laager, &c.

Mr. Howat, Post and Telegraph Master, with his staff, namely-

Messrs. Campbell, Simpson, and McLeod did invaluable work in connecting up, and in keeping in communication with head-quarters the whole of the defence works by telephone. Their duties were unceasing, by night as well as by day, and were frequently carried out under heavy fire and at great personal risk. The zeal, energy, and willingness displayed by these officers was most conspicuous throughout the siege, and their work had a large share in bringing about the successful issue of the siege.

Mr. Heal, the jailer, carried out most arduous and difficult duties most loyally and efficiently. In addition to ordinary prisoners, he had in his charge military offenders, and also a large number of Dutch suspects, spies, and Irish traitors.

He was unfortunately killed by a shell, 12th May, at his post in the jail.

Serjeant Stewart, Cape Police, rendered valuable service as head of the civil police during the siege.

Mr. Millar, head of the refugees' laager, displayed much zeal and did excellent work in the management of the refugees' laager and defences, &c,

4. Non-commissioned Officers and Men.

Trooper (local Serjeant-Major) Hodgson, Cape Police, acted as Serjeant-Major to the Army Service Corps, and was of the greatest help to Captain Ryan. He proved himself to be a most thoroughly reliable, sober, and upright man, clever at his work, and particularly active and zealous in its performance.

Serjeant Cook, Bechuanaland Rifles, specially recommended for clever and plucky scouting, and for gallantry in action (*vide* separate letter).

Serjeant-Major Moffat, Signalling Staff, for gallantry in action, in bringing a serjeant out of action under heavy fire. Also for good work as a signaller (*vide* separate letter). Serjeant-Major Taylor, Colonial Contingent, for gallantry and general good work in the Brickfields, scouting, blowing up a kiln occupied by the enemy, &c.

This non-commissioned officer was killed in action.

Conclusion.

I should like to add that the conduct of the rank and file of the garrisons throughout the 31 weeks' siege, was beyond all praise. In all the long strain of privations, due to short rations and to the entire absence of all luxuries, as well as to living in the trenches month after month, there was no complaining, and the men took their hardships smiling. When there was fighting to be done they showed unexceptionable pluck and steadiness.

The Town Guard, formed of all the civilians capable of bearing arms, took to their duties as soldiers, and submitted themselves to military discipline with most praiseworthy readiness and success.

The self-devotion and good work of the ladies who acted as nurses in the hospitals, have already been alluded to, but the bravery and patience of all the women and elder children, under all the cruel dangers, anxieties, and privations to which they were exposed, were most exemplary.

The natives took their share in the defence of their Stadt, and showed great patience under their trials.

The notable feature of the siege was that the whole community was pervaded by a spirit of loyal endurance and cheery good feeling, under which all the usual local and private differences were sunk in the one great idea of maintaining Her Majesty's supremacy to the end. With such spirit to work on, the task of conducting the defence was an easy one.

R.S.S. BADEN-POWELL.

From Major-General Baden-Powell, Commanding North-West Frontier Forces, to the Chief Staff Officer to Field-Marshal Lord Roberts, V.C.

Ottoshoop,
SIR,   6th June, 1900.

WITH reference to the recommendations of Officers for good service in the siege of Mafeking, as submitted in my report on the operations, I venture to recommend for special recognition the following from among those Officers:-

Major Godley.
Major Vyvyan.
Captain Ryan.
Major Lord E. Cecil.
Lieutenant-Colonel Walford.

Major Panzera.

All of whom did exceptionally good service.

Captain FitzClarence, for personal gallantry, recommended for the V.C.
Captain Marsh, good service in action.
Captain Ashley-Williams, good service in action.
Lieutenant Lord C. Bentinck, good service in action.
Major Anderson, medical services.
Major Goold-Adams, civil and political services.
Mr. C.C.H. Bell, civil and political services.
Mr. F. Whiteley (Mayor of Mafeking), eminent civil services. His reward would be highly appreciated by the townspeople, as recognition of their share in the defence.

In addition to the above, the following ladies for hospital services, viz.:-

Miss Hill.
Mother Teresa.
Lady Sarah Wilson.
Miss Craufurd.

The latter also for attending wounded Boers under fire on the 12th May.

I have, &c.,
R.S.S. BADEN-POWELL,
Major-General.

* These numbers are quoted from Transvaal newspapers, but must, I think, be exaggerated. I think that about 600 killed and wounded would be nearer the mark.
† ?Godley.

10

THE RELIEF OF MAFEKING

From Colonel B. Mahon to Lieutenant-General Sir Archibald Hunter, K.C.B., Commanding 10th Division.

IN accordance with orders received from you I left Barkly West on 4th May, 1900, in command of Flying Column for relief of Mafeking. We reached Spitz Kop on 5th May and from the top of a hill there I could see your engagement to the east near Rooidam, a party of the Boers you were engaged with seemed to be moving north-west in the direction of our road, I moved the Imperial Light Horse and Royal Horse Artillery so as to intercept them, but they turned east and we did not come in contact.

I despatched Captain Rickman with one squadron Kimberley Mounted Corps to join you.

The next Boers we came across were at Taungs, where a patrol of ours chased them as they were leaving, and picked up a portfolio, which one of them dropped, with their latest telegrams, one of which stated that Young Cronje with his commando was moving north to intercept us at Pudimoe.

From Pudimoe there was a Boer commando marching parallel to us on our right flank. In the Pudimoe district we arrested several rebels and seized a number of rifles, also sheep, cattle, and some horses; between Pudimoe and Vryburg no Boers were seen, but we made some more prisoners and seized several rifles and some stock.

At Vryburg I left Mr. C. St. Quintin in charge and gave him powers of acting magistrate, and Mr. P. Gethin as his assistant. I left our sick at Vryburg under charge of Dr. Nugent.

I also left the live stock we had captured and our sick horses and mules under charge of Mr. P. Gethin. No Boers were encountered until the 13th May between Brodie's and Wright's Farms, north-west of Koodo's Rand; the Boers here had an ambush in thick scrub, which was strongly supported from Koodo's Rand (at Koodo's Rand Nek they had several guns in position); they made a determined attack, but we beat them off after 45 minutes' fighting; all troops behaved excellently.

From what I have since heard there were 900 Boers there with four guns, viz., 500 who had marched up parallel to us, and 400 which had come from Mafeking to intercept us; the two forces joined on the 12th.

We crossed the Marotzani at Dr. Smart's Farm and had difficulty in watering, as we had to dig in the dry bed of the river for it; but, although it took 8 hours to water the force, we managed it all; we marched from Marotzani direct to Jan Masibi on the night of the 14th and reached the Molopo (lots of running water) at Jan Masibi at 5.30 A.M. on the 15th, and there met Colonel Plumer's column, which had also just arrived after a night march.

We all rested on the 15th, as both men and animals required it.

I formed the force into two brigades, 1st Brigade under Lieutenant-Colonel Plumer, 2nd Brigade under Lieutenant-Colonel Edwardes.

We advanced at 6.30 A.M. towards Mafeking, along the north or right bank of the Molopo, in two parallel columns at half a mile interval, the convoy in the centre and slightly in rear.

Plumer's brigade on the right and Edwardes' on the left. At Sani's Post, about 12.30 P.M., firing was heard on the left front, and I advanced Edwardes' brigade; Plumer's at the same time advancing along the river; the convoy following on the road in rear of and between the two brigades. As we advanced I found that the Boers had taken up positions all around us, and had five guns and two pompoms in positions in different places.

The convoy rather impeded my movements, as it was under shell fire, and the Boers were trying to attack it from both flanks and also from the rear, so I had to strengthen both my flank and rear guards, at the same time I continued my advance on Mafeking; the Boers retiring from our front and keeping up with us on the flanks. Our Artillery, especially the Royal Horse Artillery, were making very good practice. At 4.40 P.M. I ordered Colonel Edwardes to bring up his left and turn the Boer right flank, this movement was entirely successful. At 4.40 P.M. I had a message from Colonel Plumer to say his advance was checked on the right by a gun and pompom fire from the White Horse (Israel's Farm). I ordered the Royal Horse Artillery to shell the house. They soon silenced the gun, but not the pompom. I then sent Captain Carr with the Infantry to take the house, which they did, and captured one wagon and a lot of pompom ammunition. It was by this time getting dark, or I think they would have got the pompom.

At 5.45 P.M. all firing, except stray shots of the rear guard, had ceased, and the Boers had retired from all parts. I advanced two miles nearer Mafeking, and formed up the force, with the exception of infantry, which I reinforced with 50 New Zealand Infantry, and left holding the White House. The Boer fire was very heavy at times, and their guns very accurately laid. I attributed the smallness of our casualties to our very wide front and loose formation, and to the excellent way in which our Artillery was served, especially the Royal Horse Artillery, as they never gave the Boers an opportunity of getting fixed tenure in any positions which allowed them a close range fire, and partly to the defectiveness of the Boer shells, very few of which burst.

At 11 P.M., after first ascertaining by patrol that the road was open, I ordered an advance on Mafeking. We started at 12.30 AM., and marched seven miles to Mafeking, which place we entered at 3.30 A.M. on the 17th of May, 1900. Shortly after daylight it was reported that the Boers were clearing out of all their laagers on the east of the town. At 8 A.M. Colonel Baden-Powell ordered out the troops, and we shelled and pressed for a short way, but the horses were too beat to do much. However, we captured one gun and a large quantity of ammunition and other stores, and by 11 A.M. there was not a Boer near Mafeking.

I cannot say what the Boer losses were in either engagement, but from what I have since heard I believe they were fairly heavy. I saw one man at Kraaipan who assisted in burying 22 Boers on the 14th May.

I estimate the number of Boers engaged against us on the 17th of May at about 2,000.

I cannot speak too highly of the behaviour of all ranks, more especially the Royal Horse Artillery and Imperial Light Horse, both during the march, which was long and tiring, and during both engagements. The march was rendered the more fatiguing by having an active enemy on our flank always looking for an opportunity to delay and harass us, and thus rendering scouting more necessary, and extra work on men and horses.

The following farmers were very useful to us and rendered us every assistance, viz., Mr. Keely, Mr. Lamb, Mr. Brodie, and Mr. Wright. The latter had our wounded (25) from the engagements on the 13th May, 1900, in his house, and was most kind in many ways to them. All the above live in the Marotzani district.

I brought into Mafeking five wagon loads of provisions and hospital stores, equalling 10,500lbs.; also 17 bags of flour and 81 head of cattle (these latter, viz., flour and cattle, were captured on the march), and handed them over to Ordnance Corps Stores, Mafeking. I at the same time sent for 200 more cattle and 1,000 sheep to Vryburg: they duly arrived, and I handed them over about the 23rd May.

B. MAHON, Colonel,
Commanding Mafeking Relief Column.
Mafeking, 23rd May, 1900.

11

THE RELIEF OF LADYSMITH

No. 2.

From Field Marshal Lord Roberts to the Secretary of State for War.

Army Head-quarters, South Africa,
Government House, Bloemfontein,
MY LORD,   28th March, 1900.

In continuation of my Memorandum of the 18th ultimo, I have the honour to submit for your Lordship's information a despatch, dated 23rd March, 1900, from Lieut.-General Sir George White, V.C., G.C.B., G.C.S.I., G.C.I.E., describing the defence of Ladysmith, which was invested by the enemy from 2nd November, 1899, until 1st March, 1900, and including the operations of the two days preceding the siege.

2. In the second and third paragraphs of the despatch, Sir George White gives his reasons for deciding to remain at Ladysmith, instead of falling back on the line of the Tugela River. If the question were regarded from an abstract point of view, arguments might be advanced in favour of the latter course; but the existing state of affairs when Sir George White landed in Natal, political exigencies, and the estimate then current of the resources and fighting strength of the Boers must be taken into consideration.

Sir George White arrived at Durban on the 7th October, 1899, where he was met by the late Major-General Sir A.P. Symons. He found most of the troops in Natal already distributed between Glencoe and Ladysmith, Major-General Symons being confident that he could drive back any hostile force which might cross the frontier. Sir George White proceeded at once to Maritzburg, and on 10th October discussed the military and political situation with the Governor of Natal. At this interview he expressed disapproval of the forward position which had been taken up near Glencoe, the force at his disposal, in his opinion, too weak to admit of its defence, together with that of Ladysmith, against superior numbers, and the troops being liable to be cut off, should the Boers advance from the Orange Free State through the passes of the Drakensberg Range. The Governor deprecated a voluntary withdrawal from the position, as being almost certain to lead to a rising among the Dutch, and possibly the native population, not only in Natal, but in Cape Colony. In face of this objection, Sir George White resolved to postpone the concentration of his force at Ladysmith.

On 11th October Sir George White proceeded to Ladysmith, Major-General Symons going on to Dundee. That evening the Boers crossed the frontier, but beyond a slight affair of outposts in the direction of the Drakensberg, no fighting took place until the 20th. The interval was occupied by Sir George White in organizing his troops and examining the Ladysmith position. On 20th October a Boer force, which had entered Natal from the Vryheid district of the Transvaal, and crossed the Buffalo River, was attacked near Glencoe by Sir A.P. Symons. The General was mortally wounded, and, though the enemy's advance was checked for a time, reinforcements came up which necessitated a retirement. Our troops fell back first in the direction of Helpmakaar to Beith, and thence to Ladysmith, which was reached on 27th October.

On the 19th October the enemy, advancing from Newcastle, cut the railway line at Elandslaagte; on the 20th the ground was reconnoitred from Ladysmith, and the next day an action was fought in which the Boers were signally defeated. But here again no permanent advantage was gained, as the reported arrival of a strong column of the enemy from the Orange Free State at Bester's Station led to the immediate withdrawal of our troops to Ladysmith. On the 24th Sir George White moved out some 7 miles to the north-east of Ladysmith in order to cover the march of the force returning from Glencoe, under the command of Major-General Yule, and engaged the enemy at Rietfontein, returning to Ladysmith the same evening. He again attacked the Boers on the 30th at Lombard's Kop, the action being without decisive result. By the 2nd November Ladysmith had been invested, and railway communication between it and Colenso interrupted.

3. From the foregoing narrative it is apparent that Sir George White was placed in an extremely difficult position in being called upon to decide, immediately after his arrival in Natal, whether he should concentrate his whole force at Ladysmith, and, subsequently, when the enemy had shown their strength, whether he should attempt to withdraw that force behind the Tugela.

As regards the first question, I think that he would have done better had he ignored the political objections which were urged by the Governor of Natal and concentrated at Ladysmith. The retention of a portion of his force at Glencoe at once involved him in military complications which he foresaw and ought to have avoided. Nor, indeed, was the political situation improved by his being eventually compelled to order a retirement which could have been effected without risk or loss before the enemy had arrived within striking distance.

As regards the second question, I am of opinion that under the existing circumstances, and having regard to the information then available, Sir George White's decision to make a stand at Ladysmith was correct. A position on the Tugela would to some extent have been more secure, as the country is more open, and the reinforcement of the troops holding the river alignment would have presented fewer difficulties. But, as Sir George White explains in his despatch, the Tugela, at the time of the year, was not a formidable defensive obstacle, and if Ladysmith had been evacuated, the Boers would have pressed on, enveloped the British force, and cut off its communication by rail with Maritzburg. The same process might have been repeated if Sir George White had fallen back on Maritzburg. Moreover, a withdrawal to the Tugela would have enabled the enemy to over-run a much larger portion of the Colony, and so encouraged the disloyal Dutch population throughout South Africa that a general rising might not improbably have taken place.

Undoubtedly the protracted siege of Ladysmith caused grave anxiety, and the necessity for its relief diverted a large body of troops from Cape Colony, and thus delayed the concentration of a force sufficient to undertake offensive operations in the enemy's country. But for these consequences Sir George White cannot justly be held responsible, his main obligation being to defend Natal against a Boer invasion. They may be ascribed to several causes. First, the enemy greatly out-numbered the British force available in Natal when Ladysmith was invested. Secondly, the sharp salient angle formed by the frontier line along the north of Natal, and the convergence on Ladysmith of the railways from the Orange Free State and Transvaal, gave the invaders a decided strategical advantage. This advantage was increased by the general configuration of the country, consisting of a series of rocky terraces sloping gradually downwards from the Drakensberg to the sea. Thirdly, although Ladysmith, had been selected as our advanced military station and depot of supplies in Northern Natal, its liability to attack does not seem to have been recognised, and no steps had been taken before the war began to construct the works and provide the armament which would have materially facilitated its defence.

The foregoing review of the situation, as it must have presented itself to Sir George White, shows that he had strong grounds for deciding not to withdraw behind the Tugela, his decision was approved by General Sir Redvers Buller and though the relief of Ladysmith was an arduous operation which cost many lives, the presence of a strong British garrison at this point prevented the enemy from penetrating further south than Estcourt, and protected the capital and southern portion of the Colony.

4. The behaviour of the Ladysmith garrison through the four months during which it was exposed to continual bombardment, as well as to the privations of a protracted siege, reflects the greatest credit on all ranks. I have much pleasure in bringing to the favourable notice of Her Majesty's Government the resolution and resource displayed by the General Officer in Chief Command, and the cheerful spirit which pervaded the troops, in spite of repeated failures to relieve the town from the south; and I cordially support Sir George White's recommendations on behalf of the Officers (naval and military), the Warrant, non-commissioned, and petty officers, and the men, whose names he has brought forward as specially deserving of recognition.

Praise is also due to the civilians and nursing sisters, who rendered valuable assistance.

5. It is gratifying to observe that, in his account of what occurred on 6th January, when the enemy's determined attack on Ladysmith was gallantly repulsed, a Colonial corps, the Imperial Light Horse, has been singled out by Sir George White for special commendation. By their conduct on this and other occasions during the present war our Colonial kinsmen have proved their readiness to share with their comrades in Her Majesty's Regular Forces the honourable duty of upholding the rights and furthering the interests of the British Empire

I have, &c.,
ROBERTS, Field-Marshal,
Commanding-in-Chief, South Africa.

From Lieut.-General Sir George White, V.C., G.C.B., G.C.S.I., G.C.I.E., late Commanding the Ladysmith Garrison, to the Chief of the Staff to the Field-Marshal Commanding-in-chief in South Africa.

Cape Town,

Sir,   23rd March, 1900.

In my despatch dated 2nd December, 1899, addressed to the Secretary of State for War, and forwarded through you, I brought down the history of events relating to the force under my command to the evening of 30th October, 1899. On the morning of the following day, General the Right Honourable Sir Redvers Buller, V.C., G.C.B., K.C.M.G., arrived at Cape Town and assumed command of the whole of the forces in South Africa. On the 10th January, 1900, Field-Marshal Lord Roberts took over the chief command. I have now the honour to report, for his Lordship's information, the events which have taken place from that date until the 1st March, 1900, on which day Sir Redvers Buller arrived in Ladysmith, having successfully carried out the relief of this long besieged town.

2. It will be remembered that during October, 1899, the forces of the Orange Free State and the South African Republic had been gradually converging on Ladysmith from west and north, and that, although my troops had success-fully encountered portions of the enemy's armies at Talana, Elandslaagte, and Rietfontein, the battle of Lombard's Kop on 30th October had proved that the numbers and mobility of the Boer forces, when once concentrated, were too great to admit of any prospect of victory should I continue with inferior numbers to oppose them in the open field. The task before me was the protection from invasion by the Boers of as large a portion as possible of the Colony of Natal, and especially of Pietermaritzburg, the capital of that Colony and the seat of its Government; and I had now to consider how this could be best insured. On 31st October General Sir Redvers Buller telegraphed to me as follows:- "Can you not entrench and await events, if not at Ladysmith then behind the Tugela at Colenso?" On the same date I replied, stating my intention to hold on to Ladysmith, and on 1st November I received Sir Redvers Buller's approval of this course in a telegram which commenced as follows:- "I agree that you do best to remain at Ladysmith, though Colenso and line of Tugela river look tempting."

3. It may be well to state here shortly the reasons which governed my choice of this position. Ladysmith is the most important town in Northern Natal, and there was reason to believe that the enemy attached very great and per-haps even undue importance to obtaining possession of it. It was suspected then, and the suspicion has since been confirmed that the occupation of that town by the Boer forces had been decided on by the disloyal Dutch in both Colonies as the signal for a general rising; as, in fact, a material guarantee that the power of the combined Republics was really capable of dealing with any force the British Empire was able to place in the field against them. Our withdrawal would, therefore, have brought about an insurrection so wide-spread as to have very materially increased our difficulties. Strategically the town was important as being the junction of the railways which enter Natal from the Transvaal and the Orange Free State, and until the Republics could gain possession of that junction their necessarily divergent lines of supply and communication prevented their enjoying to the full the advantages of com-bined action. Tactically the place was already partially prepared for defence and offered a natural position of some strength; and although the perimeter which must be occupied was very great for the number of troops available, yet it afforded a possibility of maintaining a protracted defence against superior numbers. On the other hand, the mere fact of a retirement behind the Tugela would have had a moral effect at least equal to a serious defeat, and would have involved the abandonment to the enemy of a large town full of an

English population, men, women, and children; and of a mass of stores and munitions of war which had been already collected there before my arrival in South Africa, and had since been increased. The line of the Tugela from the Drakensberg to the Buffalo River is some 80 miles long, and in a dry season, such as last November, can be crossed on foot almost anywhere. Against an enemy with more than double my numbers, and three times my mobility, I could not hope to maintain such a line with my small force, and any attempt to prevent their turning my flanks could only have resulted in such a weakening of my centre as would have led to its being pierced. Once my flank was turned on the line of the river the enemy would have been nearer Maritzburg than I should have been, and a rapid withdrawal by rail for the defence of the capital would have been inevitable. Even there it would have been impossible to make a prolonged defence without leaving it open to the enemy to occupy the important port of Durban, through which alone supplies and reinforcements could arrive, and for the defence of which another retreat would have become eventually essential; thus abandoning to the enemy the whole Colony of Natal from Lang's Nek to the sea. On the other hand, I was confident of holding out at Ladysmith as long as might be necessary, and I saw clearly that so long as I maintained myself there I could occupy the great mass of the Boer armies, and prevent them sending more than small flying columns south of the Tugela, which the British and Colonial forces in my rear, added by such reinforcements as might be shortly expected, could deal with without much difficulty. Accordingly, I turned my whole attention to preparing Ladysmith to stand a prolonged siege.

4. With this object in view, I employed my troops during 31st October and 1st November in improving and strengthening the defences of the various positions surrounding Ladysmith, which together enclosed the area which I had determined to hold. During these days the Boers gradually pushed round from north and west to the south and east of the town, which underwent a slight bombardment on 1st November. On 31st October, General Koch, of the Army of the South African Republic, who had been wounded and taken prisoner at Elandslaagte, died, and his widow was permitted to remove his body for burial in the Transvaal. Before leaving she expressed her gratitude for the courtesy and kind treatment which both her late husband and herself had received at our hands. On the same date, I despatched the 2nd Bn. Royal Dublin Fusiliers and Natal Field Battery by rail to Colenso to assist in the defence of the bridges over the Tugela. During the night of 1st–2nd November, the Boers brought several new guns, into position, and although the Naval Brigade, under Captain The Hon. H. Lambton, R.N., opened fire from one of the naval 4.7-inch guns on the morning of 2nd November, the

bombardment of the town became much more severe than on the previous days. At about 4 a.m., the 5th Dragoon Guards, 5th Lancers, 18th Hussars, Natal Mounted Volunteers, and 69th Battery, Royal Field Artillery, moved out south into the Long Valley to reconnoitre the enemy and to endeavour to surprise one of his camps in the direction of Onderbrook. Major-General French, who was in command, left Colonel Royston with the Natal Mounted Volunteers and two guns to hold the Nek between Wagon Hill and Middle Hill, and with the remainder of his force passed round the southern end of End Hill (where he left a squadron of the 5th Lancers to hold a ridge, dismounted), and gaining the plateau pushed on about 3,000 yards and opened an effective fire on the Boer camp. The enemy evacuated their camp and took up a position on a ridge to which they brought up field guns. Major- General French, having fulfilled his mission, withdrew his force, reaching camp by 10 a.m. Our casualties were one man wounded.

As he returned to Ladysmith a telegram was received from General Sir Redvers Buller, desiring that Major-General French and his staff might be sent to the Cape. Communication by wire and rail were still open, and although trains were constantly fired upon, advantage had been taken of the fact to send southward as many of the civil population of Ladysmith as were willing to depart. Major-General French and his staff left by train about noon on 2nd November, and a telegraphic report was received here that, although the train had been heavily fired on near Pieters Station, it had reached Colenso in safety. Immediately afterwards the wires were cut by the enemy, and railway communication was interrupted. Ladysmith was thus isolated from the world outside it, and from this date the siege may be held to have commenced.

5. On 3rd November, four squadrons, Imperial Light Horse, under Major Karri Davis who were reconnoitring to the south, found a body of the enemy, with one gun, on Lancer's Hill, and asked for reinforcements to drive them off. The 5th Dragoon Guards, 18th Hussars, 19th Hussars, and 21st Battery, Royal Field Artillery (the whole under Brigadier General J.F. Brocklehurst, M.V.O.), were accordingly sent down the Long Valley to their assistance. The 19th Hussars seized Rifleman's Ridge and endeavoured to turn the enemy's left, while the 18th Hussars covered the right rear; two companies of Infantry, detached from Caesar's Camp, occupied Wagon Hill, and a Mounted Infantry company seized Mounted Infantry Hill to protect the left rear; while the 5th Dragoon Guards and 21st Field Battery were moved straight down the Long Valley. Meantime two squadrons, Imperial Light Horse, were holding Middle Hill, while the remaining two squadrons were facing the enemy on Lancer's Hill. The squadrons on Middle Hill were opposed to a considerable

body of the enemy, who were moving up from the east. The 21st Field Battery opened fire on Lancer's Hill and quickly silenced the enemy's gun. Believing that the enemy were evacuating the hill the two squadrons, Imperial Light Horse, made a gallant but somewhat ill-advised attempt to occupy it, but though they seized and held a portion of the hill the enemy was in too great strength for further progress. In the meanwhile I had sent out the Natal Mounted Volunteers and the 42nd and 53rd Field Batteries to join Brigadier-General Brocklehurst, and to cover his retirement, if necessary. General Brocklehurst sent the Natal Mounted Volunteers to reinforce the Imperial Light Horse squadrons on Middle Hill, and brought both batteries into action in the Long Valley. Finding, however, that the numbers of the enemy in his front and on both flanks were continually increasing, and that he could not hope to press his reconnaissance further without serious loss, he determined to withdraw. With the assistance of a dismounted squadron, 5th Dragoon Guards, under Major Gore, the squadrons, Imperial Light Horse, on Lancer's Hill were retired under cover of Artillery fire till they reached the main body, when the whole force engaged was gradually withdrawn to camp. Our loss was two Officers and two non-commissioned officers and men killed. Three Officers and 23 non-commissioned officers and men wounded, and one man missing. The enemy's loss is reported to have been considerable, chiefly from our Artillery fire.

In the afternoon the enemy made demonstrations of an attack in force on Devonshire Post, which was reinforced as a measure of precaution, but the attack was not seriously pressed, and was repulsed with ease. The bombardment this day was very heavy, a large number of shells falling into the town, and specially in and around the hospitals, which were in various churches and public buildings near the centre of the town. In the evening a deputation of civilian residents of Ladysmith waited on me with the request that permission might be obtained for them to pass through the enemy's lines and proceed to the south. The Principal Medical Officer of the Force also represented that the effect of the bombardment on the large number of wounded in his hospitals was very bad, and asked that, if possible, an agreement might be arrived at for the hospitals to be placed outside the town. Next morning I sent Major Bateson, R.A.M.C., under flag of truce, with a letter to General Joubert, asking that these requests might be agreed to on grounds of humanity to sick, wounded, and non-combatants. In reply, General Joubert agreed to my hospitals being moved out of Ladysmith to a point on the flats, 4 miles down the railway and close to the Intombi Spruit. He refused to allow the civil inhabitants to go south, but permitted them to accompany the sick and wounded to the Intombi Camp. Food and all other requisites for this camp were to be supplied from Ladysmith, and, for this purpose, one train was to be allowed to run each way daily, and by daylight only, under flag of truce. On this same day General Joubert sent into Ladysmith six Officers of the Royal Army Medical Corps, 10 Assistant Surgeons, and 98 of our wounded from Dundee; together with a number of Indian hospital attendants. There was a threatening of attack on Caesar's Camp on this night, 4th November, but it was not pressed. Our first communications by pigeon post to Durban were sent off on this date.

6. 5th November was Sunday. Throughout the siege Sundays have generally been observed by both sides, as far as possible, as days of rest from fighting. There has been no special arrangement on the subject, but a kind of tacit understanding came into existence that neither side would fire unless specially provoked to do so by the construction of fortifications or other signs of movement on the opposite side. 5th November was no exception to this rule, and advantage was taken of the day to send our sick and wounded and all such civilians, men, women, and children, as elected to go, to the Intombi Camp.

7. The defences of Ladysmith were, for the purposes of command, divided into four sections, "A," "B," "C," and "D." "A" section, under Colonel W.G. Knox, C.B., commenced at Devonshire Post and extended to the point where the Newcastle Road passes between Junction Hill and Gordon Hill. "B" section included all the defences from Gordon Hill round to Flagstone Spruit, and was commanded by Major-General F. Howard, C.B., C.M.G., A.D.C. "C" section, under Colonel Ian Hamilton, C.B., D.S.O., comprised the ground from Flagstone Spruit to the eastern extremity of Caesar's Camp. "D" section, under Colonel Royston, Commandant of the Natal Volunteers, included the thorn country north of Caesar's Camp and the Klip River Flats. The troops, which were allotted to these sections, and to the general reserve, and the variations in these arrangements which were, from time to time, found necessary.

8. On 6th November, 2nd Lieutenant R.G. Hooper, 5th Lancers, reached Ladysmith with despatches. Arriving in Natal too late to join his regiment before communication was cut off, he most gallantly made his way through the Boer lines at night, and on foot, accompanied only by a Kaffir guide. All the provisions in the shops and stores in the town were taken over on this date and administered as part of the general stock, all civil residents being placed on rations which were issued free or on payment according to their means.

9. Next day, 7th November, Caesar's Camp was subjected to a heavy fire of shells and long rangs musketry. Although no actual attack was made, it was found advisable to send the Imperial Light Horse to reinforce this point; while the 42nd Battery Royal Field Artillery, under Major Goulburn, was

placed in position on the plateau during the night, the horses returning to the camp. A number of natives of India were sent into Ladysmith by the Boers.

10. On 8th November a 6-inch gun opened fire from the top of the Bulwana Mountain. Throughout the siege this gun has proved most troublesome to the defence. On the same day a number of refugees from Dundee, both English and Indian, were sent into Ladysmith by the Boers, and were located by us in the Intombi Camp.

11. 9th November was ushered in by a very heavy fire at dawn on all sides of our defences from the enemy's artillery, which included several new guns, which now opened for the first time, and whose exact positions it was very hard to locate. This was followed by a general advance of their infantry and the development of a severe musketry action at Caesar's Camp, in the thorn bush north of that ridge, at Devonshire Post and Observation Hill. The steady front shown by our troops prevented the enemy from trying to close, and although on Caesar's Camp, where the 1st Bn. Manchester Regiment, under Lieut.-Colonel A.E.R. Curran, rendered very valuable service, the action lasted until darkness set in, yet elsewhere it had mostly died away at 12 noon. At that hour I proceeded, with my Staff, to the Naval Battery on Gordon Hill, when a salute of 21 shotted guns, in honour of the birthday of the Prince of Wales, was fired at the enemy by Captain the Hon. H. Lambton, R.N., and three cheers were given for His Royal Highness, which were taken up by the troops both in camp and on the defences. A message of congratulation, to be telegraphed to His Royal Highness, was despatched by pigeon post to Durban. Our casualties during the day amounted to 4 men killed, 4 Officers and 23 men wounded. It is difficult to form any accurate estimate of the enemy's losses, but they certainly considerably exceeded our own.

12. From 10th to 13th November, inclusive, very little of importance occurred, the fire both of guns and rifles being much less severe than usual. An Irish deserter from the Boers gave himself up on the 12th November. From him we learnt that the total force then surrounding us here numbered about 25,000 men, that they were mounting more guns, and expected to be reinforced shortly.

13. On 14th November, I sent Brigadier-General J.F. Brocklehurst, M.V.O., with two regiments of Cavalry, two batteries of Artillery the detachments of the Imperial Light Horse and Natal Volunteers, across the Klip River, to try and work out on one or both sides of Rifleman's Ridge into the more open country beyond, to find out the enemy's strength in that direction, and, if possible, to capture one of their wagon convoys, of which several had recently been seen passing at a distance of some miles. The Natal Mounted Volunteers

and Imperial Light Horse seized Star Hill, but after shelling Rifleman's Ridge for some time General Brocklehurst decided that it was too strongly held for him to leave it in his rear, while an attempt to storm it would have been more costly than the occasion would justify. He, therefore, returned to camp. On this night the Boers commenced for the first time to shell the town and camps at night, opening fire from their heavy guns about midnight for a few minutes, a practice which they maintained nightly for about a week, and then discontinued.

14. From this time nothing worth record took place until 19th November, when the Boers sent into Intombi Camp six privates of the 2nd Bn. Royal Dublin Fusiliers, who had been wounded in the attack on an armoured train near Colenso, on 15th November.

15. 20th November was marked by an unusual number of casualties from shell fire, chiefly among the 18th Hussars and Gordon Highlanders.

16. Next day General S. Burger sent in a letter under a flag of truce, complaining that we had been running trains at night to the Intombi Camp, contrary to our agreement with General Joubert – a complaint for which there was no foundation whatever. He also inquired why a Red Cross flag was flying on the Town Hall although our hospital was at Intombi. I replied, on 22nd November, by giving my personal assurance that trains never had been, and never would be, run to Intombi at night, and explaining that the Red Cross flag was hoisted on the Town Hall because that building was in use as a hospital for ordinary cases of sickness, and for slightly wounded men whom it was not worth while to send to Intombi. Before my answer could reach him the Boer guns were deliberately turned on the Town Hall, which was several times struck.

17. On 23rd November the enemy endeavoured, under flag of truce, to send into Ladysmith 230 Indian coolies. It became evident that the intention was to send in here as many non-combatants as could be collected who would be useless for defence, but would help to consume our supplies. For this reason I refused to receive them, and requested that they might be sent to the Officer commanding our forces south of the Tugela. I understand that this course was eventually adopted. Copies of the correspondence attached as Appendix B. The same evening an attempt was made to wreck the only engine which the enemy possessed on the Harrismith line. With this object an old locomotive was selected from those in the railway yard here and was sent off down the line, at night, with a full head of steam and with the safety valve screwed down. The Boers had, however, provided against such an attempt by destroying a culvert on our side of their temporary terminus, and here our engine was

derailed and upset. The enemy evidently feared that it carried a cargo of explosives, as they did not approach it next morning until they had sent a number of shells into it from their artillery.

18. On the 24th November we had the misfortune to lose 228 oxen, which were captured by the enemy. Owing to lack of rain the grazing within our lines had become insufficient for all our animals, and a number of our cattle had to be grazed outside our defences, wherever a re-entrant gave them some protection from capture. Owing to the carelessness of certain civilian conductors, these oxen were allowed to stray too far out and seeing this the Boers commenced bursting shells on our side of the cattle in order to hasten their movements. In this they were successful, the Kafirs in charge abandoning their animals in order to seek shelter. As soon as the occurrence was noticed, the Mounted Infantry Company of the 1st Bn. Leicestershire Regiment, under Captain C. Sherer, was sent out to try and head them back, but it was then too late, and though Captain Sherer did all that was possible and drove back a considerable number, under a heavy musketry fire from the enemy, yet, as already mentioned, the enemy obtained possession of 228 head.

19. Beyond the usual daily bombardment nothing worth recording took place till 27th November, which was marked by the unmasking of a new 6-inch gun on Middle Hill, and a very evident increase in the number of Boers in our immediate vicinity. An attack on our positions seemed likely, and all precautions were taken accordingly, but next day news arrived of Major-General Hildyard's fight at Mooi River, and the consequent withdrawal of the Boers to the north of the Tugela, which fully explained the increased numbers visible from Ladysmith.

20. On the 28th November, two 6.3-inch howitzers were sent to occupy emplacements which had been prepared for them on the reverse slope of Wagon Hill; a naval 12-pr. was also placed on Caesar's camp. From this position they opened fire next day, and proved able to quite keep down the fire from the enemy's 6-inch gun on Middle Hill, which some days afterwards was withdrawn from that position. I arranged an attack on Rifleman's Ridge for the night of 29th November, but was compelled to abandon it, as just at sunset the enemy very strongly reinforced that portion of their line. There can, I think, be no doubt that my plan had been disclosed to them, and indeed throughout the siege I have been much handicapped by the fact that every movement or preparation for movement which has taken place in Ladysmith, has been at once communicated to the Boers. The agents through whom news reached them, I have, unfortunately, failed to discover. I have sent away or

locked up every person against whom reasonable grounds of suspicion could be alleged, but without the slightest effect.

21. Two civilians, who had volunteered to blow up the Sunday's River railway bridge, started on their perilous journey on 29th November, and returned here on 1st December. They reached the bridge without mishap, and duly placed the charges, but owing to not fully understanding the use of the fuze, only one out of four charges exploded.

22. On 29th November also we observed flashing signals on the clouds at night from Estcourt and were able to read a portion of a message. At a later period of the siege no difficulty was experienced in reading such messages, but we were without means of replying in similar fashion.

23. 30th November was a day of very heavy bombardment, a new 6-inch gun opening fire from Gun Hill and doing much damage. One shell in particular entered the Town Hall which we had hitherto used as a hospital, killing and wounding 10 persons. It was found necessary to evacuate the building and place the hospital under canvas in a gorge where the protection from shell fire was better. This severe bombardment continued throughout 1st and 2nd December, but fortunately proved comparatively harmless. On the latter date heliographic communication via Weenen was restored after having been interrupted for a long period.

24. On 3rd December General Joubert sent me a letter alleging that we had made unfair use of the Intombi Camp, and proposing that it should be broken up. In reply, I dealt in detail with the points raised, none of which had any foundation in fact, and as a result the breaking up of the camp was not pressed.

25. On 5th December, at 1.30 a.m., two companies of the 2nd Bn. Rifle Brigade moved out, under Captain J.E. Gough, to surprise Thornhill's Farm which the enemy were in the habit of occupying with a picket at night. The enterprise was very well conducted, but the farm was unfortunately found unoccupied.

26. On the night of 7th December, Major-General Sir A. Hunter, K.C.B., D.S.O., made a sortie for the purpose of destroying the Boer guns on Gun Hill, which had been giving us much annoyance. His force consisted of 500 Natal Volunteers, under Colonel Royston, and 100 men Imperial Light Horse, under Lieut.-Colonel A.H.M. Edwards, with 18 men of the Corps of Guides, under Major D. Henderson, D.A.A.G. for Intelligence, to direct the column, and four men Royal Engineers and 10 men No.10 Mountain Battery,

Royal Garrison Artillery, under Captain Fowke and Lieut, Turner, Royal Engineers, with explosives and sledge hammers for the destruction of the guns when captured. Sir A. Hunter's arrangements were excellent throughout, and he was most gallantly supported by all his small force. Gun Hill was taken, a 6-inch Creusot and a 4.7-inch howitzer destroyed, and a Maxim captured and brought into camp. Our loss was only one Officer and seven men wounded. I consider that Major-General Sir A. Hunter deserves the greatest credit for this very valuable service for which he volunteered. He brings to my notice specially the gallant behaviour of Colonel W. Royston, Commanding Volunteers, Natal, Lieut.-Colonel A.H.M. Edwards (5th Dragoon Guards), Commanding Imperial Light Horse, Major D. Henderson, D.A.A.G. for Intelligence (wounded), Major A.J. King, Royal Lancaster Regiment, Major Karri Davis, Imperial Light Horse, Captain G.H. Fowke, R.E., and Lieutenant E.V. Turner, R.E., whose names I have much pleasure in bringing forward for favourable consideration.

27. The same night three companies of the 1st Bn. Liverpool Regiment, under Lieut.-Colonel L.S. Mellor, seized Limit Hill, and through the gap in the enemy's outpost line thus created, a squadron 19th Hussars penetrated some 4 miles towards the north, destroying the enemy's telegraph line and burning various kraals and shelters ordinarily occupied by them. No loss was incurred in this enterprise. At the same time five companies 1st Bn. Leicestershire Regiment, under Lieut.-Colonel G.D. Carleton, visited Hyde's and McPherson's farms, usually occupied by the enemy as night outposts, but found them evacuated.

28. The slight opposition met with by these various operations of the night of 7th–8th December made it appear probable that the enemy had unduly weakened his force to the north of us in order to strengthen that opposing Sir Redvers Buller on the Tugela. Recognising that if this proved to be the case there might be an opportunity for my Cavalry to get far enough north to damage the enemy's railway, I ordered Brigadier-General J.F. Brocklehurst, M.V.O., to move out at dawn with 5th Lancers, 5th Dragoon Guards, and 18th Hussars and 53rd Battery, Royal Field Artillery, along the Newcastle Road, to feel for the enemy and discover his strength and dispositions. The reconnaissance was carried out in a very bold and dashing manner by the 5th Lancers and 18th Hussars, the 5th Dragoon Guards being in reserve. The enemy, however, proved to be in considerable strength, and having obtained the information I required I directed Brigadier-General Brocklehurst to withdraw his brigade. The effect of these various enterprises was shortly evident in the return from the line of the Tugela next day of some 2,000 Boers.

29. On the 10th December, Lieut.-Colonel C.T.E. Metcalfe, Commanding 2nd Bn. Rifle Brigade, volunteered to carry out a night enterprise against a 4.7-inch howitzer on Surprise Hill. The undertaking was one of very considerable risk, as to reach that hill it was necessary to pass between Thornhill's and Bell's Kopjes, both of which were held by the enemy. Lieut.-Colonel Metcalfe moved off about 10 p.m., with 12 Officers and 488 men of his battalion, together with a destruction party under Lieutenant Digby Jones, R.E., and succeeded in effecting a complete surprise, his advance not being discovered until he was within 4 or 5 yards of the crest line, which was at once carried, and the howitzer destroyed. The retirement, however, proved more difficult, since the enemy from Bell's and Thornhill's Kopjes, consisting apparently of men of various nationalities, closed in from both sides to bar the retreat. Lieut.-Colonel Metcalfe, however, fixed bayonets, and the companies, admirably handled by their captains, fought their way back to the railway line, where a portion of the force had been left in support, and from which point the retirement became easy. A number of the enemy were killed with the bayonet, and his total casualties must have been very considerable. Our own loss amounted to 1 Officer and 16 men killed, 3 Officers and 37 men wounded, and 6 men missing. The affair reflects great credit on Lieut.-Colonel C.T.E. Metcalfe and his battalion, and I have much pleasure in bringing to your notice, in a subsequent portion of this despatch, the names of the Officers who particularly distinguished themselves on this occasion.

30. My attention was now chiefly directed to preparations for moving out a flying column to co-operate with General Sir Redvers Buller. All these preparations, including the movement of a 4.7-inch and a 12-pr. gun, both belonging to the Royal Navy, were completed by 15th December. Meanwhile the enemy had moved his 6-inch gun from Middle Hill to Telegraph Hill, and on 12th December I moved down the 6.3-inch howitzers to near Ration Post to oppose it.

31. The firing of Sir Redvers Bullers guns from the direction of Colenso had been audible for some days, and was especially heavy on 15th December. On 16th, Sir Redvers heliographed that he had attacked Colenso on the previous day, but without success. Although this news was naturally disappointing to the hopes of immediate relief which they had entertained, yet it was received by both soldiers and civilians without any discouragement, and with a cheerful readiness to wait until the necessary reinforcements should arrive. From this time up to the close of the year few other events of importance occurred, but on Christmas day a telegram was received from Her Majesty and most gratefully appreciated by the garrison of Ladysmith. At this period a few of the many shells daily fired into our camps were especially destructive, one

shell, on the 18th December, killed and wounded 10 men and 12 horses of the Natal Volunteers. Another, on 22nd December, killed 8 and wounded 9 of the Gloucestershire Regiment, and, on the same day a single shell wounded 5 Officers and the serjeant-major of the 5th Lancers. On 27th December, again, one shell killed 1 Officer of the Devonshire Regiment and wounded 8 Officers and 1 private of that regiment. During this period, also, fresh complaints regarding the Intombi Camp were made by the enemy; and, by agreement with General S. Burger, Major-General Sir A. Hunter was sent to that camp to hold an inquiry. A few minor irregularities were discovered and corrected, and a copy of Sir A Hunter's report was sent to General Burger, who was apparently satisfied that the complaints were without serious foundation.

32. At the close of the year my chief source of anxiety lay in the heavy and continuous increase in the number of the sick, which had risen from 475 on 30th November to 874 on 15th December, and to 1,558 on the last day of the year. Enteric fever and dysentery were chiefly responsible for this increase, there being 452 cases of the former, and 376 of the latter under treatment on 31st December.

33. The Boers opened the new year by a fire of heavy guns at midnight, but beyond the daily long-range bombardment, nothing of importance occurred until 5th January, when we shelled, by indirect fire, two Boer camps, one behind Bell's Kopje, and one near Table Hill on the Colenso Plateau. In the latter case the fire probably had little effect, as the range was too great even for the naval gun employed, and the only possible observing station was very inconveniently placed. It was subsequently ascertained from the Boers themselves that the shells falling into the camp behind Bell's Kopje had been very effective, stampeding the horses and compelling the enemy temporarily to vacate the camp and seek shelter elsewhere.

34. On the 6th January the enemy made a most determined but fortunately unsuccessful attempt to carry Ladysmith by storm. Almost every part of my position was more or less heavily assailed, but the brunt of the attack fell upon Caesar's Camp and Wagon Hill. On the night of the 5th – 6th January, Caesar's Camp was held by its usual garrison, consisting of the 1st Bn. Manchester Regiment; the 42nd Battery, Royal Field Artillery; a detachment of the Royal Navy, with a 12-pr. gun and a detachment Natal Naval Volunteers. Wagon Hill was held as usual by three companies, 1st Bn. King's Royal Rifle Corps, and a squadron, Imperial Light Horse. A detachment Natal Naval Volunteers, with a 3-pr. Hotchkiss gun, had been sent there on the evening of the 5th January, and two Naval guns, one a 4.7-inch and the other

a 12-pr., were in process of transfer to the hill during the night. These guns were accompanied by naval detachments and a working party of Royal Engineers and Gordon Highlanders, who were consequently on Wagon Hill when the attack commenced at 2.30 a.m. on the morning of 6th January. This attack was first directed on the centre of the southern face of Wagon Hill, whence it spread east and west. It fell directly on the squadron of Imperial Light Horse, under Lieutenant G.M. Mathias, and the Volunteer Hotchkiss Detachment under Lieutenant E.N.W. Walker, who clung most gallantly to their positions, and did invaluable service in holding in check till daylight the Boers who had gained a footing on the hill within a few yards of them. The extreme south-west point of the hill was similarly held by a small mixed party of Bluejackets, Royal Engineers, Gordon Highlanders, and Imperial Light Horse, under Lieutenant Digby Jones, R.E. The remainder of the hill was defended by the companies of 1st Bn. King's Royal Rifle Corps. Shortly after 3 a.m. An attack was developed against the south-east end of Caesar's Camp (which was garrisoned by the 1st Bn. Manchester Regiment), and on the thorn jungle between that hill and the Klip River, which was held by the Natal Mounted Volunteers. As soon as the alarm reached me, I ordered the Imperial Light Horse, under Lieut.-Colonel A.H.M. Edwards, to proceed as rapidly as possible to Wagon Hill, and the Gordon Highlanders to Caesar's Camp. Shortly afterwards, four companies, 1st Bn. King's Royal Rifle Corps, and four companies, 2nd Bn. King's Royal Rifle Corps, were ordered to march at once on Wagon Hill, and the 2nd Bn. Rifle Brigade on Caesar's Camp. This section of my defences was under the command of Colonel Ian Hamilton, C.B., D.S.O., who, judging that Wagon Hill was the point most seriously threatened, proceeded there himself, where he arrived about dawn, bringing with him a company of the 2nd Bn. Gordon Highlanders under Major Miller Wallnutt. Perceiving that the close and deadly nature of the fighting made it impossible for one Officer to adequately command on both hills, I directed Colonel Hamilton to devote his attention to Wagon Hill, while I entrusted the defence of Caesar's Camp to Lieut.-Colonel A.E.R. Curran, 1st Bn. Manchester Regiment, who had been stationed there with his battalion ever since the commencement of the siege, and was specially acquainted with the locality. I ordered Major W.E. Blewitt's battery of Royal Field Artillery, escorted by the 5th Dragoon Guards, to move out by Range Post and endeavour to prevent reinforcements reaching the enemy from the west. Major A.J. Abdy's battery of Royal Field Artillery I sent to Colonel Royston, Commanding Natal Mounted Volunteers, to take up position on the Klip River Flats and shell the south-eastern corner of Caesar's Camp, where the enemy had effected a lodgment.

The Imperial Light Horse reached Wagon Hill at 5.10 a.m., and were at once pushed into action. They pressed forward up to and over the western edge of the flat crest of the hill to within a few yards of the enemy, who held the opposite edge of the crest. They thus afforded a most welcome relief to the small garrison of the hill, but they themselves suffered very severely in occupying and maintaining their position. The company of 2nd Bn. Gordon Highlanders, which arrived with Colonel Hamilton, was sent under cover of the western slopes to reinforce the extreme south-west point of the hill, and to endeavour to work round so as to outflank the enemy, but were unable to do so owing to the extreme severity of the fire kept up by the Boers from Mounted Infantry Hill and from every available scrap of cover in Bester's Valley, which they occupied in great numbers. At 7 a.m., four companies 1st Bn. King's Royal Rifle Corps and four companies 2nd Bn. King's Royal Rifle Corps arrived, and about 8 a.m., one of these companies, followed shortly afterwards by another, was sent to reinforce the extreme south-western point of the hill, but although gallantly holding their own under a rain of shells and bullets, no progress could be made either there or on the main ridge. Meanwhile the 21st and 42nd Batteries, Royal Field Artillery, and the naval 12-pr. on Caesar's Camp, were in action against Mounted Infantry Hill and the scrub on either side of it, and were of great assistance in keeping down the violence of the enemy's fire. Colonel Hamilton, seeing plainly that the only way of clearing out those of the enemy's marksmen who were established on the eastern crest of Wagon Hill, within a few yards of our men, was by a sudden rush across the open, directed Major Campbell to tell off a company of the 2nd Bn. King's Royal Rifle Corps to make the attempt, which however failed, Lieutenant N.M. Tod, who commanded, being killed, and the men falling back to the cover of the rocks from behind which they had started. The fighting continuing stationary and indecisive, at 10 a.m. I sent the 5th Lancers to Caesar's Camp and the 18th Hussars to Wagon Hill, two squadrons 19th Hussars having been previously posted on the ground near Maiden Castle to guard against any attempt of the enemy to turn Wagon Hill from the west.

For some time the fighting slackened considerably, the Boers being gradually driven down below the crest line, except at a single point where they were favoured by excellent cover, with a flat open space in front of it. At 1 p.m., however, a fresh assault was made with great suddenness on the extreme south-west point of the hill, our men giving way for a moment before the sudden outburst of fire and retiring down the opposite slope. Fortunately the Boers did not immediately occupy the crest, and this gave time for Major Miller Wallnutt, 2nd Bn. Gordon Highlanders, Lieutenant Digby Jones, R.E., Lieutenant P.D. Fitzgerald (11th Hussars), Adjutant Imperial Light

Horse, Gunner W. Sims, R.N., and several non-commissioned officers, Imperial Light Horse, to rally the men; while Major E.C. Knox, Commanding 18th Hussars brought up a portion of his regiment, which was in reserve at the foot of the hill, to act dismounted.

The top was reoccupied just as the three foremost Boers reached it, the leader being shot by Lieutenant Digby Jones, R.E., and the two others by No. 459 Trooper H. Albrecht, Imperial Light Horse. Had they survived I should have had great pleasure in recommending both Lieutenant Jones and Trooper Albrecht for the distinction of the Victoria Cross. I regret to say that both were killed before the conclusion of the action.

At 3.30 p.m., a storm of wind and rain of extraordinary severity set in and lasted for 3 hours. During its continuance the 5th Dragoon Guards, 5th Lancers, and 1½ squadrons 19th Hussars reinforced Wagon Hill, acting dismounted. About 4.45 p.m., when the storm was at its worst, the portion of our troops holding the extreme south-west point of the hill were again driven from their position, but were rallied and reoccupied it; 2nd Lieutenant R.E. Reade, 1st Bn. King's Royal Rifle Corps, rendering himself conspicuous by his gallant service at this period.

At 5 p.m., Lieut.-Colonel C.W. Park arrived at Wagon Hill with three companies 1st Bn. Devonshire Regiment, which I had ordered up as a reinforcement, and was at once directed by Colonel Hamilton to turn the enemy off the ridge with the bayonet. The Devons dashed forward and gained a position under cover within 50 yards of the enemy. Here a fire fight ensued, but the Devons were not to be denied, and, eventually, cheering as they pushed from point to point, they drove the enemy not only off the plateau but cleared every Boer out of the lower slopes and the dongas surrounding the position. Lieut.-Colonel Park went into action with four Officers, but he alone remained untouched at the close. The total loss of the Devons was nearly 28 per cent. of those engaged, and the men fired only 12 rounds per rifle. Captain A. Menzies, 1st Bn. Manchester Regiment, with a few of his men, accompanied the Devons throughout. He also was wounded.

I desire to draw special attention to the gallantry displayed by all ranks of the Imperial Light Horse, some of whom were within 100 yards of the enemy for 15 hours exposed to a deadly fire. Their losses were terribly heavy, but never for one moment did any of them waver or cease to show a fine example of courage and determination to all who came in contact with them.

I have already mentioned that about 3 a.m., the south-east end of Caesar's Camp was also attacked, as well as the pickets of the Natal Volunteers in the thorn scrub to the north of that hill. During the darkness the enemy succeeded in establishing themselves on part of that end of Caesar's Camp, but the precise details of what occurred have not been made clear, as nearly all the defenders of this portion have been killed. It is believed, however, that taking advantage of a general similarity of dress to that of the Natal Volunteers and Police, and many of them having a perfect command of the English language, the Boers succeeded in deceiving the pickets as to their identity, and were thus able to effect a surprise. As already stated, I sent the 53rd Battery, Royal Field Artillery, under Major A.J. Abdy, to Colonel Royston, Commanding Natal Volunteers; and these guns, most ably handled, came into action on the Klip River flats, and, though exposed to the fire of several Boer guns (including a 6-inch Creusot gun on Bulwana Mountain), to which they had no means of replying, shelled the south-east portion of Caesar's Camp with great effect, and inflicted very heavy losses on the enemy. The 2nd Bn. Gordon Highlanders and 2nd Bn. Rifle Brigade were sent to Lieut.-Colonel A.E.R. Curran, who was in command here, and were gradually pushed into the fight, company by company, wherever their services were most required. Gradually the Boers were pushed back over the crest line, but held on most stubbornly to the slopes, being continually reinforced or relieved from the dongas below and from the adjacent hills, whence a fire of very great intensity was kept up, while the whole of the plateau was swept by the Boer long-range guns from distant eminences. At last, after 15 hours of stubborn resistance by our men, and of continual effort on the part of the Boers, the enemy were driven off at all points during the same storm in which Wagon Hill was also cleared as already described, their retreat being hastened by the heavy fire poured on them as they retired.

Another attack was made before dawn on the 6th January on Observation Hill West, occupied by ½ battalion 1st Bn. Devonshire Regiment, under Major M.C. Curry. The enemy gained some dead ground near our works during the darkness, and at 9.30 a.m., and again at a later hour, they attempted to storm the works under cover of the fire of these men and of guns and rifles from all the surrounding kopjes. These, however, were repelled with no great difficulty by the wing 1st Bn. Devonshire Regiment, and the Artillery allotted to this portion of the defence, consisting of Royal Field Artillery and naval guns. The enemy, however, held on to the dead ground originally occupied all day, and only withdrew during the storm in the afternoon. The remainder of Section "B" and the whole of Section "A" of the defences were subjected to a heavy fire of guns and rifles all day, but no other attempt to press home an attack was made on these portions of our line.

Our losses, I regret to say, were very heavy, consisting of 14 Officers and 135 non-commissioned officers and men killed, and 31 Officers and 244 men wounded. I have not been able to ascertain the actual loss to the Boers, but 79 bodies found within our lines were returned to them next day for burial, and native spies report that their total casualties could not be less than 700.

35. On 8th January a thanksgiving service in commemoration of the repulse of the enemy on 6th idem was held by Archdeacon Barker, and very largely attended by such officers and men as could be spared from duty. From this time until the end of the siege, no further effort to carry Ladysmith by assault was made by the Boers, whose attention was fully occupied by the various attacks made by Sir Redvers Buller on the line of the Tugela, though the town and camps were exposed to a daily bombardment from the enemy's guns, and skirmishing between our outposts and those of the Boers went on all day and every day, and caused us small but continuous losses. During this period I shall only refer to a night enterprise undertaken by 2nd Lieutenant H.C.W. Theobald, and 15 non-commissioned officers and men, 1st Bn. Gloucestershire Regiment. The object was to set fire to the abbattis which the enemy had constructed at the foot of Gun Hill, and was carried out in a manner reflecting credit on the young Officer in command, and without loss; while creating a considerable scare among the Boers who fired heavily in the darkness for a considerable time.

36. On 1st March I sent Colonel W.G. Knox, with the 1st Bn. Liverpool Regiment, 1st Bn. Devonshire Regiment, 2nd Bn. Gordon Highlanders, 5th Dragoon Guards, and the 53rd and 67th Batteries, Royal Field Artillery, to move out along the Newcastle Road to harrass as much as possible the enemy whom we could see retiring before the successful advance of Sir Redvers Buller's force. Colonel Knox carried Long Hill and Pepworth Hill and opened fire with his guns on Modder Spruit Railway Station and the large Boer camp there, which the enemy at once evacuated. Both men and horses were too weak for rapid or prolonged operations, but several of the enemy's camps were captured, and the force returned after having very successfully carried out their object to as great a distance as their weakness permitted them to pursue. Our casualties were 2 Officers and 6 non-commissioned officers and men wounded.

37. Colonel Lord Dundonald with a body of Colonial troops rode into Ladysmith on the evening of 28th February, and on 1st March General Sir Redvers Buller himself arrived, and the siege came to an end.

38. During the period from 6th January to 1st March, our struggle became one against disease and starvation even more than against the enemy. Our worst foes in this respect were enteric fever and dysentery, the former especially committing great ravages among the young soldiers of the garrison. Our deaths by disease from 2nd November, 1899, to 28th February, 1900, amounted to 12 Officers and 529 non-commissioned officers and men. The Officers of the Royal Army Medical Corps, the Army Nursing Sisters, the many ladies who voluntarily offered their services as nurses, and the hospital

staffs of all ranks, maintained throughout the siege a brave and protracted struggle against sickness under almost every possible disadvantage, their numbers being most inadequate for the work to be done, and the supplies of drugs and of suitable food for invalids being entirely insufficient for so many patients for so long a period.

39. Even more important was the regulation and augmentation of the food supplies, as will be realized from the simple statement that 21,000 mouths had to be fed for 120 days; and the admirable manner in which all arrangements were made and carried out by the Officers of the Army Service Corps and Indian Commissariat Department under the able and untiring super-intendence of Colonel E.W.D. Ward, C.B., my A.A.G. (B), will be evident from the fact that at the date of the relief we still possessed resources capable of maintaining this great number on reduced rations for another 30 days.

At the commencement of the siege, it became necessary to augment as far as possible all food supplies, and, with this view, one mill and subsequently two, were taken over and worked under military supervision and with labour and mechanics obtained from the employees of the Natal Government Railway, who remained voluntarily with the garrison. From these mills we produced during the siege mealie flour, mealie bran and crushed mealies. The mills were worked under the personal supervision of Lieut.-Colonel Stoneman, A.S.C., D.A.A.G., assisted by Major D.M. Thompson, Assistant Commissary-General, Indian Commissariat Transport Department.

When grazing and forage became scarce and the supply of cattle approached within a measurable distance of extinction, it was necessary to utilize for food the horses which would otherwise have died from exhaustion and weakness. From these slaughtered horses very considerable additions to the food supply were made by the establishment of a factory from which were made: (i.) "Chevril," a strong meat soup issued nightly to the troops; (ii.) a condensed form of "Chevril" which took the place in the hospitals of various meat extracts which had been expended; (iii.) a jelly similar to calf-foot jelly for the sick and wounded; (iv.) "Chevril paste" made of boiled meat and jelly and issued as a ration to the men, and which being similar to the potted meats manufactured at home was much appreciated by the troops; and finally (v.) "neats-foot oil," which was used for lubricating the heavy Naval Ordnance. The boiled meat was given to the soldiers at the rate of ½ lb. per man.

The whole of this factory was under the management of Lieut. C.E.J. MacNalty, A.S.C., whose untiring energy, ingenuity, and intelligence are deserving of high commendation. Captain J.R. Young, R.E., R.S.O., converted a railway locomotive shed into a factory, and displayed very great skill in improvising the various appliances necessary for the manufacture of the different foods.

With the object of still further improving the rations a sausage factory was established which converted the horse-flesh into excellent sausages, issued to the men at the rate of ¼ lb. per head. This factory was most efficiently worked under the supervision of Mr. R. Beresford Turner.

As a safeguard against any serious loss of animals by disease or from other causes with a consequent reduction of our power of continuing the defence, a reserve of "biltong" was prepared, under the superintendence of Captain A. Long, A.S.C., who undertook it in addition to his onerous duties of Local Transport Officer.

The very large number of enteric and dysentery patients rendered it necessary to utilise all available sources of milk supply. All milch cows were requisitioned, and a dairy system established which provided milk, on medical certificate, for the sick, both military and civilian.

The feeding of the civil population was carried out by the Army Service Corps, a staff of civilian assistants being organised for distribution, and a large shed specially converted for the purpose. The two foregoing duties were carried out under the direction of Lieut.-Colonel Stoneman, D.A.A.G., and Major Thompson, A.C.G.

40. On the investment of Ladysmith, the main was broken by the enemy, and the water supply for the camp and town became dependent upon the Klip River. A system of filtration by Berkfeld filters was commenced, which answered well so long as the limited supply of alum lasted; as soon as it was expended the muddy condition of the water clogged the filters, and this method became unreliable. Three condensers were then constructed out of improvised materials by Mr. Binnie, Maintenance Manager, Natal Government Railway, under the able direction of Engineer C.C. Sheen, R.N., H.M. Ship "Powerful." As a further means of obtaining pure water, apparatus for clearing water was constructed out of barrack sheeting placed on wooden stands, and having a deposit of wood ashes, through which the water was strained. It thus became possible to use the filters and also to provide all units with clearing arrangements. It was possible, so long as the coal lasted, to supply at least 12,000 gallons of condensed of filtered water daily. The management of the water supply was carried out by Lieutenant H.B. Abadie, 11th Hussars, who performed the duties of Staff Officer for Water Supplies, and whose work is deserving of much praise.

Mr. W. King, District Inspector, Public Works Department, Mr. R. Brooke and the officials of that department, rendered most valuable assistance in every way possible.

41. With the object of reducing the number of orderlies employed in the conveyance of letters, a postal system, which included all the defences and the camp and town, was organised and most efficiently carried out by Captain P.C.J. Scott, A.S.C.

42. In order to supply the deficiency of hay, a corps of grass-cutters was formed and placed under the charge of Major W.J.R. Wickham, Assistant Commissary-General, Indian Commissariat Transport Department. This corps, which consisted of Indian refugees and Kaffirs, did excellent work, and collected grass under conditions of considerable difficulty.

43. I take this opportunity of publicly expressing my deep sense of the gallantry and patient endurance of hardships displayed by all ranks of all corps under my command. The Naval Brigade of H.M. Ship "Powerful," under Captain the Honourable Hedworth Lambton, R.N., have rivalled the best of our troops in gallantry and endurance, and their long-range guns, though hampered by a most serious want of sufficient ammunition, have played a most prominent part in the defence, and have been most successful in keeping the enemy from bringing his guns to the ranges at which they would have been most efficient.

The Cavalry have not only performed their regular duties, but when their horses became non-effective have served as infantry, being re-armed with rifle and bayonet, and taking their regular share in holding the fortifications.

The Artillery have displayed their usual skill and gallantry, whether as mobile batteries or when used as guns of positions in fixed emplacements as became increasingly necessary during the latter portion of the investment.

The Royal Engineers, both Officers and men, have sustained the grand traditions of their corps, and whether engaged on the defences, in maintaining telegraphic and telephonic communication between all sections of the defences, in ballooning, or in any other work required of them, have done everything which they were called upon to perform in a manner which has afforded me the highest satisfaction.

The work of the Infantry especially, exposed day and night to all weathers on our lines of defence, almost continually under fire, and living latterly on a ration consisting of little more than a proportion of horse flesh with ½ lb. per man of inferior and scarcely eatable mealie bread, has been of the most severe and trying nature, and has been carried out without a murmur and with the most cheerful steadfastness.

Of the Imperial Light Horse, specially raised in Natal at the commencement of the war, I have already expressed my opinion. No praise can be too great for the gallantry and determination which all ranks of this corps have invariably displayed in action.

The Natal Volunteers have performed invaluable service. Their knowledge of the country has been of the very greatest use to me, and in every action in which they have been engaged they have shown themselves most forward and daring. The Natal Naval Volunteers have proved themselves worthy comrades of the land forces of the Colony.

44. The civil inhabitants of Ladysmith, of all ages and both sexes, have uncomplainingly borne the privations inseparable from a siege, and have endured the long-continued bombardment to which they have been exposed with a fortitude which does them honour.

45. In conclusion, I trust I may be allowed to give expression to the deep sense of gratitude, felt not only by myself but by every soldier, sailor and civilian who has been through the siege, to General Sir Redvers Buller and his gallant force, who, after such severe fighting, so many hardships, and notwithstanding very severe losses, have triumphantly carried out the relief of my beleaguered garrison.

46. Finally, I desire to bring prominently to your notice the following Officers, Warrant Officers, non-commissioned officers, sailors, soldiers, volunteers, and civilians, who have rendered specially good service during the four months of the siege.

Major-General Sir Archibald Hunter, K.C.B.,D.S.O., who acted as my Chief of the Staff, is an Officer of well-known reputation. I cannot speak too highly of him, whether for the performance of Staff duties or for bold leading in the field. He is a most loyal and efficient Staff Officer, and I recommend him for advancement with the utmost confidence, being well assured that such a step would be for the good of the State.

Captain the Honourable Hedworth Lambton, R.N., commanding the Naval Brigade, reached Ladysmith in the nick of time, when it became evident that I was not strong enough to meet the enemy in the open field. He brought with him two 4.7-inch and four 12-pr. guns, which proved to be the only ordnance in my possession capable of equalling in range the enemy's heavy guns. Although the ammunition available was very limited, Captain Lambton so economised it that it lasted out to the end of the siege, and under his direction the naval guns succeeded in keeping at a distance the enemy's siege guns, a service which was of the utmost importance. Captain Lambton personally has been the life of the garrison throughout the siege.

Major-General F. Howard, C.B., C.M.G., A.D.C., Commanding the 8th Brigade and in charge of Section B of the defences, has proved himself a careful and able administrator. The works constructed in his section were exceptionally strong and well maintained.

Colonel I.S.M. Hamilton, C.B., D.S.O., Commanding 7th Brigade and in charge of Section C of the defences, has, during the whole of the operations of the defence, been in charge of the most exposed and most extended front, including the immense position of Caesar's Camp and Wagon Hill, over 4 miles in perimeter. I cannot speak too highly of his indefatigable zeal in organising the defence of his front, and in keeping up the hearts of all under him by his constant and personal supervision. His leadership on 6th January was the most marked factor in the success of the defence.

Colonel W.G. Knox, C.B., Colonel on the Staff in charge of Section A of the defences, exercised the command entrusted to him with great zeal and skill. The works constructed on his front were models of semi-permanent entrenchment, laid out from the commencement on a plain which enabled him to strengthen them day by day until they became practically impregnable. He is an Officer of fine nerve and a strong disciplinarian. I trust his services may be adequately rewarded.

Colonel W. Royston, Commanding Natal Volunteer Forces and in charge of Section D of the defences. I can only repeat the high praise which I had the pleasure to bestow on Colonel Royston in my despatch of the 2nd December, 1899. He commanded Section D of the defences in an admirable manner, and with his force, though much reduced in numbers by casualties and disease, continued to the end to perform invaluable service. He is an Officer exceptionally suited to his important position as Commandant of the Natal Volunteer Forces, and I trust that he may receive some suitable reward.

Major-General J.F. Brocklehurst, M.V.O., continued to command the Cavalry Brigade until the horses became useless from starvation. In all Cavalry actions round Ladysmith his personal gallantry was conspicuous.

Colonel C.M.H. Downing, Commanding Royal Artillery, did all that a highly-trained specialist could do to assist me in the defence, both as regards the employment of his batteries as mobile units, and also in their distribution and action when it became necessary to demobilise them, and place the guns in fixed epaulments. He is an Officer in whose knowledge and judgment in artillery matters I have every confidence.

Major S.R. Rice, Commanding Royal Engineers, was indefatigable in his exertions both by day and night, and showed considerable skill in laying out works and in giving to the Commanders of Sections of the defences that advice and assistance in their construction which the trained Officers of the Royal Engineers can so ably afford.

Brevet-Colonel E.W.D. Ward, C.B., Army Service Corps, Assistant-Adjutant General, for "B" duties. As the siege continued and the supply difficulties constantly increased, Colonel Ward's cheerful ingenuity met every difficulty with ever-fresh expedients. He is unquestionably the very best

Supply Officer I have ever met, and to his resource, foresight, and inventiveness the successful defence of Ladysmith for so long a period is very largely due. He is exceptionally deserving of reward, and I trust that he may receive the advancement which his services have merited.

Colonel B. Duff, C.I.E., Indian Staff Corps, Assistant Military Secretary, performed the duties of his office with his characteristic ability and zeal. He also took a prominent part in the general Staff duties of head-quarters, in which his services were equally valuable. This Officer is fitted for the highest posts.

Colonel R. Exham, Royal Army Medical Corps, did all that a Principal Medical Officer could do in organising the medical services under circumstances of exceptional difficulty, and with personnel and materiel both inadequate for a siege of such long duration, accompanied by such a great amount of sickness.

Lieut.-Colonel R.W. Mapleton, Royal Army Medical Corps, in charge of Intombi Hospital Camp, was placed in a most exceptional position, in charge of a neutral camp where the maintenance of discipline in the ordinary way was impossible, but in the face of all difficulties he did everything possible to maintain the sanitation of the camp, and to ensure the well-being of the sick and wounded.

Veterinary Lieut.-Colonel I. Matthews, Army Veterinary Department, Principal Veterinary Officer, did excellent work in maintaining, so far as the want of proper forage would admit, the efficiency of all animals belonging to the Force. He was a very valuable adviser on veterinary matters both to myself and to the General Officer Commanding the Cavalry Brigade.

Brevet Lieut.-Colonel Sir Henry S. Rawlinson, Bart., Coldstream Guards, Deputy-Assistant Adjutant-General, who officiated throughout the siege as Assistant Adjutant-General (A), is a Staff Officer of great ability and activity, with a wonderful eye for the topography of the country. His constant observations of the enemy's positions and movements were of much value to me in forecasting their intentions. He is an officer well worthy of advancement.

Brevet Lieut.-Colonel H.M. Lawson, R.E., additional Assistant Adjutant-General (A), is a Staff Officer of the highest ability and the soundest judgment, and rendered me most valuable service throughout the siege.

Major E.A. Altham, Royal Scots, Assistant Adjutant-General for Intelligence, has had to contend with all the difficulties inseparable from intelligence work under the limitations imposed by siege conditions. All that was possible under these conditions he has done, and I consider him an excellent Intelligence Officer in every respect. Brevet-Major H. Henderson, Argyll and Sutherland Highlanders, Deputy-Assistant Adjutant-General for Intelligence.

Towards the latter end of the siege, Major Altham was attacked by enteric fever, and Major Henderson assumed charge of the Field Intelligence Department. He is a bold and accurate reconnoitrer, and the intelligence he brought back was always reliable. Whether as a subordinate or as head of the Field Intelligence Department, he has always afforded me the greatest assistance. I recommend him for reward.

Major C. de C. Hamilton, R.A., Deputy-Assistant Adjutant-General (A), has done a good deal of most useful work, and has shown himself a Staff Officer of high promise.

Major W.F. Hawkins, R.E., Director of Army Telegraphs, was indefatigable in maintaining electric communication between my headquarters and all portions of the defence. The service thus rendered was of the highest value, and conduced greatly to the successful defence of Ladysmith.

Major G.M. Heath, R.E., in charge of Balloon Section, is a bold and enterprising aeronaut, and rendered useful service during the siege; the constant watch which he kept on the enemy's movements being a source of much disquiet to them.

Major W.C. Savile, R.A., Senior Ordnance Officer, conducted the duties of his department with zeal and ability.

Colonel J.G. Dartnell, C.M.G., Chief Commissioner, Natal Police, possesses an exceptional knowledge of the Colony of Natal and of native character. I am greatly obliged to him for the advice and assistance which he has always been ready to afford me, of which I have availed myself freely, and which I have found of the highest value.

Mr. T.R. Bennett, Resident Magistrate of Ladysmith, was placed by me in charge of the Civil Camp at Intombi, and performed much good service in strictly enforcing the conditions on which I was permitted by Commandant-General Joubert to maintain that camp.

Mr. D.G. Giles acted as Resident Magistrate at Ladysmith during Mr. Bennett's absence, and was of great assistance in maintaining discipline amongst the civil population, both European and Native.

The Reverends E.J. Macpherson, O.S. Watkins, T. Murray and Father Ford, the senior chaplains of the Church of England, Wesleyan, Presbyterian and Roman Catholic denominations respectively, showed the greatest zeal and self-sacrifice in their attention to the sick and wounded, as well as in their ministrations to those in health. I regret that the calls on them for aid and comfort by the dying were only too constant.

I have, &.c.,
GEO. S. WHITE, Lieut-General,
Late Commanding Ladysmith Garrison.

NO. 3.

From Field-Marshal Lord Roberts to the Secretary of State for War.

Army Head-quarters, South Africa,
Government House, Bloemfontein,
28th March, 1900.

My Lord,

I have the honour to submit for your Lordships information a despatch, dated 14th March, 1900, from General Sir Redvers Buller, V.C., G.C.B., K.C.M.G., describing the operations of the force under his command from the 29th January up to the 1st March, 1900, the day succeeding that on which the relief of Ladysmith was effected.

2. I concur with Sir Redvers Buller in his admiration of the courage and tenacity displayed by the troops. Undeterred by previous failures, and regardless of fatigue, exposure, and the heavy losses which decimated their ranks, they gallantly assaulted one position after another until they found or made a way into Ladysmith. I trust that Her Majesty's Government will agree with me in thinking that credit is due to the General Officer in Chief Command, to the subordinate General and other Officers, and last but not least, to the brave soldiers who marched and fought almost without cessation from the 15th January to the 28th February.

3. I observe that the account given by Sir Redvers Buller of what occurred on 1st March differs in one respect from that contained in paragraph 36 of Sir George White's despatch of 23rd March, which was forwarded to your Lordship with my letter, dated 28th idem. Sir Redvers Buller states that the whole country round for 10 miles was clear of the enemy, and that, as they had moved their laagers between the 20th and 24th February, pursuit was useless. On the other hand, Sir George White reports that he sent out along the Newcastle Road a force consisting of one Cavalry regiment, two Field Batteries, and three battalions of Infantry to harass the enemy who could be seen retiring in that direction. From enquiries which I have made, I am led to believe that Sir Redvers Buller must have been misinformed. The principal Boer laagers do not appear to have been broken up until the 28th February, and many of the enemy's wagons were within a few miles of Ladysmith on the morning of the 1st March.

I have, &c.,
ROBERTS, Field Marshal,
Commanding-in-Chief, South Africa.

From the General Officer Commanding, Natal, to the
Secretary of State for War.
(Through the Field-Marshal Commanding in South Africa.)

The Convent, Ladysmith,
14th March, 1900.

Sir,

1. Ever since the enemy occupied positions round Ladysmith they have always maintained a very strong force on the south bank of the Tugela, east of Colenso, about the Hlangweni Mountain.

2. I examined this position several times in December, as, had I been able to take it, it was evident its possession would confer great advantages. I decided that its capture was a task altogether beyond the powers of the force I then commanded.

3. On the 29th January, after the engagement round Spion Kop, I told my men that their efforts, though unsuccessful, had found for me the key of the Ladysmith road. In these days of fighting I had learned to estimate, at its full value, the extraordinary tenacity of British Infantry, and the manoeuvring power that tenacity gave me, and thoughts of a possible chance at Hlangweni occurred to me.

4. But before leaving the Upper Tugela I resolved to try an attack on Val Krantz or Mongers Hill, as it was evident that if I could succeed in advancing on Ladysmith from the west such a success would be far more disastrous to the enemy than anything that could be obtained from an advance from the south. The position, according to my then information, offered a fair prospect of success, and, moreover, I hoped that, even if I did not succeed, I should, by an attack near Doorn Kloof, and by leaving a force behind at Springfield, be able to tie a very considerable number of the enemy to the Upper Tugela.

5. On the 7th, finding the position at Val Krantz too strong, I telegraphed to Sir George White that I was moving to attack Hlangweni, and if fortunate there should advance on Umbulwani Mountain.

6. I left an entrenched force of Infantry, two naval 12-prs., a brigade of Cavalry, and a battery of Horse Artillery at Springfield. I have reason to think that this force retained nearly 4,000 of the enemy about Potgieter's and Skiet Drifts. The rest of my force was concentrated at Chieveley by the 11th February. In the meanwhile I obtained, by the kindness of Admiral Sir R. Harris, a reinforcement of heavy guns, in one naval 6-inch, mounted on travelling carriage by Captain Scott, R.N., and two naval 4.7-inch mounted

on platform carriages, and Lord Roberts sent me two more 5-inch guns from the Cape.

7. On the 12th I reconnoitred the Hlangweni position, which I found occupied by the enemy. The 13th was so intensely hot that I did not move the troops.

8. On the 14th February I moved out from Chieveley with the force detailed in Annexure "A," and after slight opposition, occupied Hussar Hill, opposite the centre of the enemy's position.

9. On the 15th I extended my position to the right by the occupation, after some opposition, of Moord Kraal, and commenced an Artillery fire.

10. On the 16th my Infantry outposts were pushed down to the line of the Gomba Stream, and the eastern end of Cingolo Hill was occupied by the 2nd Cavalry Brigade.

11. The 14th, 15th and 16th were so hot that no Infantry movements on any scale were possible, but a steady bombardment was kept up; the enemy, who were being reinforced, replying with some six guns.

12. On the 17th the 2nd Division, under General Lyttelton, advanced to the Gomba Valley, and the 2nd Brigade moved up and occupied Cingolo Hill with the Royal West Surrey Regiment, who bivouacked that night on its northern crests; the 4th Brigade occupied a position about half-way up between the Gombo Spruit and the Nek, and two batteries of Royal Field Artillery were, with some difficulty, got into position between the brigades.

13. The whole country is thick bush intersected by deep dongas studded with precipitous kopjes dividing large underfeatures of the Cingolo and Monte Cristo Hills.

14. On the 18th the 2nd Cavalry Brigade moved forward along the eastern slopes of Cingolo and the 2nd Brigade crossed the Nek and assaulted Monte Cristo, the steep crags of which were brilliantly carried after considerable resistance by the West Yorkshire and Queen's Regiments. Captain T.H. Berney, West Yorkshire Regiment, a most gallant Officer, led the assault and was the first man up. He was, I regret to say, shot through the head as he got to the top. As soon as Monte Cristo was gained General Lyttelton advanced the 4th Brigade, and the Rifle Brigade worked forward along the western slopes of Monte Cristo to the back of the left of the enemy's position, and General Warren throwing the 6th Brigade forward, the position was well carried by the Royal Scots Fusiliers and abandoned precipitately by the

enemy, who left a large quantity of material, many dead and wounded, and a few prisoners behind.

15. Through this attack, which was made in echelon from the right, the naval guns, under Captain Jones, R.N., and Royal Artillery, under Colonel Parsons, R.A., rendered the greatest possible service, shelling the successive positions till the Infantry closed on them.

16. By half-past four we had taken the main position and had three brigades and two batteries right across its centre, but there was a very strong position on Hlangweni Mountain facing us, about 2 ¼ miles to our front, and on our right the river bank, a very difficult country.

17. The troops wanted water, roads had to be made, and owing to the nature of the country, intercommunication between units was very difficult. The troops, therefore, bivouacked as they stood, the rest of the force and the guns being brought up during the night.

18. On the 19th, General Hart advanced from Chieveley on Colenso, and the 2nd and 5th Divisions moved forward up the south bank of the Tugela against Hlangweni, which was taken by the 6th Brigade; our heavy guns moved to the northern end of Monte Cristo. The enemy made considerable opposition, but was gradually forced back.

19. On the 20th, we found that the enemy had, during the night, abandoned all his positions south of the Tugela, and also his main position in Colenso. We occupied Hlangweni, and Thorneycroft's Mounted Infantry swam the river, and entered the Colenso position, but were driven out.

20. On the 21st we threw a bridge across the Tugela (the river was very rapid, the bridge 98 yards long), and after a rather severe opposition from the north, the Colenso position was occupied by General Coke and the 10th Brigade.

21. On the 22nd, the 11th Brigade, supported by the 2nd Division, took possession of the hills which covered the railway bridge over Onderbrook Spruit, and commanded the country between that and Langerwachte Spruit. The fighting was very severe. Our principal objective was a long hog-backed hill running north and south, which completely commands the valley of the Langerwachte Spruit. It was taken, but our men were driven off by severe enfilade and reverse fire; they managed, however, to get and retain a lodgment at the south end, which, though it did not give us the hill, completely denied it to the enemy.

22. The fire, which made the hill untenable, came from some sangars on a low ridge, the continuation of and about 150 yards in front of the right of the hill

we had taken in the Onderbrook Valley. These were taken, but were found untenable, as they were exposed to enfilade and reverse fire from some sangars about 1,200 yards off, and 500 yards in front of our left; these were then taken, but could not be held, as they were completely commanded by the slopes of Grobelaar's Hill, about 1,400 yards to the west.

23. This rendered it impossible for us to obtain full command of the Onderbrook Valley, but at the end of the day we had obtained a footing upon the two most important hills in it, and had made these positions as secure as was possible against enfilade fire by hastily-erected sangars and traverses.

24. The positions thus won, after hard fighting, covered the line of railway across Onderbrook Spruit up to the Langerwachte Valley. This valley is full of dongas and small isolated kopjes, more or less covered with bush; in fact, an ideal place for the methods of defence employed by the enemy. Its eastern side is closed by a high steep hill, which was evidently the enemy's main position, and which was very strongly fortified and protected by extremely strong flank defences.

25. It was now clear that this hill must be taken before we could advance further. During the night of the 22nd, the 11th Brigade were relieved in the positions about Onderbrook by the 2nd Brigade and two battalions of the 6th Brigade, and the sangars were improved as much as was possible.

26. But, even then, the men had to lie crouched on the hill sides, sheltered by hastily piled stones, with an active keen-sighted enemy within 150 yards of one flank and 500 yards of the other. During the day the front line could scarcely move, for anyone who exposed himself was shot. They were under constant fire, both rifle and artillery, both night and day, and they were three times heavily attacked; but for 5 days and nights they unflinchingly maintained this position. It was wonderful!

27. During the afternoon of the 22nd and morning of the 23rd, the enemy's positions near the Langerwachte, and all the dongas leading thereto, were thoroughly searched by shell fire, and on the afternoon of the 23rd, General Hart advanced with the 5th Brigade, supported by two battalions of the 4th Brigade, to attack the position east of the spruit.

28. It had been my intention that this attack should be made by five battalions, but the advance up the railway was necessarily slow, and, in some places, the enemy brought a heavy fire upon it, both rifle and Maxim-Nordenfelt, causing many casualties and checking the advance considerably. It was getting late, and General Hart attacked the hill when two battalions only were up, thinking his supports would follow. For the reason I have mentioned, the

supports arrived but slowly, and the attack was made by two battalions, supported by a ½ battalion only – the Royal Inniskilling Fusiliers, the Connaught Rangers, and ½ the Royal Dublin Fusiliers.

29. The attack was delivered with the utmost gallantry, but the men failed to reach the top of the hill. The regiments suffered severely, but their loss was not unproductive, their gallantry secured for us the lower sangars and a position at the foot of the hill, which ensured our ultimate success.

30. That night the enemy made a heavy attack on our left. There was hard fighting, a good deal of it hand to hand, prisoners being taken and retaken, and several bayonet charges being delivered. The Rifle Reserve Battalion, a scratch regiment made up by combining the drafts for the three rifle battalions in Ladysmith, under command of Major Stuart-Wortley, behaved very well. The men withheld their fire, and, waiting in their sangars till the enemy were within 20 yards, went in with the bayonet.

31. The enemy also attacked in the evening the position taken during the day by General Hart, but in both cases our positions were held and the enemy repulsed.

32. We had now been fighting continuously for 72 hours, had obtained a position in front of Onderbrook Spruit, which divided the enemy, and forced him to make a long detour if he wished to reinforce his forces to the east of us from those on Grobelaars Kloof and the Ladysmith road, while the advance of General Hart's Brigade gave us a position in front of the enemy's extreme left. I saw that if I could effect a crossing nearer to the east of the position occupied by General Hart, I should be able to turn the enemy's left and drive him from his positions.

33. On the 24th, the rugged crests of the south bank of the Tugela from Hlangweni to Monte Cristo were searched for a roadway, and a Kaffir path was found by Lieut.-Colonel Sandbach, R.E., which gave access to the river below the cataract, exactly at the back of General Hart's position. Road making was at once commenced on both sides of the river. I withdrew the garrison from Frere, reduced that at Chieveley, and called up every gun and man I could muster for the final assault.

34. After the fighting of the 23rd, which continued on both flanks long into the night, we brought in, all the dead and wounded we could find in the dark, but as soon as it was light the enemy fired upon our stretcher bearers, and also upon Medical Officers who bravely went out to tend the wounded, and we were obliged to leave them lying unattended the whole day in the sun. Among them were also some of the enemy's own men.

35. During the 24th the Artillery duel continued, the enemy constantly bringing guns into position, and removing them directly our guns found their position. They also kept up a constant and annoying long-range rifle fire upon our position.

36. On the 25th, Sunday, I directed my guns not to fire unless attacked, and proposed to the enemy a cessation of hostilities to bury dead and bring in wounded, many of whom on both sides had been lying unattended for 40 hours or more. This the Commandants, who were, I believe, Botha and Lucas Meyer, at length assented to, but they insisted on taking as prisoners all the men not very badly wounded. I attach a copy of a statement made by one of our men, "B."

37. Throughout the 25th work at the new roads was being pressed, and the baggage of the 11th Brigade, and all the heavy guns were passed over the pontoons back to Hlangweni. At 8 p.m. the enemy emphasised the recommencement of hostilities by opening a tremendous rifle fire from all his positions, but little damage was done. The rest of the night was quiet.

38. During the 26th the guns were got into position, and a slow bombardment was kept up, so that every battery and every gun got the exact ranges of all the targets within their respective zones.

39. By 6 p.m. the approaches to the new bridge were complete, and during the night of 26th-27th, the pontoons were taken up, brought round, and by 10.30 a.m. the 27th, the new bridge was ready for traffic. At this moment I received from Lord Roberts a "clear the line" telegram, announcing the surrender that morning of General Cronje and his force. The good news was communicated to the troops as they were moving to attack and, received with loud cheers, added an extra fillip to their already intense desire for victory.

40. On the left, General Coke and the 10th Brigade occupied the Colenso kopjes, and had the 73rd Battery, Royal Field Artillery, in position firing north-west, commanding the Ladysmith road, and the avenues by which any force could approach our left.

41. General Lyttelton, with the Royal Fusiliers and Royal Welsh Fusiliers of the 6th Brigade, and the Devonshire Regiment, Royal West Surrey, two companies West Yorkshire, and two companies East Surrey, of the 2nd Brigade, with four companies Scottish Rifles of the 4th Brigade, under General Hildyard, held the hills between the Onderbrook and Langerwachte Valleys. These Brigades were sadly mixed, but the necessity of supporting General Hart's advance, and the impossibility of withdrawing men from the firing line during daylight, had rendered this unavoidable.

42. General Lyttelton was supported by the 28th and 78th Batteries, Royal Field Artillery, placed on the south side of the Tugela, on the western spurs of Hlangweni, the 28th Battery firing west up Onderbrook Spruit, and the 78th north up Langerwachte. On the high crest of the northern spur of Hlangweni were the 64th Battery Royal Field Artillery, two naval 4.7-inch guns and four naval 12-pr. Q.F. guns. East of them were four guns of the 4th Mountain Battery, then two naval 4.7-inch on platform mountings, then "A" Battery, Royal Horse Artillery, the 63rd Battery, Royal Field Artillery, then on Green Hill the 19th Battery, Royal Field Artillery, under cover of Green Hill the 61st Howitzer Battery, and behind them on Fussy hill four 5-inch guns of the 16th Company Royal Garrison Artillery. On the extreme left were two Mountain Battery guns and four 12-pr. naval guns mounted high up on the northern slopes of Monte Cristo. There was thus a battery of 76 guns on a front of about 4½ miles. Every sangar and important point of the enemy's position had been given a name, the gun positions were connected up by signallers, and special observers were posted at the principal points. At Chieveley were one naval 6-inch Q.F. gun, three naval 4.7-inch and two naval 12-prs. These guns covered the Colenso – Ladysmith road and the deep kloofs on each side of it which were very strongly held by the enemy, who, I think, really expected us to attack on that side.

43. The whole south bank of the Tugela from opposite the junction of the Onderbrook Spruit to Monte Cristo was lined by the Border Regiment and the Rifle Reserve Battalion with all the machine guns we could muster, to keep down sniping, and to prevent any of the enemy being able to watch our movement to the right.

44. The attacking party consisted of the Royal Welsh and Royal Scots Fusiliers and the Royal Dublin Fusiliers under General Barton; the Royal Lancaster, the South Lancashire, the York and Lancaster, and the West Yorkshire under General Kitchener, and the 4th Brigade, the whole under command of General Warren.

45. General Hart held the tete du pont on the north bank of the Tugela with the Connaught Rangers, the Royal Inniskilling Fusiliers and the Imperial Light Infantry.

46. The position occupied by the enemy consisted of three rocky hills rising abruptly from the Tugela to a height above it of about 600 feet. The westermost hill, called by us Terrace Hill, is separated from the middle hill and from the rugged crests of the north bank of the Tugela, by a valley which, rising steeply from the Langerwachte, ends in a shallow nek between the two hills over which the Colenso – Nelthorpe track passes. The middle hill, called by

us Railway Hill, is separated from the eastern, called Pieter's Hill, by a deep ravine along the western side of which the railway to Pieters winds through deep cuttings. Pieter's Hill rising steeply on the west from this ravine, falls by gentler gradients to the north-east towards the Klip River, the valley of which is intersected by dongas clothed in thick mimosa and camel thorn scrub.

47. Terrace Hill was a formidable position, it was strongly fortified with three tiers of trenches and flanked by trenches running down the Langerwachte Spruit on one side, and up almost to the crest of Railway Hill on the other. The crests of these hills were about 1,700 yards distant from the river, which here flows through a deep gorge, the sides of which on the north are almost precipitous to about 400 feet, the ground from the crest of this gorge to the crest line of the hills presenting an excellent field of fire for a force occupying the crests. Within this field of fire sangars had been constructed in every suitable spot. Pieter's Hill was not so strongly held, but a very considerable force was, as we found out later, concealed in the ravine between it and Railway Hill. Our approaches to the position were of the worst possible description; there was no road, and the attacking column had to scramble up an almost precipitous rocky cliff to gain the crest of the ravine. We had, though, one great advantage, our Artillery positions were excellent, and from the length of our line the enemy's positions were in almost all cases partly enfiladed as well as met by frontal fire.

48. At 10.30 a.m. General Barton's force crossed the pontoon bridge, and scrambling about 1½ miles down the edge of the Tugela, ascended the steep cliffs of Pieter's Hill unopposed, the rifle and machine gun fire from the south bank having cleared the north bank.

49. As the troops passed over the crest they were met by a heavy fire in front from the enemy in the ravine between Pieter's and Railway Hills, and also in flank from a reinforcement which came from Bulwana into the ravine on the east. These last were, to some extent, kept back by our guns on Monte Cristo, but owing to the fact that General Kitchener's advance was somewhat delayed, General Barton's force had to bear a heavy attack for a considerable time single-handed. His dispositions were extremely good; his three regiments were very well handled; his men fought most gallantly, and stubbornly maintained their position.

50. General Kitchener's Brigade followed General Barton over the pontoon bridge, and diverting slightly to their right, scaled the shoulder of the ravine, and gained the railway cutting. General Kitchener then directed the West Yorkshire and the Royal Lancaster Regiments to attack Railway Hill, but the men of the latter seeing the main position, Terrace Hill, on their left front

went straight at it, and were stopped by a heavy fire from the sangars in the valley. General Kitchener at once remedied the mistake, and directed the South Lancashire on the right of the Royal Lancaster, between them and the West Yorkshire, who were then gaining the crest of Railway Hill.

51. During the delay thus caused General Barton's force was, as has been said, left exposed, but directly the West Yorkshire took Railway Hill, they dislodged the enemy from the ravine and captured a Maxim gun. Meanwhile the South Lancashire pressed forward, and, aided by the Artillery fire, captured the sangars in the valley, taking a few prisoners and killing many of the enemy, who were practically confined to their trenches by the severity of the Artillery fire.

52. The fire of the naval guns here was particularly valuable, their shooting was admirable, and they were able to keep up fire with common shell long after the Royal Field Artillery were obliged to cease their shrapnel. Indeed, Lieutenant Ogilvy, H.M. Ship "Terrible," kept up fire on the largest sangars till the infantry were within 15 yards of them. His guns must have saved us many casualties. No one who watched the operations can have the slightest doubt that Artillery, cooperating with Infantry in an attack on a prepared position, ought to have a considerable proportion of common shell.

53. The sangars in the valley were soon taken, though I regret to say, at the cost of the life of Colonel McCarthy O'Leary, who fell while gallantly leading his regiment, and the Royal Lancaster and South Lancaster pressing on, well supported by the York and Lancaster on the right, and the 4th Brigade on the left, soon gained the summit of the hill, and the day was won.

54. The enemy fled in all directions, but as they were driven off the hills to the west they were able to keep up so strong a fire from the broken ground in the Langerwachte Valley, that it was impossible that evening to bring up the Cavalry and Artillery.

55. By 8 p.m. firing had ceased, and at daylight the enemy had disappeared from our front and flanks.

56. On the 28th, General Lyttelton's Division marched unopposed along the railway line and Boer road to the position captured the previous day, and the Cavalry and Artillery were sent forward.

57. I assigned the frontal advance to Lord Dundonald, as I was anxious the Colonial troops should, if possible, be the first to enter Ladysmith. He was opposed by some 200 of the enemy near Nelthorpe, but a few rounds of shrapnel dispersed them, and, pushing forward, he entered Ladysmith about 6 p.m. The 1st Cavalry Brigade went to the right across the southern slopes of

Bulwana, and found the enemy's rearguard posted in a strong position in a very rugged country, with three guns.

58. On the 1st March, I was moving to attack Bulwana, when I found it had been evacuated in the night, so I moved the force to Nelthorpe and rode into Ladysmith.

59. The whole country round was absolutely clear of the enemy for 10 miles. They had retreated in the greatest haste, but as they had moved their laagers between the 20th to the 24th, pursuit was useless.

60. During the whole of these 14 days, the 1st and 2nd Cavalry Brigades had kept our rear and flanks, their patrols extending from Greytown to Hongers Poort and Gourton,

61. So was accomplished the relief of Ladysmith. It was the men who did it. Danger and hardship were nothing to them, and their courage, their tenacity and their endurance, were beyond all praise.

62. During the period from the 15th January to the 28th February, this force has been engaged over 30 days, and during that period many Officers and men have distinguished themselves. I propose to make them the subject of another despatch, as I thought this, already over long, would be less confused if that course were adopted.

63. I enclose a sketch of the ground, I regret to say that Captain Kenney-Herbert was seriously injured before he could finish it.

64. I also enclose a summary of casualties, which of itself, shows the severity of the fighting.

I have, &c.,
REDVERS BULLER, General.

12

THE BATTLE OF DIAMOND HILL AND THE CAPTURE OF JOHANNESBURG AND PRETORIA

No. 6.

From Field-Marshal Lord Roberts to the Secretary of State for War.

Head-quarters of the Army in South Africa,
Kroonstad, 21st May, 1900.

MY LORD,

MY despatch of the 15th March, 1900, ended with a description of the entry of the Headquarters of the Army in South Africa into Bloemfontein.

In the present letter I propose to give a brief account of events from that time up to the 12th May, on which date the force under my immediate command occupied Kroonstad, which had been made the temporary headquarters of the Orange Free State Government.

2. Our rapid advance from the most western portion of the Orange Free State and the seizure of their capital had greatly dispirited the Boers, and the forces which fell back in front of our main army retired towards Kroonstad, while those which were in the northern districts of Cape Colony crossed the Orange River, and retreated in a northerly direction along the Basutoland border and the fertile district of Ladybrand.

3. As these forces cleared off, the southern portion of the State appeared to be settling down. Many Burghers surrendered their arms and horses, and took an oath to abstain from further hostilities against the British Government. Had I then been able to follow the enemy up and take advantage of this condition of affairs, the task of bringing the Orange Free State to terms would have been a comparatively easy one.

4. I found, however, it was impossible to do so. Cape Town, our main depôt for supplies, is 750 miles distant from Bloemfontein, with which it is connected by a single line of railway, and communication with Cape Colony had been interrupted by the destruction by the enemy of both the bridges over the Orange River.

From the country itself we were able to get scarcely anything in the shape of food except meat, and every mile we advanced took us further away from the only place where a sufficiency of supplies was obtainable. More-over, the army needed rest after the unusual exertions it had been called upon to make and by which its mobility had been greatly impaired.

5. The enemy knew exactly how we were situated. They had accurate information as to the condition of our supplies, our transport, and our artillery and cavalry horses; they regained courage by our prolonged and enforced halt at Bloemfontein, and their retrograde movement was arrested. They showed considerable strategical skill by reoccupying Ladybrand, and by concentrating a large force between Brandfort and Thabanchu. This gave them free access to the south-eastern districts of the Orange Free State, and prevented me from moving until they had been forced back north of the Thabanchu – Ladybrand line.

6. I may here mention that, as soon as railway communication with Cape Colony had been restored, the 3rd Division, under the command of Lieutenant-General Sir V. Gatacre, was directed to move up along the railway from Pethulie, viâ Springfontein, towards Bloemfontein, while the column under Major-General Clements, which had previously dislodged the enemy from Colesberg and Norval's Pont, marched through Fauresmith and Petrusburg, joining my head-quarters on 2nd April. Meanwhile I had occupied Glen Station and Karee Siding, and on the 29th March a force under Lieutenant-General Tucker as detailed in the margin,* attacked the enemy and drove them back to Brandfort, afterwards holding and entrenching a position which effectually protected the siding and the railway bridge under reconstruction at Glen.

7. On the following day, in consequence of a report that a large hostile force had collected near Thabanchu, I found it necessary to withdraw the Cavalry outpost at that town towards Bloemfontein. During its retirement to the Waterworks, 21 miles east of Bloemfontein, the Boers rapidly followed it up, and, by means of a cunningly laid ambush near Sannah's Post, to which I shall refer in a separate despatch, succeeded in capturing seven 12-pr. guns, with the entire personnel of a Horse Artillery battery and many other prisoners, besides inflicting heavy loss on the troops engaged, and seizing a convoy which accompanied them. Encouraged by this success, the Boer commanders moved southward and came in contact with a weak detachment which had been sent to Dewetsdorp by Lieutenant-General Sir W. Gatacre, and was being withdrawn by my orders. The enemy surrounded the detachment, and, before assistance could arrive, it had surrendered to superior numbers, and the Officers and men composing it had been removed, as prisoners of war, to Kroonstad.

8. The enemy then occupied Dewetsdorp, while a considerable force attacked Wepener, where a column of Colonial troops, under Lieutenant-Colonel Dalgety had arrived a few days previously.

Retiring from the town to a defensible position 3 miles to the west, which commanded an important bridge over the Caledon River, Lieutenant-Colonel Dalgety entrenched his force, and for 16 days he succeeded in keeping the Boers in check, despite the fact that they far outnumbered the small body of about 1,600 men under his command, and had also a considerable superiority in artillery, under pressure from the south and west caused them to withdraw northward along the Basutoland border.

9. While these events were taking place, the state of my mounted troops prevented me from attempting any operation which demanded rapidity of movement. I was determined, moreover, to adhere, if possible, to my plan of campaign, and not to be led into diverting from it, for operations of subsidiary importance, the troops which I required to attain my main objective, namely, to advance in adequate strength through the northern portion of the Orange Free State on Johannesburg and Pretoria. I had to content myself, therefore, with carefully guarding the line of railway, and with collecting a force strong enough to drive the enemy north of the Brandfort – Thabanchu line. For this purpose I brought the 3rd Division up to its full strength by the addition of some Militia battalions, and concentrated it, as well as the newly arrived 8th Division, at Edenburg. I had previously, on the 5th April, requested General Sir Redvers Buller to transfer the 10th Division, under Lieutenant-General Sir Archibald Hunter, together with the Imperial Light Horse, to Cape Colony, additional troops being urgently required to effect the relief of Mafeking, the state of affairs in Natal justifying some reduction in the force quartered there. I utilized Major-General Hart's Brigade of this division for the relief of Wepener, in conjunction with the main body of the Colonial troops under Brigadier-General Brabant, the remainder of Sir Archibald Hunter's Division proceeding to Kimberley. I increased and re-organized the Mounted Infantry, supplementing it by several battalions of Imperial Yeomanry, and these troops, together with the 4th Cavalry Brigade, which had recently arrived from England, I collected in the neighbourhood of Bloemfontein.

10. My dispositions for protecting the railway and expelling the enemy from the south-eastern districts of the Orange Free State had the desired effect, and on the 24th April Wepener was relieved and Dewetsdorp occupied by a body of troops under the command of Lieutenant-General French. The enemy finding themselves thwarted in the south-east portion of the Orange Free State, took up a position between Thabanchu and Ladybrand, from which

they were gradually pushed back by the 8th division under Lieutenant-General Sir Leslie Rundle, Brigadier-General Brabant's Colonial Division, and a force under the command of Major-General Ian Hamilton.†

11. On the 28th and 29th April our troops were engaged with the enemy in the neighbourhood of Thabanchu, and on the 1st May the enemy was signally defeated at Houtnek with comparatively small loss on our side, thanks to the admirable dispositions made by Major-General Ian Hamilton. It would doubtless have been more satisfactory had the troops employed at Dewetsdorp and Wepener been able to cut off the enemy's retreat and capture their guns; but, as I have already explained, they were limited in number, and during the recent operations the Boers moved with hardly any baggage, each fighting man carrying his blankets and food on a led horse. Being intimately acquainted with the resources of the country, and where grain and cattle were abundant, the enemy were not obliged to take their supplies with them, and could march at a pace which our troops could not hope to equal. It followed, therefore, that they were able to escape without suffering any other loss than that inflicted by our troops when dislodging them from the various positions they occupied.

12. By the beginning of May I had all the strategical points in the south-eastern districts securely held, and I was no longer anxious for the safety of the railway. The condition of the Cavalry, Artillery, and Mounted Infantry had materially improved, and a considerable number of remounts had arrived; sufficient supplies had been collected at Bloemfontein, and the arrangements for the transport had been completed. Under these circumstances I felt justified in ordering a forward movement towards Kroonstad. I left Bloemfontein by train for Karee Siding; to this point I had previously despatched the 11th (Pole-Carew's) Division. The 1st (Hutton's) Brigade of Mounted Infantry had moved to Brakpan, 10 miles to the west, while Lieutenant-General Tucker with the 15th (Wavell's) Brigade of the 7th Division was 2 miles to the east of the siding; the 14th (Maxwell's) Brigade was at Vlakfontein, 5 miles further east. On the morning of this day, Major-General Ian Hamilton's force was at Isabellafontein.

13. Brandfort was occupied the same afternoon, the Boer forces under General Delaroy making but a feeble resistance as soon as their right flank had been turned by Hutton's Mounted Infantry.

14. The following day the 7th and 11th Divisions with the 1st Brigade of Mounted Infantry remained in the vicinity of Brandfort, while Major-General Ian Hamilton engaged and drove back the enemy's rear guard at Welkom about 15 miles south of Winburg. On this occasion the junction of the two

Boer Forces was frustrated by a well-executed movement of the Household Cavalry, the 12th Lancers, and Kitchener's Horse, under the command of Lieutenant-Colonel the Earl of Airlie. The enemy fled after the encounter, leaving their dead and wounded on the field.

15. On the 5th May the force which I was accompanying marched to within 3 miles of the Vet River, the north bank of which was held by the enemy in considerable force. For three hours the action was chiefly confined to artillery on both sides, our Field and Naval guns making excellent practice, but just before dark the Mounted Infantry executed a turning movement, crossing the river 6 miles west of the railway bridge, which, like other bridges over the rivers along our line of advance, had been previously destroyed by the enemy. In this affair the Canadian, New South Wales, New Zealand Mounted Infantry, and the Queensland Mounted Rifles, vied with each other in their efforts to close with the enemy. We captured one Maxim gun and 26 prisoners, our losses being slight.

16. On this day Major-General Ian Hamilton captured Winburg after an engagement at Bobiansberg in which the 2nd Battalion Black Watch under Lieutenant-Colonel Carthew-Yorstoun greatly distinguished themselves.

17. During the night the enemy retired northwards to the Zand River, and on the 6th May the main force crossed the Vet River unopposed and occupied Smaldeel Junction. The drifts in the river bed were so bad that considerable delay occurred in getting the baggage and supply convoy across the Vet, and I was consequently obliged to halt at Smaldeel for two days. The Mounted Infantry, however, pushed on to Welgelegen, and Major-General Ian Hamilton's force moved some 10 miles north of Winburg, its place there having been taken by the Highland Brigade.

18. I was joined on the 8th May by Lieutenant-General French with the 1st (Porter's), 3rd (Gordon's), and the 4th (Dickson's) Brigades of Cavalry, and the following day the whole force marched to Welgelegen, the 1st and 4th Cavalry Brigades and the Mounted Infantry moving on to the south bank of the Zand, opposite Dupreez Laager. That evening a squadron of the Scots Greys succeeded in crossing the river near Verneulen's Kraal and holding the drift at that point. The 7th Division bivouacked near Merriesfontein, and Major-General Ian Hamilton marched to Bloemplaats, and pushed on the 1st Battalion Derbyshire Regiment to Junction Drift.

19. On the morning of the 10th May the enemy could be seen holding the north bank of the Zand in considerable strength. At daybreak Lieutenant-General French with two Cavalry brigades crossed the river and made a wide

turning movement past the diamond mine at Dirksburg, supported by the 1st Mounted Infantry Brigade under Major-General Hutton. I directed Ross' and Henry's Mounted Infantry battalions to seize the drift near the railway bridge. This they succeeded in doing by 7 A.M., and were followed across the river by the 3rd Cavalry Brigade and the 11th Division. The 7th Division crossed by Junction Drift. Major-General Ian Hamilton pushed forward the Cavalry Brigade across the same drift followed by the 21st Brigade under Major-General Bruce Hamilton, and the 19th Brigade under Major-General Smith-Dorrien. The enemy on his flank, as well as in front of Lieutenant-General French, offered a stubborn resistance, but by11.30 A.M. they were driven from the positions they had taken up, and withdrew towards Kroonstad, blowing up the railway bridges and culverts as they fell back.

20. My head-quarters with the 11th Division pressed on that day to Riet Spruit, 8 miles north of the river. The 7th Division bivouacked at Deelfontein Noord, and Major-General Ian Hamilton's column halted about 4 miles east of that place. During the afternoon Lieutenant-General French with the 1st and 4th Cavalry Brigades, and Hutton's Brigade of Mounted Infantry, reached a point 4 miles west of Ventersburg Road Station.

21. On the 11th May I marched with the 11th Division some 20 miles to Geneva Siding, 14 miles from Kroonstad, and 8 miles from Boschrand, where the Boers were holding an entrenched position to cover the town. Gordon's Cavalry Brigade advanced to within touch of the enemy, supported, on the left, by Hutton's Mounted Infantry. Lieutenant-General French, with the 1st and 4th Cavalry Brigades, marched to the Valsch River Drift, 10 miles northwards of Kroonstad, with instructions to cut the railway line. The 7th Division halted a short distance south-east of Geneva Siding, with Major-General Ian Hamilton's column a little further to the east.

22. During the night the enemy evacuated their entrenchments at Boschrand and retreated northwards, and on the 12th May I entered Kroonstad, with the 11th Division, without encountering any opposition.

President Steyn had left the town on the evening of the 11th May, after having previously proclaimed Lindley to be the seat of the Orange Free State Government. Commandant-General Botha and Commandant De Wet accompanied the Transvaalers in their retreat northwards.

23. Turning now to the operations in other directions, I may remark that during the period dealt with in this letter nothing calling for special notice occurred in Natal. The Boers continued to entrench themselves on the Biggarsberg, and held the Drakensberg Passes, but they attempted no offensive action. Sir Redvers Buller remained at Ladysmith, and beyond keeping

the enemy under observation did not risk any serious engagement. In this he was acting in accordance with my wishes, for, as he did not feel himself strong enough to force the Drakensberg Passes, he could not afford me any material assistance until I was in possession of Kroonstad and prepared to advance on the Transvaal.

24. In the vicinity of Kimberley the course of events has been as follows:- On the 16th March, Lord Methuen reconnoitred as far as Fourteen Streams, returning the same evening to Warrenton. He subsequently visited Barkly West, and repaired the railway line between Kimberley and Warrenton. On the 3rd April he proceeded to Boshof with the force marginally named.‡ On the 5th April, with the Imperial Yeomanry, Kimberley Mounted Corps, and 4th Field Battery, he surrounded a small Boer commando near Boshof. Colonel de Villebois Mareuil and seven of the enemy were killed, eight were wounded, and the remainder, numbering 54 Boers, Frenchmen, and Germans, were taken prisoners.

25. On this day, a message, dated 17th March, was received from Colonel Baden-Powell to the effect that the enemy were still besieging Mafeking, though in somewhat reduced numbers. A reinforcement under Colonel Plumer was approaching from the north, but it seemed doubtful whether it could break through the Boer lines. I had previously enquired from him how he stood as regard supplies, and he informed me in reply that they would, in all probability, only last until the 18th May.

26. On the 17th April, I gave orders for the formation of a flying column of mounted troops about 1,100 strong, with mule transport, for the relief of Mafeking. I placed Colonel B.T. Mahon, 8th Hussars, in command of this force, which consisted of 900 mounted men, including the Imperial Light Horse, four Horse Artillery guns with 100 men, 100 picked infantry soldiers to guard the wagons, 52 wagons with 10 mules each, and nearly 1,200 horses. The column was to take with it rations for 16 days and forage for 12 days. Medicines and medical comforts for the Mafeking garrison were also to be taken. Food and other stores for Colonel Baden-Powell's force were to be sent on by railway as soon as the line could be repaired. The flying column was ordered to start not later than the 4th May.

27. On the 24th April I instructed Lieutenant-General Hunter to have everything in readiness for an immediate advance, and to co-operate with Lord Methuen in distracting the enemy's attention until the flying column had crossed the Vaal and had obtained a good start. On the 29th April, Lieutenant-General Hunter reported that he hoped to force the passage of the Vaal on the 2nd May, and to send on the flying column on the 4th May. It

started on the day specified, and while penning these words the gratifying news reaches me that Mafeking was relieved on the 18th May after an heroic defence of over 200 days.

28. On the 5th May, Major-General Barton's Brigade engaged the enemy 2,000 strong, 2 miles north of Rooidam, and inflicted considerable loss on the Boers, who retired northward. On the 7th May, Lieutenant-General Hunter occupied Fourteen Streams without opposition, the enemy retreating in great disorder, and abandoning their ammunition, clothing, and personal effects. This result was in a great measure due to the able dispositions of Major-General Paget, who brought a powerful artillery fire to bear on the Boer position.

29. The repair of the railway bridge at Fourteen Streams was at once taken in hand, and a strong entrenched post to be held by one battalion was constructed. The force under Sir A. Hunter occupied Christiana, and is now moving along the railway line towards Mafeking, while that under Lord Methuen is marching from Hoopstad to join me.

30. It only remains to say that, since our entry into Bloemfontein on the 13th March, the pacification of the Prieska district has been completed. The arrangements for this were initiated by Major-General Lord Kitchener with his characteristic energy, and carried out by Brigadier-General Settle, Colonel Sir C. Parsons, and Lieutenant-Colonel Adye.

31. Tranquillity has been restored in the northern districts of Cape Colony, where a large number of rebels had joined the Boers.

32. Progress has also been made in organizing a provisional administration in that portion of the Orange Free State which is occupied by the British troops; District Commissioners, under the control of the Military Governor of Bloemfontein, having been appointed, and a police force being in course of formation.

33. I enclose a list of casualties.

I have, &c.,
ROBERTS, Field-Marshal.

List of Casualties which occurred in the Force serving in the Orange Free State, South Africa, between the 13th March and the 20th May, 1900.

Operations near the Glen and Karee Siding.-

Killed, 2 Officers, 19 other ranks; wounded, 14 Officers, 165 other ranks; missing, 11 other ranks; prisoners, 5 other ranks.

At Sannah's Post. – Killed, 3 Officers, 12 other ranks; wounded, 15 Officers, 108 other ranks; missing, 17 Officers, 413 other ranks.

Reddersburg. – Killed, 2 Officers, 8 other ranks; wounded, 2 Officers, 33 other ranks; prisoners, 8 Officers, 538 other ranks.

Siege of Wepener. – Killed, 3 Officers, 25 other ranks; wounded, 11 Officers, 130 other ranks.

To east of the line of railway. – Killed, 4 Officers, 29 other ranks; wounded, 32 Officers, 224 other ranks; missing, 3 Officers, 69 other ranks; prisoners, 1 Officer, 6 other ranks.

To west of the line of railway. – Killed, 3 Officers, 9 other ranks; wounded, 4 Officers, 67 other ranks; missing, 6 other ranks; prisoners, 11 other ranks.

Advance on Kroonstad. – Killed, 3 Officers, 29 other ranks; wounded, 13 Officers, 149 other ranks; missing, 2 Officers, 35 other ranks; prisoners, 3 Officers, 8 other ranks.

Total. – Killed, 20 Officers, 131 other ranks; wounded, 91 Officers, 876 other ranks; missing, 22 Officers, 534 other ranks; prisoners, 12 Officers, 568 other ranks.

No. 7.
From Field-Marshal Lord Roberts to the Secretary of State for War.

Army Head-Quarters, South Africa,
MY LORD,   Pretoria, 14th August, 1900.

IN my last despatch dated the 21st May, 1900, I brought my narrative of the war in South Africa up to the occupation of Kroonstaad on the 12th May. I shall now endeavour to describe the course of events after that date which led to the seizure of Pretoria and to give an account of the several military operations which have been carried out in South Africa up to the 13th June.

2. Before going into details, a brief reference may be made to the general attitude of the enemy during the period under review. A portion of the Boer commandoes, especially those raised in the Orange River Colony, on being driven back by our advance, during which we occupied Thabanchu and Ladybrand, collected in the north-eastern part of the Colony, whence it seemed probable that they would endeavour to cut our line of communication by rail, as soon as the main force under my immediate command had crossed the Vaal River. These commandoes blocked the passes of the Drakensberg Range and were likely to oppose any attempt on the part of the Natal force to co-operate with me through Laing's Nek. A considerable number of the enemy were also disposed along the line of railway for the purpose of holding

the several defensive positions and river crossings between Kroonstad and Pretoria. The southern and western districts of the Orange River Colony were settling down, and I had good reason to hope that no important concentration of the enemy was to be anticipated in the western portion of the Transvaal, as the possession of the railway junctions at Johannesburg and Pretoria and the restoration of the line from Kimberley to Mafeking, would render any such concentration unlikely, if not impossible.

3. My object then was to push forward with the utmost rapidity, while providing as far as my resources would admit for the safety of the main line of communication by occupying strategical points to the east of the railway at Winburg, Senekal, Lindley, and Heilbron. I calculated that, as soon as Mafeking had been relieved, a large proportion of the troops under the command of Lord Methuen and Sir Archibald Hunter would be available to co-operate on my left flank and I hoped Sir Redvers Buller would be able to assist by an advance westward to Vrede, or north-westward in the Standerton direction. But whether these anticipations could be realized or not, I felt that the enormous advantage to be gained, by striking at the enemy's capital before he had time to recover from the defeats he had already sustained, would more than counterbalance the risk of having our line of communication interfered with – a risk which had to be taken into consideration.

4. I had to halt at Kroonstad from the 12th to the 22nd May for the repair of the railway upon which I was dependent for my supplies.

5. On the 14th May I directed Lieutenant-General Ian Hamilton's column to march from Kroonstad to Lindley and on the 17th that town surrendered to Brigadier-General Broadwood.

6. Lord Methuen, whom I had ordered to move on the 14th May from Boshof to Hoopstad and there await further instructions, reached Hoopstad on the 17th May. I had thought of his force taking part in the Transvaal operations, but with regard to the probability of disturbances on the line of railway I determined to place it in the neighbourhood of Kroonstad, to which place it was accordingly directed to proceed.

7. On the 20th May, Lieutenant-General French with the 1st and 4th Cavalry Brigades marched from Jordan Siding, north of Kroonstad, to the north-east of Rhenoster Kop, while Major-General Hutton with the 1st Brigade of Mounted Infantry (exclusive of the 4th and 8th Corps, which under Colonel Henry were attached to Army Head-Quarters) advanced to the south of the same place and Lieutenant-General Ian Hamilton's column started from Lindley on the road to Heilbron.

8. On the 22nd of May my head-quarters with the 7th and 11th Divisions left Kroonstad and advanced to Honing Spruit Siding, while General Ian Hamilton's column reached and occupied Heilbron. The enemy disputed his passage of the Rhenoster and our loss might have been heavy had not Major-General Smith-Dorrien, Commanding one of Hamilton's brigade's (the 19th), been moved on the previous day to a position from which he was able to deliver at the right moment an unexpected attack upon the Boer flank.

9. On the 23rd May I marched past Roodeval Station to the Rhenoster River with the 7th and 11th Divisions, Colonel Henry with the two corps of Mounted Infantry being in advance on the east of the railway. No opposition was met with, although the hills north of the river furnished a strong defensive position and all preparations had been made by the enemy to give us a warm reception. It must be concluded that they felt their line of retreat was threatened from the east by General Hamilton's column at Heilbron and from the west by the Cavalry and Mounted Infantry under Generals French and Button, which had effected a crossing lower down the stream.

10. On the 24th May I marched with the 11th Division to Vredefort Road Station. The 7th Division bivouacked near Prospect on the west of the railway, four miles in rear, and the 3rd Cavalry Brigade four miles east of the station. The troops under Generals French and Hutton moved to the northwest, the 1st and 4th Cavalry Brigades crossing the Vaal at Parys and Versailles. General Ian Hamilton's column halted at Eerstegehik, seven miles north of Vredefort Road Station and to the east of the railway.

11. In view of the probability of opposition at the crossing of the Vaal River and of the advantages which a turning movement to the west appeared to afford, I directed Lieutenant-General Ian Hamilton to move his column across the railway on the morning of the 25th May, and to march in the afternoon to Wonderheuval and thence to the Vaal at Wonderwater Drift. By this move the enemy were completely deceived.

They had expected Hamilton's column to cross the Vaal at Engelbrecht's Drift, east of the railway, and collected there in some force to oppose him. My head-quarters with the 11th Division advanced this day to Grootvlei and the 7th Division to Wittlepoort. The 4th and 8th Corps of Mounted Infantry proceeded to Steepan on the railway, 10 miles north of Grootvlei, and 3rd Cavalry Brigade to Welterseden to guard our right flank. Generals French and Hutton moved up the Vaal to a drift near Lindaque.

12. On the 26th May I marched with the 7th and 11th Divisions to Taaibosch Spruit, while Colonel Henry's Mounted Infantry reached the Vaal at Viljoen's Drift and, after occupying the coal mines and railway station on the

south bank, crossed the river and held the drift and bridge, one span of the latter having been blown up by the Boers. The 3rd Cavalry Brigade continued to guard my right and General Ian Hamilton's Column my left at Wonder-water Drift, which was crossed this day by Brigadier-General Broadwood's Cavalry Brigade. Generals French and Hutton advanced across the Riet Spruit encountering but slight opposition and the Highland Brigade, with the head-quarters of the 9th Division, was ordered from Lindley to Heilbron.

13. On the 27th May I crossed the Vaal with the 7th and 11th Divisions and 3rd Cavalry Brigade and bivouacked at Vereeniging. Generals French and Hutton moved to Rietfontein and General Ian Hamilton to Rietkuil.

14. On the 28th May my head-quarters, with the 11th Division, proceeded to Klip River Station; the 7th Division to Witkop, south of the station; the 3rd Cavalry Brigade to the east, and Colonel Henry's Corps of Mounted Infantry to the north. The troops under Generals French and Hutton, strengthened by the 2nd Cavalry Brigade, advanced to the north-west of Johannesburg, and those under Ian Hamilton to Syperfontein 15 miles to the south-west of that town.

15. On the 29th May, I continued my march to Johannesburg, arriving oppo-site the Germiston Railway Junction at 3.30 P.M. The 11th Division, with the 7th Division on its left, moved along the railway and occupied Germiston after some slight resistance. Colonel Henry, whose Mounted Infantry preceded the main body, met with opposition at Natal Spruit Junction early in the day and later on at Boksburg. Forcing the enemy back, he moved round by his left to the north of Germiston, supported on the right by Gordon's Cavalry Brigade. General Ian Hamilton, who was advancing to a point about 12 miles west of Johannesburg, found his way blocked at 2 P.M. by a con-siderable force of the enemy at Doornkop. They had with them two heavy guns and several field guns and pompoms, and were holding a strong position on a long ridge running east and west. Hamilton decided to engage with the enemy at once. The right attack was led by the 1st Battalion Gordon Highlanders, who captured the eastern end of the ridge and, wheeling round, worked along it until after dark. The City Imperial Volunteers led on the left flank and behaved with great gallantry; but the chief share of the action and casualties fell to the Gordon Highlanders, who lost 1 Officer killed and had 9 Officers wounded. The enemy, who had fought obstinately, retired during the night. Our casualties in this engagement were 2 Officers and 24 men killed and 9 Officers and 106 men wounded. General French also was opposed throughout his march on the 28th and 29th May, but he had suc-ceeded by dark on the latter day in working round the very extended right

flank of the enemy, thereby facilitating the progress of Ian Hamilton's column. French's losses were slight, 2 Officers being wounded and 2 men killed and 17 wounded.

16. The next morning I halted to the south of Germiston, the force being distributed as follows:-

The 11th Division, with the heavy guns, near my head-quarters.

The 7th Division, 3rd Cavalry Brigade, and Colonel Henry's Mounted Infantry on the heights to the north of Johannesburg.

Lieutenant-General Ian Hamilton's Column at Florida, three miles west of the town.

The troops under Generals French and Hutton a few miles north-east of Florida.

On this day I had an interview with Dr. Krause who had been left in temporary charge of Johannesburg and who agreed to surrender the town to me the next morning. In the course of the day the Queensland Mounted Rifles captured a Creusot field gun, a gun wagon, 11 wagons loaded with military stores and ammunition and 23 prisoners.

17. Meanwhile, on the 29th May, I had received information that the Highland Brigade was being hard pressed by the enemy at Roodepoort, 18 miles south of Heilbron. The Irish Battalion of Imperial Yeomanry had been ordered to proceed from Ventersburg-road Station to join this brigade at Lindley. It had, however, failed to reach that place before the Highlanders left for Heilbron and Lieutenant-General Sir H. Colvile, in command of the troops, had started without it. This was very unfortunate, as Colvile was much in need of mounted troops. On this news reaching me, I directed Lord Methuen to despatch Douglas's Brigade from Kroonstad to Colvile's assistance. This order had scarcely been issued when I heard from Lieutenant-General Rundle, at Senekal, that the Irish Yeomanry, which had arrived at Lindley only a few hours after the departure of the Highland Brigade, had found that place in the hands of the enemy. Lieutenant-Colonel Spragge, who commanded the Yeomanry, accordingly halted 3 miles west of the town, and sent messengers to Colvile and Rundle apprising them of his dangerous position, which was aggravated by his having only one day's provisions in hand. Spragge was at first opposed by only a small force, but, on his defenceless position becoming known to the Boers, their numbers rapidly increased. General Rundle could not go to Spragge's relief, as he had been called upon to support Brigadier-General Brabant in the direction of Hammonia, nor could he leave Senekal until the arrival of Major-General Clements, who, with a portion of his brigade, was proceeding to that place from Winburg.

Under the impression, however, that he might indirectly relieve the hostile pressure on Lieutenant-Colonel Spragge's detachment, General Rundle, with a force of six companies of Yeomanry, two Field Batteries, Major-General Campbell's Brigade, and the 2nd Battalion Royal West Kent Regiment, moved out four miles on the Bethlehem road and encountered the enemy, who were in considerable strength at Kuring Kraus. After an engagement, which had no decisive result, General Rundle fell back on Senekal, his casualties amounting to 30 killed and 150 wounded.

18. General Colville, with the head-quarters of the 9th Division and the Highland Brigade, reached Heilbron on the 29th May. During the latter part of the march the brigade was but slightly troubled by the enemy, the greater part of whom had turned their attention to the Imperial Yeomanry.

On this day Lord Methuen left Kroonstad in obedience to my instructions to assist the Highland Brigade. On the third march out he received a message from Lieutenant-Colonel Spragge, dated the 29th May, reporting that he was heavily pressed by the enemy and was short of food and ammunition, but hoped that he would be able to hold out until the 2nd June. This message Lord Methuen repeated to me by telegraph and I at once ordered him to push on to Lieutenant-Colonel Spragge's assistance, and on the 1st June, half an hour after the receipt of my reply, he started off with his mounted troops, Imperial Yeomanry, a Field battery, one section of pompoms, and reached Lindley at 10 o'clock the following morning, having covered 44 miles in 25 hours. Unfortunately he was too late, as Lieutenant-Colonel Spragge had found it necessary to surrender two days before. Methuen, on nearing Lindley, attacked the Boer force, which had increased from 300 to 3,000 strong, and, after a running fight which lasted five hours, completely defeated them and occupied the town. I then directed him to leave one of his Infantry brigades (Paget's) and to march with the other (Douglas's) to Heilbron with supplies for Sir H. Colville's force.

19. To return to the operations at Johannesburg. I received the formal surrender of the town early on the 31st May and entered it at noon with the 7th and 11th Divisions, the Union Jack being hoisted with the usual salute in the main square. After the ceremony, I established my head-quarters at Orange Grove, three miles north of Johannesburg on the Pretoria road, the 11th Division bivouacking four miles further north and the 14th Brigade of the 7th Division a short distance to the west. The 15th (Wavell's) Brigade was detailed to garrison the town and Lieutenant-Colonel C.J. Mackenzie, Seaforth Highlanders, was appointed Military Governor.

20. On the 1st and 2nd June my headquarters remained at Orange Grove, while Lieutenant-General Ian Hamilton's column moved from Florida to

Bramfontein, four miles west of Orange Grove, and the 1st, 3rd, and 4th Cavalry Brigades, with Hutton's Mounted Infantry, were distributed ten miles to the north of the same place.

21. During these two days, disquieting news continued to reach me regarding the activity and numbers of the enemy who had opposed us in the Orange River Colony and who were now closing in behind us, threatening the single line of railway leading to Cape Colony, upon which I was dependent for provisioning the army. This information was the more disconcerting, as, owing to our rapid advance and the extensive damage done to the railway, we had practically been living from hand to mouth and, at times, had not even one day's rations to the good. It was, therefore, suggested to me that it might be prudent to halt at Johannesburg until the Orange River Colony should be thoroughly subdued and the railway from Natal opened. But, while fully recognizing the danger attending a further advance, I considered the advantages of following up without delay the successes we had achieved, and not giving the enemy time to recover from their several defeats, or to remove the British prisoners from Pretoria quite justified the risk being run. Accordingly I advanced on the 3rd June with Pole-Carew's division and the head-quarters and Maxwell's Brigade of the 7th Division to Leeuwkop, a distance of 12 miles, Colonel Henry, with his corps of Mounted Infantry, moving to a point 4 miles to the north, Brigadier-General Gordon, with the 3rd Cavalry Brigade, 6 miles to the east, Lieutenant-General Ian Hamilton with his column to Diepsloot, 15 miles south of Pretoria, and the troops under Generals French and Hutton to Rooikrans, 13 miles south-west of Pretoria.

22. On the 4th June I marched with Henry's Mounted Infantry, four Companies Imperial Yeomanry, Pole-Carew's Division, Maxwell's Brigade and the naval and siege guns to Six Mile Spruit, both banks of which were occupied by the enemy. The Boers were quickly dislodged from the south bank by the Mounted Infantry and Imperial Yeomanry, and pursued for nearly a mile, when our troops came under artillery fire. The heavy guns were at once pushed to the front, supported by Stephenson's Brigade of the 11th Division, and the enemy's fire was soon silenced. They then moved to the south along a series of ridges parallel to our main line of advance with the object of turning our left flank, but in this they were checked by the Mounted Infantry and Imperial Yeomanry, supported by Maxwell's Brigade. As, however, the Boers continued to press on our left flank and thus threatened our rear, I ordered Ian Hamilton, who was moving three miles to our left, to incline to his right and close the gap between the two columns. As soon as Ian Hamilton's troops

came up, and De Lisle's Mounted Infantry pushed well round the enemy's right flank, they fell back on Pretoria. It was now dusk, and the troops had to bivouac in the positions which they were occupying, the Guards Brigade near the most southern of the forts defending Pretoria, and within four miles of the town, Stephenson's next to the Guards on the west, and Ian Hamilton's column still further to the west, French with the1st and 4th Cavalry Brigades and Hutton's Mounted Infantry towards the north of the town, Broadwood's Cavalry between French and Ian Hamilton, and Gordon's Cavalry to the east, near the Irene Railway Station.

23. Shortly before dusk Lieutenant-Colonel De Lisle, whose Mounted Infantry had followed up the enemy to within 2,000 yards of Pretoria, sent an officer under a flag of truce to demand in my name the surrender of the town. To this no reply was given, but about 10 P.M. Mr. Sandberg, Military Secretary to Commandant-General Botha, with a General of the Boer Army, brought in a letter from the Commandant-General proposing an armistice for the purpose of arranging the terms under which Pretoria would be handed over to the British force. I replied that the surrender must be unconditional and requested an answer before 5 o'clock the following morning, as my troops had been ordered to advance at daybreak. At the time named on the 5th June I received the reply from Commandant-General Botha to the effect that he was not prepared further to defend the place and that he entrusted the woman, children, and property to my protection. I, therefore, ordered Pole-Carew's Division with Henry's Mounted Infantry to move within a mile of the town and at 9 A.M. I proceeded myself to the railway station. At 2 P.M. I made a ceremonious entry, the British flag being hoisted on the Raadzaal, and Pole-Carew's Division and Ian Hamilton's Column marching past. That evening I established my head-quarters at the British Agency. The 14th Brigade was detailed to garrison Pretoria and Major-General J.G. Maxwell was appointed Military Governor.

24. The prisoners found here on our arrival numbered 158 Officers and 3,029 men, but about 900 men had been removed by train the previous day in the direction of Middleburg.

25. It may be here mentioned that the forts surrounding the town were undefended, and that their armament had been dismounted and carried off. The place was quiet and the population orderly; and, though most of the gold in the banks, and all the public treasure had been taken away, no damage had been done to private property. The wives of President Kruger and Commandant-General Botha remained in Pretoria when their husbands left and are still here.

26. The enemy had retired during the night of the 4th June in an easterly direction, but not to any great distance, and as the presence of a considerable Boer force (calculated at 12,000) was having a very disquieting effect on the town, I determined to drive them further away. The position they were holding was a strong one along a range of hills at Pienaars Poort, 15 miles from Pretoria; the attack commenced early on the 11th June, Pole-Carew's Division, with the naval and siege guns, moving to Christinen Hall, opposite the Poort, with Ian Hamilton's column on the right and Broadwood's and Gordon's Cavalry Brigades still further to the right in touch with each other and with Hamilton's column. Henry's corps of Mounted Infantry was directed to close the gap in the hills at Frankpoort, to the north of Eerstefabriken Railway Station; while French, with Porter's and Dickson's Cavalry Brigades and Hutton's Mounted Infantry, was to work round to the north-east of the enemy's position. The centre of the Boer alignment at Pienaar's Poort was so strong naturally, that to have assaulted it by direct attack would have involved a useless loss of life. I, therefore, determined to develop flanking operations, knowing by experience that the enemy would retire as soon as their rear was seriously threatened; but the long distances to be traversed, and the defensive advantages which the nature of the ground afforded the Boers impeded our advance. Moreover, as I have since learnt, the Boer leaders had intended to follow our tactics and try and outflank us; consequently, their centre was but lightly held, whilst the wings of their army were so strong that French and Button on our left, and Broadwood and Gordon on our right, informed me by signal that they were only just able to hold their own. Broadwood was indeed, at one time, hardly pressed, being under a heavy artillery fire from his front and left, whilst he was simultaneously attacked on his right rear by a commando from Heidelburg. The enemy came on with great boldness and, being intimately acquainted with the ground, were able to advance unseen so close to "Q" Battery, Royal Horse Artillery, that it was with some difficulty they were kept off, while at the same time another body made a separate attack on Broadwood's right flank. To help the guns and drive off this second body, Broadwood ordered the 12th Lancers and Household Cavalry to charge. Both charges were successful, inasmuch as they relieved the immediate pressure on the guns and Broadwood's right flank, and caused the enemy to revert to artillery and long-range rifle fire; but I regret to say that these results were obtained at the cost of some 20 casualties, amongst them being Lieutenant-Colonel the gallant Earl of Airlie, who fell at the head of his regiment, the 12th Lancers. Meanwhile, Ian Hamilton's Infantry was pressing on as fast as it could to the assistance of the Cavalry, and as each battalion came up, it deployed for attack and very soon became hotly engaged. From my own position I could clearly

see (though Ian Hamilton could not) a large number of Boers galloping away in great confusion from a long low ridge some ¾ mile in front of his Infantry, and about 1½ mile short of Diamond Hill near Rhenosterfontein. Diamond Hill appeared to me to be the key of the formidable position taken up by the Boers on this flank and I saw there was every probability of our troops shortly capturing the subsidiary ridge and thereby gaining certain facilities for a further advance on the morrow against Diamond Hill itself. I, therefore, determined to press the attack home at this point next day, and ordering all the troops along our 25 miles of battle front to bivouac on the ground they held, I made arrangements to reinforce Ian Hamilton by the Guards Brigade under Major-General Inigo Jones and two naval 12-prs. under Captain Bearcroft, Royal Navy.

27. On the morning of the 12th June, I directed Ian Hamilton to continue his advance on Diamond Hill and then to move towards the railway at Elands River Station, with a view to his threatening the enemy's line of retreat should they continue to oppose us.

Hamilton told off Gordon's Cavalry Brigade with one Infantry battalion to guard his right rear and Broadwood's Brigade with a party of Mounted Infantry to contain the enemy on his right, whilst he attacked Diamond Hill with the 82nd Field Battery, the 1st Battalions of the Sussex and Derbyshire Regiments and City Imperial Volunteer Battalion. The troops advanced under Artillery fire from both flanks, as well as heavy Infantry fire from the hill itself. The steadiness with which the long lines moved forward, neither faltering nor hurrying, although dust from bullets and smoke from bursting shells hung thick about them, satisfied me that nothing could withstand their assault.

The position was carried at 2 P.M., by the troops above named, the Guards Brigade being in close support. Fighting continued until dusk, the Boers having rapidly taken up a fresh position near the railway.

28. On the morning of the 13th June it was found that the enemy had withdrawn during the night towards Middleburg and Ian Hamilton at once took up the pursuit, his Infantry moving to Elands River Station, while his mounted troops pushed on towards Bronkhorst Spruit Station. Generals French and Hutton moved east to Doornkraal, but finding that the enemy had disappeared returned to Kameelfontein. The enemy having been dispersed, our troops returned the next day to the neighbourhood of Pretoria, the mounted corps requiring a large number of remounts to restore their efficiency.

29. While the force under my immediate command was thus occupied near Pretoria, the enemy in the Orange River Colony under Commandant

Christian De Wet continued their attacks on our lines of communication south of the Vaal. On the 2nd of June a convoy of 50 ox-wagons left the Rhenoster River Station for Heilbron with an escort of details proceeding to join the Highland Brigade. The following afternoon the convoy was surrounded by the Boers in greatly superior numbers, but was obliged to surrender before reinforcements from the Vredefort Road Station could reach it.

Early on the morning of the 7th June the enemy attacked the post on the Rhenoster railway bridge held by the 4th Battalion Derbyshire Regiment, 70 men of the Railway Pioneer Regiment, and a few men belonging to the Imperial Yeomanry. Pickets had been posted on the kopjes commanding the railway bridge and camp, but these were driven in by the heavy artillery and rifle fire brought to bear on them from the more distant hills. The engagement continued up to 11 A.M., by which hour 5 Officers and 32 men had been killed and 100 men wounded out of a total strength of 700. The Boers having six guns, to which the defenders of the post could not reply, and outnumbering the latter in the proportion of six to one, the garrison had to surrender, as further resistance would have been useless.

30. The possibility of such mishaps had been clearly foreseen by me when I determined to advance on Pretoria, for I knew I was not sufficiently strong in numbers to make the railway line absolutely secure and at the same time have a force at my disposal powerful enough to cope with the main army of the Transvaal supported by forts and guns of position. Now, however, that I was in possession of the Capital and the majority of our prisoners had been recovered, I took immediate steps to strengthen the posts along the railway. The liberated prisoners were armed and equipped and despatched to Vereeniging and other stations south of the Vaal, and as soon as more troops could be spared, they were distributed along the line between Pretoria and Kroonstad. I deputed Lieutenant-General Lord Methuen to superintend these arrangements and on the 11th June he attacked and defeated the commando under Christian de Wet at the Rhenoster River. The Imperial Yeomanry Field Hospital, which had fallen into the hands of the Boers when the Derbyshire Militia surrendered a few days previously, was recovered, together with the Officers and men who had been wounded on that occasion. Other desultory attacks were subsequently made on the railway line and the trains employed for reconstruction purposes, but the enemy were on each occasion repulsed without serious loss on our side and in the course of a few days railway and telegraphic communication were restored.

31. Turning now to the western side of operations, I have the satisfaction to record that Mafeking was relieved by the flying column under Colonel

Mahon's command on the 17th May. Hearing no doubt of the approach of this column, the Boers made a daring attempt to capture the place on the 12th May. Before dawn on that morning a storming party 250 strong, led by Commandant Eloff, rushed the pickets on the west and got into the Staat and Protectorate camp, a severe musketry demonstration being simultaneously made against the eastern part of the defences. The western pickets closed in and prevented the enemy's supports from following up, thus cutting off Eloff's line of retreat, while the town guard stopped his further advance. Fighting went on all day and in the evening two parties surrendered, while the third was driven out of the Staat camp under heavy fire. Ten of the enemy were killed, 19 of their wounded were left behind, and 108 prisoners were taken, including among the latter Eloff and 9 Officers. 17 Frenchmen and a good many Germans. Our casualties amounted to six men killed and 2 Officers and nine men wounded.

32. On the 15th May Mahon joined hands with Colonel Plumer's column at Jan Massibis, 30 miles west of Mafeking, and moving north the next day to the Molopo he was stubbornly opposed by the local Boer Force augmented by a commando from Klerksdorp under General Delarey, which had taken up a strong position nine miles from the town. The Canadian Field Battery from Buluwayo joined Colonel Mahon early that morning, having pressed on by forced marches, and rendered valuable assistance. The enemy were defeated and the combined column entered Mafeking at 4 A.M. on the 17th May. Being there reinforced by the garrison, they marched out after a short rest and attacked the enemy's main laager, capturing one gun and a quantity of stores and ammunition. The Boers retreated into the Transvaal, most of them dispersing to their farms.

Steps were at once taken to restore railway communication with Mafeking from the north and south. The line from Buluwayo was completed on the 26th May and that from Kimberley was nearly finished on the 6th June. On the 20th May Zeerust was occupied without opposition by a flying column under Colonel Plumer, and a few days afterwards troops were quartered in Ottoshoop and Polfontein.

33. Lieutenant-General Hunter moved from Fourteen Streams into the Transvaal on the 15th May, and the next morning entered Christiana unopposed, the Boers 3,000 strong under Du Toit having retired to Klerksdorp. Hunter then returned to Fourteen Streams and marched up the railway line, reaching Vryburg on the 24th May. On the 26th, I directed him to form an advance base at Doornbult Siding and to concentrate at Holfontein, marching thence to Lichtenburg.

The force at his disposal consisted of Mahon's Flying Column, less the Kimberley Mounted Corps which I left with Major-General Baden-Powell, the Scottish Imperial Yeomanry, a brigade-division of field artillery, and six battalions of infantry. Hunter's advanced troops occupied Lichtenburg on the 1st June and his whole force was collected there on the 7th June. On the 8th he started viâ Ventersdorp for Potchefstroom, in order to get into railway communication with Klerksdorp and Johannesburg.

34. In the western districts of Cape Colony Lieutenant-General Warren and Colonel Adye have operated against the rebels with considerable success. On the 21st May Warren surprised the enemy at Douglas, capturing their wagons, tents, and cattle. The Boers retreated northwards. On the 30th May Adye had an engagement near Khees in the Prieska district, our casualties being 1 Officer and 3 men killed and 4 Officers and 16 men wounded. On this occasion over 5,800 head of cattle and sheep were captured with large number of wagons and tents and much personal property. On the 3rd June Warren advanced against the enemy at Campbell and dispersed them. He reported the Herbert district to be then clear of rebels and that he proposed shortly to occupy Griquatown.

35. In the Orange River Colony bands of marauders were reported by the Military Governor to be raiding the country in the vicinity of Abraham's Kraal, and on the 13th May I desired Lieutenant-General Kelly-Kenny to despatch three companies of Imperial Yeomanry from Bloemfontein with the object of dispersing them, and at the same time of repairing the telegraph line between Bloemfontein and Boshof. This duty was satisfactorily performed, the Yeomanry detachment returning to Bloemfontein on the 22nd May, after having quieted the disturbed district and collected nearly 100 rifles rand 3,000 rounds of ammunition. Up to the 24th May 400 Burghers had surrendered to the Officer Commanding at Boshof, including Commadant Duplessis and Field-Cornets Botha and H.J. Duplessis.

36. During the period dealt with in this letter an important advance has been made by the troops in Natal. Between the 10th and 13th May the force under General Sir Redvers Buller's command moved by Sunday's River Drift to Waschbank Station, the enemy retiring to the nek in front of Helpmakaar. On the night of the 13th, Helpmakaar was evacuated, and on the 15th our troops occupied Glencoe and Dundee, the Boers falling back on Laing's Nek. The Cavalry reached Newcastle on the 17th and Sir Redvers Buller with the 3rd Division entered the town the next day. The railway was found to be much damaged and it was necessary to repair it before attempting to cross the Drakensberg. The delay thus caused enabled the enemy to concentrate in

greater strength at Laing's Nek and in front of the Botha and other passes, and local commandoes were reported to be threatening the railway line from the east. Sir Redvers Buller decided first to clear his right flank and on the 27th May he despatched a column to Utrecht. On the 29th, Utrecht surrendered to Lieutenant-General Hildyard, while Lieutenant-General the Honourable Neville Lyttelton was marching on Vryheid, which also surrendered a couple of days later. Railway communication was restored to Newcastle on the 29th May. On the 4th June Sir Redvers Buller reported that he would be ready to force Laing's Nek by a turning movement on the 6th and that the enemy, though probably 4,000 to 5,000 strong with a considerable number of guns, were much disheartened.

While deprecating a direct attack which might entail heavy loss of life, I suggested enough men should be left to occupy the enemy's attention at Laing's Nek and that with the rest of his force Sir Redvers Buller should move rapidly through Botha's or some neighbouring pass, thus obliging the enemy to withdraw from their strong position at the Nek. On the 8th June Sir Redvers Buller attacked and defeated the Boers at Botha's Pass, and moving northwards again came in touch with them on the 10th at Gansvlei. The enemy were driven back along the ridge, which they held till dusk. During the night they withdrew to a range of hills six miles north-east of Gansvlei, through which the Volksrust road passes at a point called Allemann's Nek. On the 11th June Sir Redvers Buller advanced against this position, and, after some severe fighting, the brunt of which fell on the 2nd Battalion Dorsetshire Regiment, seized Allemann's Nek and occupied the crest of the hills, the Boers retreating all along the line. The 3rd Cavalry Brigade was also heavily engaged on the right flank. Our casualties amounted altogether to 142 killed and wounded. The same night the Boers evacuated Laing's Nek and Majuba, Sir Redvers Buller establishing his head-quarters at Joubert's Farm, four miles north of Volksrust.

37. To the north of the Transvaal some delay has occurred in concentrating General Carrington's force owing to the small carrying capacity of the railway from Beira to Marandellas; but the congestion of traffic has lately been relieved and the greater part of the troops have reached Mafeking, where their co-operation will be very valuable.

38. In conclusion, I desire to record my high opinion of the conduct and endurance of the troops during the operations summarized in this letter. Their powers of marching and their gallantry when engaged with the enemy were equally admirable; and it is particularly gratifying to me to bring to notice the services rendered by the Colonial Corps, the Imperial Yeomanry and the City Imperial and other Volunteers, who have proved themselves

most efficient soldiers. My acknowledgments are also due to the Militia Battalions, which have done excellent work in the Orange River Colony, in the western districts of Cape Colony, and on the lines of communication.

I have, &c.

ROBERTS, Field-Marshal.

Commanding-in-Chief, South Africa.

* 7th Division, 3rd Cavalry Brigade, Le Gallais' Mounted Infantry.

† This consisted of the 2nd Cavalry Brigade under Brigadier-General Broadwood, the 2nd Brigade of Mounted Infantry under Brigadier-General Ridley, Brigadier-General Smith-Dorrien's Brigade of the 9th Division, and a newly-formed brigade (21st) composed of 1st Battalion Sussex, 1st Battalion Derbyshires, the 1st Battalion Cameron Highlanders and the City Imperial Volunteer Battalion, under the command of Major-General Bruce Hamilton.

‡ Three field batteries, a section of a Howitzer battery, seven companies of Imperial Yeomanry, Kimberley Mounted Corps, 600 strong, the 9th Infantry Brigade, and two battalions of the 20th Brigade.

13

BATTLE OF BLOOD RIVER POORT

TUESDAY, DECEMBER 3, 1901.

War Office, December 3, 1901.

THE following Despatches have been recently received from General Lord Kitchener, G.C.B., &c., Commanding-in-Chief, South Africa.

From Lord Kitchener to the Secretary of State for War, London, S.W.

Pretoria,

SIR,

October 8th, 1901.

1. In continuation of my despatch, dated 8th September, 1901, I have the honour to report that during the past month there has been a general recrudescence of activity on the part of the enemy, which has made itself felt more particularly in the extreme south-east portions of the Transvaal. The immediate cause of this was, undoubtedly, the necessity felt by the Boer leaders to tide over the 15th September, the date fixed by the Proclamation of 7th August as the limit of time within which by voluntarily surrendering, the leaders might avoid certain penalties threatened by that Proclamation. In this they have succeeded. There has been no general surrender, but the device to which the Commandant-General resorted for turning the thoughts of his burghers in another direction has probably cost him and his cause more heavily than a simple pursuance of the usual evasive tactics would have entailed.

Operations on the Natal Frontier.

2. I alluded in my last despatch to the indications of a concentration in the Ermelo district, and to rumours of designs on Natal, and to the preliminary steps taken to meet this contingency.

On the 4th September, Lieut.-General the Hon. N.G. Lyttelton assumed command in Natal, in succession to Lieut.-General Sir H. Hildyard, who proceeded home on leave of absence. General Hildyard arrived from England at the commencement of the war in command of the 2nd Brigade, and has since then continued, without interruption, to exercise command in various positions of great responsibility. Much as I regret the loss of his valuable services, I am glad that he should now be able to enjoy a well-earned rest.

General Lyttelton having assumed command, at once found it necessary to turn his attention to the enemy in the Vryheid District. The commandos which had assembled in the Ermelo District early in the month, gradually worked south by Piet Retief and Paul Pieters Burg, whilst others joined them *en route*, but it was not until the 18th September that Major Gough's reconnaissance made the situation quite clear.

For some days previous to this, mist and rain had concealed the enemy's movements from our patrols sent out from Utrecht and Vryheid, and the natives, fearing the penalty the Boers now so ruthlessly exact from them for any assistance given us, had kept to their kraals. On the 15th September Major Gough's Mounted Infantry moved out from Dundee, with Lieut.-Colonel Stewart in command of the Johannesburg Mounted Rifles, to De Jager's Drift. Colonel Pulteney's troops were at Volksrust, and Lieut.-Colonel Garratt with his column, having passed through Wakkerstroom, was moving on Utrecht.

On the 17th September, Lieut.-Colonel Stewart and Major Gough decided to push on towards the Bloed River to gain touch with the enemy, reported to be in the vicinity of Scheeper's Nek. Major Gough marched about an hour in advance of Lieut.-Colonel Stewart, and as he neared the river sent back word asking Lieut.-Colonel Stewart to remain for the present near Rooi Kop, in readiness to support him should he hear his guns in action. Half-an-hour later Lieut.-Colonel Stewart observed Major Gough's force galloping in the direction of Bloed River Poort, and he immediately pressed forward in support with his mounted men. While thus advancing, Lieut.-Colonel Stewart was met by a messenger, who informed him that Major Gough had met with a serious reverse in front, and feeling it imperative to afford protection to his own guns at Rooi Kop, as well as to Major Gough's baggage, which was following behind, he decided, after verifying the report, to fall back, at once to De Jager's Drift, thus covering Dundee.

Major Gough had galloped into a well-arranged ambush. Believing that he was in presence of only 300 Boers he had pressed forward boldly to seize a ridge which appeared to command their position. The enemy, however, numbered fully 1,000, and whilst checking Major Gough in front, they rapidly overwhelmed his right flank and assailed his guns from the rear. There was a short sharp fight at close quarters, in which our men displayed much gallantry, and then completely outnumbered and surrounded, the whole of Major Gough's small force was captured.* It is due to Major Gough to state that he has commanded in the field for the past two years under every condition, and with unvarying success, and I should be sorry to mark a solitary error of judgment in any way that might militate against the future utility of this gallant Officer.

Lieut.-Colonel Stewart in falling back when he did showed great judgment and a sound appreciation of the situation in a position of considerable difficulty.

Commandant-General Louis Botha, General C. Botha, and Commandants Opperman, Britz, and Henderson were all reported to have been present in the engagement, and it was quite evident that Dundee was momentarily menaced by a commando of considerable strength.

The troops placed at General Lyttelton's disposal were now rapidly concentrated on the threatened point. On the 18th of September Colonel Allenby's column reached Dundee, and by the 25th of the month General Lyttelton, who already held the line of the Buffalo in strength, had assembled two mobile forces at Dundee under command of Major-Generals Clements and Bruce Hamilton respectively.

A third force under Major-General Walter Kitchener moved out to Utrecht. It consisted of the column under Lieut.-Colonel Garratt, which had followed the enemy into that district from Wakkerstroom, and the troops under Major-General W. Kitchener and Colonel Campbell who had arrived at Volksrust on the 23rd September at the conclusion of their operations in the vicinity of Ermelo.

In the meantime the Boers who had halted for some days at Bloed River Poort after their success against Major Gough, were reported to be moving into the salient angle of the Vryheid District which projects southwards into Zululand between Nqutu and Ndwande. Hostile patrols were seen to the east of Vant's and Rorke's Drifts, and it became apparent that our occupation of the line of the Buffalo had compelled the enemy to seek access to Natal by a wider detour to the south. This led him towards our fortified posts of Itala and Fort Prospect on the Zululand border, a few miles to the north-west of Melmoth, and to meet it General Lyttelton pushed out the force under Major-General Bruce Hamilton from Vant's and Rorke's Drifts in a south-easterly direction. The garrison of Itala consisted of 2 guns of the 69th Battery, Royal Field Artillery, and 300 men of the 5th Division Mounted Infantry, all under the command of Captain (local Major, and now Major and Brevet Lieut.-Colonel) A.J. Chapman, Royal Dublin Fusiliers. The attack on this post, which was conducted by Commandant-General Louis Botha and other leaders, at the head of some 1,500 men, was a most determined one. Commencing at 3 a.m. on the 26th September, it was pressed almost without intermission for 19 hours, when the enemy, repulsed on all sides, withdrew under cover of dusk in an easterly and north-easterly direction. That on Fort Prospect was made by a detached Boer force about 500 strong. This post was held by 35 men of the 5th Division Mounted Infantry and 51 men of the Durham Artillery Militia, all under the command of Captain C.A. Rowley,

2nd Bn. Dorsetshire Regiment, and the attack on it was easily repulsed. The successful defence of these two places reflects the greatest credit on Major Chapman and Captain Rowley, and all ranks of the small garrisons under their respective commands.

On the 27th September the Boer commandos being fully occupied in burying their dead and collecting and tending their wounded, showed of signs of aggression, and early on the 28th, the columns under Major-General Bruce Hamilton, which had been directed on Itala, as soon as the southward movement of the enemy was confirmed, arrived at that place. They were at once interposed between the enemy, who had fallen back on their approach towards Babanango and Retief's Rust, and the Tugela, and communication with Melmoth was opened up. General Lyttelton's plans for clearing the country of the Boers, and if possible, intercepting them, had in the meantime been developed. On hearing that they had committed themselves to a southward movement towards Zululand, he arranged that while Major-General Bruce Hamilton headed them off in the direction of Itala and Melmoth, General Clements should take them in flank through Nqutu, and Major-General Walter Kitchener should move from Utrecht by the Schurveberg and Vryheid upon their rear and endeavour to block the possible avenues of escape to the north.

On the 29th September, General Kitchener reached Vryheid, and on the 30th General Clements was reported to be at Vant's Drift on the Buffalo River. On the 2nd October, General Kitchener arrived at Geluk (234) whence he pushed on a portion of his advanced troops to Toovernaar's Rust (518); . Major-General Bruce Hamilton was then in touch with the enemy in the neighbourhood of Retief's Rust, and General Clements moving on from Vant's Drift in the direction of Nqutu. On the same day Major-General Kitchener was engaged with 300 of the enemy near Pondwana Mountain. On the 4th October General Bruce Hamilton advanced north by Entonjaneni, on Inhlazatye, in communication on his left with General Clements, whose columns were directed from Nqutu upon Kromellenbog (289). The enemy's main body on this date was reported to be close to Ntabankulu with General Kitchener still to the north of it in the vicinity of Uitzicht (176). As our columns pushed on the Boers continued their retreat north to Boschoek (156), Kromellenbog (303), and Leeuwnek (15), where they were held for a time by Major-General W. Kitchener, but on the night of the 5th October the Boers were successful in breaking through to the north. Abandoning their baggage and wagons they moved rapidly round General Kitchener's left Bank from Boschoek (156), to Smaldeel (575),retreating thence with all speed over the Pivaan River, past Paul Pietersburg, in the direction of Piet Relief and the Slangapies Berg. General Kitchener followed at once in close pursuit by Waterval (310), to Nooitgedacht (246), and Bellevue (600), where he engaged a rearguard, which in a strong position covered the flight of the main body. Our columns continue their movement to the north in support of General Kitchener, but the unfinished state of a line of blockhouses from Wakkerstroom to Piet Retief, which was commenced on the 1st October by the 2nd Bn. Scots Guards and 2nd Bn. West Yorkshire Regiment, under Brigadier-General Bullock, renders it unlikely now that any large bodies of the enemy can be cut off before they escape into the Ermelo District.

It is disappointing that we were unable to gain the full advantage which this futile effort of the Boer leaders might have afforded us of striking them when concentrated, but the country in which these operations took place, at all times difficult, was rendered almost impassable by the heavy rains which continued, with one short interval of four or five days, throughout their progress and which finally forced the enemy to abandon his wagons in order to effect his escape.

Operations in the Eastern Transvaal.

3. Upon the departure of Lieut.-General Sir Bindon Blood for India, Brigadier-General Reeves assumed temporary command in the Eastern Transvaal, where the columns under Colonels Park and Benson have continued their operations north and south of the railway.

Colonel Benson, who had reached Witbank Station on 6th September, marched thence along the railway line to Middelburg. He again left Middelburg on the 10th, in a south-easterly direction, having located a party of Boers at Pullen's Hope (213), and, after a long march, on an extremely dark night, was successful in surprising and capturing 33 prisoners, with 73 horses, 515 cattle, 4 wagons, 4 carts, and a quantity of ammunition. Colonel Benson then joined his convoy and baggage, from Middelburg, at Eikeboom (218), and the following day marched to Blesbokspruit (219), from which point he passed through the valley of the Klein Olifant to Weltevreden (151). Here, on the 14th, he was informed that a band of the enemy had spent the previous night at Tweefontein (496). He accordingly started on a night march, taking with him two squadrons of the 2nd Scottish Horse, and the 19th Bn. Mounted Infantry, and, early on the 15th, took 10 Boers and 250 head of cattle, the remainder of the enemy making good their escape.

On the 16th September Colonel Benson moved on to Carolina, and the following day again left that place, having heard of a gathering of Boers at Busby (206), on the Umpilusi River, some distance to the south-east. After a 40-mile march he reached his objective, and, just as the early morning mist was lifting, charged down upon two laagers at Middeldrift (191) and Busby (206), in which he secured 54 prisoners, 48 vehicles, 1,700 head of cattle, and

242 horses. Amongst the prisoners, most of whom belong to the Carolina Commando, were P.M. Botha, late Landdrost of Pretoria and Commandant Nieuwhoudt.

Colonel Benson then returned, by Lake Chrissie, to Carolina, and, on the 28th September, moved on westward into the Bethal District, capturing 12 prisoners on the following day in the vicinity of Monson's Store, to the west of the Klein Olifant. On the 1st October, when at Kranspoort (264) he received intelligence which pointed to the presence of 100 Boers at Weltevreden (179), on the Olifant's River. He started the same evening to try to overtake this band, but found, on arrival at his destination, that they had already trekked away on the previous afternoon. Their tracks were, however, carefully followed by Colonel Benson's men, who came up with the enemy at Driefontein (235), and captured 7 prisoners, 30 horses, 12 mules, and some cattle. The remainder of the Boers fled north, hotly pursued by our troops, who covered over 50 miles in 19 hours in the course of the chase.

The westward movement was then continued, Kaallaagte (326) being reached on the 4th September, since which date Colonel Benson has operated near Bethal.

There is no doubt that the Boers in this part of the country have been so constantly alarmed and harassed by the frequent night raids made by our troops that they have for the time become thoroughly demoralised. They seldom spend two nights in one place, shift camp daily, and saddle up regularly at 3 a.m. in readiness for flight. This is highly creditable to our men, but it naturally adds to the difficulty experienced in making any substantial captures.

Colonel Park, who had arrived near Bankfontein (234), north-east of Middelburg on the 8th September, marched into the latter town on the 11th to refit his column.

On the 16th he again left Middelburg for Machadodorp, intending to operate in the vicinity of Schoeman's Kloof before returning to Lydenburg. A number of Boers had congregated in the Badfontein Valley, but, as Colonel Park approached, they dispersed and cleared away in the direction of Ohrigstad and Pilgrim's Rest. Colonel Park accordingly moved on to Lydenburg, and thence followed up the retiring enemy towards Kruger's Post, where at dawn, on 2nd October, he was successful in capturing 13 prisoners, 8 rifles, 3 wagons, some cattle and dynamite.

On the following day, Colonel Park took with him six companies of Mounted Infantry and two companies of the Manchester Regiment, and made a thorough search of all the farms between Kruger's Post and Ohrigstad. Four armed burghers were taken in this district, and large quantities of supplies, forage, and ammunition were collected and destroyed. Colonel Park then moved back towards Kruger's Post. His return march however, was not un-molested, for at Rustplaats (15) he was attacked by a very considerable force which had apparently come from the east, under General Viljoen. Fighting went on for some hours, and the Boers then withdrew, Colonel Park con-tinuing his way back to camp.

On the 7th October, Colonel Park surprised and attacked a party of Boers upon a farm at Rosenkrans (1444). The men escaped, but 40,000 rounds of Mauser ammunition, three wagons, and a quantity of mealies were left in our hands. Colonel Park then moved south to the Spekboom River.

The railway traffic to the east has been little interrupted during the last few weeks, but on 16th September an attack was made upon Belfast by a Boer commando, 100 strong, under Commandant Grobelaar, with the evident intention of obtaining supplies. The attack was easily repulsed, one man only of the garrison being wounded, but many Boer bullets fell in the refugee camp where one woman was killed, and two children wounded.

A general advance has been made in the Eastern Transvaal of the Constab-ulary posts which ran from Eerste Fabriken, through Springs and Heidelberg, to the Vaal River. This line has now been gradually pushed forward during the month by Colonel Pilkington, South African Constabulary, to the line Wilge River Station – Greylingstad, and the junction of Kalk Spruit with the Vaal, an alteration of position which has enabled us to enclose and clear a much larger area of country. The work of the Constabulary, as they moved the blockhouses to the new line, has been covered and secured by the simul-taneous advance of the troops under Lieut.-Colonels Hacket Thompson, Bewicke Copley, and Sir H. Rawlinson who operated respectively from Bronkhorst Spruit, Springs, and Heidelberg.

As the majority of the Boers in this district had accompanied General Botha towards the Natal frontier, few of them were seen by the northern and central columns, but Sir Henry Rawlinson, to whom was assigned the task of clearing the front of the Constabulary between the Standerton line and the Vaal River, came in contact with several parties of the enemy which he chased westwards towards Barnard's Kop, and southwards over the Vaal into Orange River Colony.

On the 3rd October, Sir H. Rawlinson marched into Greylingstad, whence he organised a night patrol to Barnard's Kop, which resulted in the capture of three armed burghers. On the evening of the 4th, he again left Greylingstad for Watervalshoek (204), where the laagers of Field-Cornets Hans Botha and Pretorius were reported to be. The former of these was successfuly sur-prised at daybreak on the 5th near Kaffir Spruit (199), 7 prisoners, 20 horses, 12 wagons, 12 Cape carts, and 650 cattle being captured. The other laager had already moved east before the advance of the Constabulary posts, and though Sir Henry Rawlinson followed it for some distance, he was unable to add to his captures.

Operations on the Pietersburg Line.

4. No events of importance have occurred in the Northern Transvaal during the past few weeks. Since the train-wrecking incident of the 31st of August, the Pietersburg line has been undisturbed, and General Beyer's wandering bands have kept to the hills to the west of the railway, avoiding as usual contact with our troops.

Two columns have remained in this district in observation of the enemy, one under Colonel Colenbrander acting from Warmbaths, and the other under Lieut.-Colonel Wood, who has taken Lieut.-Colonel Grenfell's place, from Nylstroom.

Night raids and long-distance marches have from time to time been undertaken when opportunity presented, and a certain number of prisoners (including Captain M. Coetzee, the leader of Beyer's Scouts) have been brought in by our troops.

Operations in the South-Western Transvaal.

5. At the date of my last despatch, the situation in the South-Western Transvaal was briefly as follows:- General Fetherstonhaugh and Colonel Kekewich completing their search for the dismounted stragglers of Kemp's force, to the south-west of Olifant's Nek. Colonel Allenby from Rustenburg, and Brigadier-General Gilbert Hamilton on their march to Pretoria and Klerksdorp respectively, and Lord Methuen's troops approaching Zeerust from the Marico Valley.

On the 11th of September, Brigadier-General Hamilton reported from Cyferkuil (47) as he approached Klerksdorp, that he had captured near Geduld (158) a Boer convoy, with 25 prisoners, 140 horses, 7 wagons, and 520 cattle.

General Fetherstonhaugh continued to search the kloofs round Leeuwfontein (339) for some days, and then on the 12th of September moved by Tafel Kop on Ventersdorp, to replenish his supplies. At Tafel Kop, he learnt that Kemp, who had escaped from our cordon in a north-easterly direction, was already working his way back to the south again, as our troops withdrew.

Colonel Kekewich, after assisting General Fetherstonhaugh in his operations to the southwest of Oliphant's Nek, returned to Naauwpoort (214) with the prisoners taken. He again left Naauwpoort on the 13th of September, and passing through Olifant's Nek, turned east to operate on the northern slopes of the Magaliesberg. On the 15th he reached Oorzaak (568), from which place he operated in conjunction with Colonel Mackenzie (1st Bn. Suffolk Regiment), who was then employed in constructing blockhouses to the south of the range between Naauwpoort (214) and Olifant's Nek. A careful search of the slopes and summits of the hills resulted in the capture of Field-Cornet Klopper, and 36 other prisoners of war. Colonel Kekewich then moved to Roodekoppies (171), whence he returned to Magato's Nek to co-operate once more with General Fetherstonhaugh against Kemp's commando, now reported to be reassembling in that neighbourhood. On the 24th Colonel Kekewich was at Rietfontein (299). Here he organised a night expedition by Bulhoek (833) and Lamoenfontein (357) to Crocodile Drift (266) on the Eland's river, at which place he surrounded and took a Boer laager, under Acting-Commandant van Rooijan, with 35 prisoners, 15 horses, 5 wagons, and several hundred cattle. Colonel Kekewich then moved to Waterval (596), whence on the 26th he marched to Lindley's Poort (102). Kemp's men on this date were reported to be on the Toelani River.

Being unable, however, to gain touch with the enemy, Colonel Kekewich on the 29th turned east to Moedwill (639), where at dawn on the following morning his camp was heavily attacked by a force of at least 1,000 Boers under Generals Delarey and Kemp, who had evidently followed up our column from the valley of the Toelani. The attack which lasted from 4.45 a.m. till 6.15 a.m. being delivered upon three sides of our camp with great vigour and a lavish expenditure of ammunition, was quickly repulsed after severe fighting, in which all ranks displayed great gallantry, the conduct of the 1st Bn. Derbyshire Regiment being especially distinguished. The enemy foiled in their attempt to rush the position were compelled to fall back, and they apparently retired in a northerly and north-westerly direction.

Our losses in this action were severe, 1 officer and 31 men being killed, and 26 officers, including Colonel Kekewich, and 127 men wounded. To give some idea of the severity of the fire to which the troops were subjected it may be mentioned that 3 piquets were practically annihilated, and that out of a party of 12 men of the Derbyshire Regiment which was guarding a drift, 8 men were killed and 4 wounded.

Upon Colonel Kekewich being incapacitated by wounds the command of the column was temporarily assumed by Lieut.-Colonel Wylly, Derbyshire Regiment. I am glad, however, to report that Colonel Kekewich has this day been able to resume his work.

In the meantime General Fetherstonhaugh had again left Ventersdorp, marching north on the 21st September to resume operations in conjunction with Colonel Kekewich. Moving by Tafel Kop he was engaged on the 24th at Doornkom (896) with a number of Boers whom he drove in the direction of the Toelani Valley. On the following day be captured a position on

Winkelhoek (280), driving the enemy towards Doornkloof (591); then failing to find any further objective, he turned back in a south-easterly direction to Waterval (68).

On the 29th September he moved to Kwaggafontein (924), and here on the 30th heard of the attack on Colonel Kekewich's camp at Moedwill. On receipt of this intelligence he at once sent Colonel Williams's column to Hartebeestfontein (514) to support Colonel Kekewich, following himself as soon as possible with the remainder of his force. By the 2nd October General Fetherstonhaugh had concentrated the whole of his troops at Moedwill, but he was unable to obtain any definite news of the enemy, who seemed to have scattered, after their unsuccessful attack, amongst the farms on both sides of the Rustenburg – Zeerust road. Between the 2nd and 6th he executed reconnaissances to the west in the hopes of being able to gain touch with Generals Delarey and Kemp, but failing to learn their whereabouts moved south on the latter date to Kosterfontein (292) on his way towards Tafel Kop. On the departure of General Fetherstonhaugh for the south, Lieut.-Colonel Wylly moved east through Magato's Nek to refit his column and draw supplies from Rustenburg.

Lord Methuen reached Zeerust on the 9th September after a series of sharp encounters with the enemy in the neighbourhood of the Marico Valley. The Boers had shown great boldness in these attacks, and persistently followed his rearguard up to Zeerust. Two days later Lord Methuen returned to Mafeking, and he utilised the remainder of the month in refitting his troops and in passing convoys into Lichtenburg and Zeerust, preparatory to a fresh movement to the east. This contemplated advance had the double object of completing the collection of the ripening crops in the Marico District, and establishing a line of blockhouses between Zeerust and the lead mines.

On the 2nd October his column marched from Mafeking to commence work, and on the 4th Lord Methuen had reached a line Wonderfontein (41) – Kleinfontin (76) – Waterkloof (148), from which points he is now moving south upon Bokkraal (300), carefully clearing the country of all scattered bands. An affair of patrols at Wilgeboom Spruit (276) on the 4th October, resulted in five burghers being killed.

Operations on the Vaal.

6. Great progress has been made during the past month in clearing the enemy from both banks of the Vaal River. The line of blockhouses from Kopjes Station to Potchefstroom, which was commenced in the first week of September by the 2nd Bn. Scots Guards and 1st Bn. Oxfordshire Light Infantry, has been completed; Heilbron has been similarly connected with Frankfort, and, east and west of Vereeniging, the drifts over the Vaal have

been permanently occupied by detachments of the Railway Pioneer Regiment under Lieut.-Colonel Capper.

To prevent any interruption of this work, and to cover its completion, the columns under Lieut.-Colonels Byng and Dawkins were brought up from the south of Orange River Colony on the 10th September to Vredefort Road Station. From this point they moved out into the area round Reitzburg – Venterskroon – Parys, where a considerable number of Boers were taken as they sought to escape from the tract of country gradually being enclosed by the blockhouse line. Many of these prisoners who had fled south from the Losberg and Gatsrand were found lurking in the bed of the Vaal River, near Rensburg Drift.

Having thoroughly searched and cleared the ground between Parys and Reitzburg, Colonel Byng marched west to Coal Mine Drift, where he heard of the assembly at Bothaville of some 500 Boers, most of whom had left the area then being included within our blockhouse system. He proceeded at once in that direction with the idea of attacking, but found as he advanced that the enemy only broke up into small parties and dispersed in the country lying between the Rhenoster and Valsch rivers. He accordingly moved back with Lieut.-Colonel Dawkins along the Valsch River to Kroonstad, where they arrived on the 3rd October, having captured 81 prisoners of war since leaving Vredefort.

To work in co-operation with our troops to the south, Major-General Mildmay Willson organised a small force under Lieut.-Colonel Hicks, 2nd Bn. Royal Dublin Fusiliers, which consisted of 250 Mounted Infantry, two field guns, and five companies of Infantry. This column, which assembled at Banks Station, moved thence on the 17th September for the country lying between the Gatsrand and the Vaal, where it was employed in establishing and provisioning Constabulary posts, and in hunting small parties of Boer snipers. 26 prisoners were taken, and on the 29th September the force returned to Potchefstroom. From there the column moved to Venterskroon, and on the 8th October Lieut.-Colonel Hicks reported by runner from Buffelshoek that the South African Constabulary troops, acting in co-operation with his column, had captured Field-Cornets George Hall and Van der Venter, 16 burghers, and a 7-pr. gun, which had been taken some weeks ago from their post at Houtkop. Colonel Rimington's Operations in Northern Orange River Colony.

7. On the 10th September, Colonel Rimington's Column, which had marched north from Kroonstad, was at Leeuwfontein, 6 miles south of Heilbron. From here, on the 14th, he made a night march on Anderkant (292), where he surprised and captured 6 Boers, 6 wagons, 9 Cape carts, and a number of

horses and mules. On the 20th he was at Jakhal's Kop, south of the Heilbron – Frankfort Road, and on the 22nd marched thence to the junction of the Vaal and Wilge rivers, where he overtook Strydom's Commando, and secured 13 prisoners, 18 wagons, 17 Cape carts, 2 Scotch carts, 1,180 cattle, and 40 horses. Colonel Rimington then returned to Heilbron, and on the 28th marched to Oploop, between the Klip and Wilge rivers, watching for an opportunity of co-operation with Sir Henry Rawlinson's Column, which was then assisting the Constabulary to the north of the Vaal. On the 2nd October his chance came, and he captured 24 prisoners and 2,000 cattle, 30 horses, 14 loaded wagons, 22 Cape carts, and 20 mules, all belonging to Buys' Commando, which had been driven south of the river by Sir Henry Rawlinson's advance from Heidelberg.

On the 3rd October, Colonel Rimington was at De Rust on Venter's Spruit, and on the 7th he entered Standerton to draw supplies preparatory to moving south of De Lange's Drift to co-operate with Brigadier-General Broadwood and Colonel De Lisle from Harrismith.

As it had been intended to reinforce Colonel Rimington by the column under Lieut.-Colonel Wilson (Kitchener's Fighting Scouts), which had been refitted at Kroonstad after its return from the Senekal district, the latter Officer was ordered to leave Kroonstad for Heilbron on 1st October. He crossed the Rhenoster River at dawn on the 4th, and almost immediately afterwards a portion of his command was attacked at Paardekraal by a considerable force of the enemy which was driven off with loss. Having repulsed this attack, Colonel Wilson resumed his march on Heilbron, where, instead of joining Colonel Rimington's command, he was temporarily assigned the duty of covering the line of blockhouses from Heilbron to Frankfort.

Major-General Elliot's Operations in Eastern Orange River Colony.

8. After two or three days' halt at Winburg, Major-General Elliot's Division again started on 10th September to march east towards the Wittebergen. It seemed desirable to revisit this district once more, with the object of endeavouring to come up with some of the parties of Boers which had evaded capture during the previous movement. Lieut.-Colonel Barker and Major Pine Coffin remained to operate from Winburg to the west of General Elliot's line of advance, whilst Major-General B. Campbell continued to maintain his position on the eastern slopes of the Wittebergen. Brigadier-General Dartnell, with the Imperial Light Horse from Bethlehem, was also ordered to assist in the operations by blocking the passes at Retief's and Slabbert's Neks.

The movement from Winburg was commenced in four columns, General Broadwood's Brigade being on the right, Colonel Bethune's on the left, and the troops of Colonel Lowe and Lieut.-Colonel De Lisle in the centre. Lieut.-Colonel De Lisle came in sight of a convoy, under Commandant Koen, which was then trekking towards the Korannaberg, and after a long gallop overtook and captured 15 prisoners, 47 wagons, 22 carts, 250 horses, and 2,500 cattle. On the 12th Colonel Bethune drove 70 Boers from a position near Wonkerkop, and on the following evening he made a night march to Rietvlei, where he was again slightly engaged.

From the 14th to the 18th September the Division was employed in searching the western slopes of the Wittebergen, moving gradually northwards upon a line parallel to that followed by Major-General Campbell inside the Brandwater Basin from Steynsberg towards Retief's and Slabbert's Neks. This combined movement yielded good results. 17 Boers were taken by Major-General Campbell, and large quantities of supplies and vehicles were found hidden away in the mountain kloofs. A continual sniping was maintained from the summits of the hills by small parties of Boers under the leadership of Commandant Prinsloo. Having accomplished all that was possible in this distinct, General Elliot pushed north from Tafel Berg on the 19th by Bethlehem to Harrismith, a destination which seemed advisable in consequence, of the development of events in Natal, and arrived there on the 26th.

The result of the operations which then closed was reported to be as follows:- 7 Boers killed, 5 wounded, 46 prisoners, 3 voluntary surrenders, 2,560 horses, 9,100 cattle, 127 wagons, 101 carts, 2,700 rounds of ammunition.

The 2nd Imperial Light Horse with General Dartnell had already been brought into Harrismith, and proceeded thence by rail and road to Eshowe, in Zululand, and on the 29th of September Colonel Bethune, with 600 men of General Elliot's Division, followed General Dartnell to the same destination.

The other brigades of General Elliot's Division remained temporarily in the eastern portion of the Orange River Colony in readiness to act against any parties of the enemy who might seek to penetrate into Natal in co-operation with General Botha's enterprise. On the 28th and 29th Colonel De Lisle, and Brigadier-General Broadwood moved north from Harrismith towards Muller's Pass and Vrede to disperse certain hostile bands which were reported to be hovering about the frontier. Colonel De Lisle was at Muller's Pass on the 2nd of October, and the same night General Broadwood bivouacked at Boschoek, a few miles to the west. Few Boers were seen, and it was evident that the parties which may have been meditating an inroad into Natal had thought better of their project, and retired west towards Witkoppies and Vrede. Our columns accordingly made a reconnaissance on the 5th in that direction trying to gain touch with the enemy, and watching for an opportunity of communicating with Colonel Rimington, who was then known to be moving east from Cornelia along the Vaal valley.

Operations in the Harrismith and Bethlehem Districts.

9. Allusion has already been made to the part taken by Major-General B. Campbell's column in operations about the Wittebergen. The remainder of Sir Leslie Rundle's Division has been occupied in blocking the passes leading into Natal between Van Reenen's and Witzie's Hoek, in relieving the garrisons upon the Albertina – Van Reenen's line which have hitherto been furnished from the Natal command, and in passing supplies by convoy into Bethlehem.

After the departure of Brigadier-General Dartnell for Zululand, the 1st Imperial Light Horse, under Lieut.-Colonel Briggs, remained to act independently from Bethlehem. This force which was especially organised with a view to mobility has already justified its existence, and some excellent long distance raids have been undertaken.

The most successful of these took place on the night of the 28th of September, when after a circuitous march of 38 miles from Bethlehem, Lieut.-Colonel Briggs surrounded the town of Reitz at dawn on the 29th. Here he captured 21 prisoners (including Landdrost Piet de Villiers), 9 Cape carts, 2 wagons, 24 horses, 9 rifles, 250 cattle and some ammunition. His return march, however, was much opposed, and several unsuccessful attempts were made at night by parties of Boers, said to be under De Wet, to surround and rush his force.

Operations in Southern Orange River Colony.

10. After Commandant Smuts had crossed to the south of the Orange River at Kiba Drift, as mentioned in my last despatch, the remainder of the Boers in the south-eastern portion of the Orange River Colony, under Commandant Kruitzinger and other leaders, broke up into a number of small commandos which have moved rapidly about, evading the pursuit of our columns in the area marked by Wepener – Dewetsdorp – Bethulie and Zastron.

On the 8th September, the positions of the different columns under Major-General C. Knox, in this district, were, approximately, as follows:- Colonel Thorneycroft at Quaggafontein and Meyerhoek, guarding the line of the Orange River to the south of Zastron; Lord Basing at Jurysbaken, patrolling thence to Commissie Bridge on the Caledon; Colonel Sir Henry Rawlinson on the march south from the Elandsberg to Aliwal; and General Plumer at Smithfield. Major Damant had already returned to Springfontein.

From Smithfield, on the 9th September, General Plumer moved up the valley of the Caledon to Arcadia and Bastard's Drifts against the Boers who had been driven north from the Elandsberg on 7th September, by Sir Henry Rawlinson. From these drifts he detached Sir John Jervis upon Wepener in pursuit of two large parties of the enemy, whilst with Colonel Colvin's Column he struck across to Runnymede on the Basuto border. On the 15th, the force reassembled at Wepener, where General Plumer learnt from prisoners that the commandos which had retired north before Sir John Jervis, were local men, and that Kruitzinger had once more doubled back to the Elandsberg. He accordingly sent Colonel Colvin in the latter direction to co-operate with Colonel Thorneycroft, whilst he himself, with Sir John Jervis's Column, moved back towards Smithfield by the right bank of the Caledon.

On the 19th September, some of Sir John Jervis's mounted men, under Captain Knight of the Buffs, had a sharp skirmish at Wessel's Rust, 8 miles north-west of Bastard's Drift, an affair in which we captured eight prisoners, including Adjutants Brand and Joubert.

On the same day Colonel Thorneycroft, relieved by General Hart of the task of watching the line of the Orange River, had moved up to Rocklands with Colonel Minchin's Column, thereby setting free Lord Basing to fill the gap between Smithfield and the railway, and Colonel Sir H. Rawlinson had advanced from Aliwal to Beestekraal and Willemsfontein to enable General Hart to devote his entire attention to the line of the river east of Klaarwater Drift.

Colonel Thorneycroft, ascertaining that Kruitzinger had moved on the 17th from the Elandsberg to Tilly, 10 miles north-east of Vecht Kop, despatched Major Copeman's Column in that direction on the night of the 18th, and himself prepared to follow through Dorcum with Colonel Minchin's troops.

On the 22nd September a party of New Zealanders, under Major Tucker, belonging to Lieut.-Colonel Colvin's Column, was engaged on the Elands-berg with 150 Boers under Field-Cornets Hugo and Bothma, both of whom, with several other prisoners, were captured.

The effect of these operations was to press some of the enemy's bands toward the Thabanchu line, where their presence had not been taken into account by the Commandant of the section. On the 19th September, a small force, consisting of some 160 mounted men and two guns of "U" Battery, Royal Horse Artillery, which had been detached without any authority or sufficiently important object by the Officer Commanding at the Bloem-fontein Waterworks, was surrounded and captured at Vlakfontein, 18 miles south-west of Sannah's Post, by a Boer commando under Commandants Coetzee and Ackermann.

On receipt of this news General Plumer was ordered to move north rapidly on Wepener, where he arrived on 26th September, and Colonel Rochfort, who had succeeded to the temporary command of Major-General Bruce

Hamilton's force when the latter was transferred to Natal, was directed to push his columns across the railway line from the west with the object of hemming in the enemy against the Thabanchu line.

Daily skirmishes occurred with one or other of the columns, and at daybreak on the 29th, Colonel Lowry Cole surprised a Boer laager under Commandant Dreyer and Field-Cornet Van Vuuren, capturing both these leaders and other prisoners.

In conjunction with these operations General Plumer despatched 200 New Zealanders under Major Andrews from Wepener to hold Mokari Drift on the Caledon. This party reached the drift on the 27, just in time to anticipate some 300 to 400 Boers who were about to cross the river to the south-east. In some sharp fighting which followed, the enemy, who were driven westward, left six dead and seven wounded on the field. The same evening General Plumer joined Major Andrews at Mokari, and the whole force then moved south by Commissie Bridge to Rouxville, without being further engaged. After two days' halt General Plumer received orders to march to the railway at Springfontein.

As previously mentioned Colonel Thorneycroft moved east from the Rouxville District on the 18th and 19th September, and passing through Corunna on the 20th, successfully attacked a Boer force at Vaunedikking's Vallei the same evening.

At the end of September Major Damant's column was withdrawn and brought by rail to Heilbron, to assist Colonel Wilson in covering the Heilbron – Frankfort line of blockhouses.

Colonel Sir Henry Rawlinson's troops were also withdrawn to Burgherdorp, and moved thence by rail to the Transvaal for operations near Heidelberg which have already been described.

To each of the columns now left on the east of the main line of railway an area was assigned with a centre from which to work. The columns thus placed are able to deal with any small bands coming within their reach, and three or four can easily combine against any more formidable gathering of the enemy. In this manner the whole district is being rapidly brought under control.

In the south-western portion of the Orange River Colony the situation has improved in a very marked degree. Only a few small scattered parties remain in this district and the work of systematic clearance has been so thoroughly carried out by the troops under Major-General Bruce Hamilton that as already shown it was found possible to withdraw, first the columns under Lieutenant-Colonels Byng and Dawkins to the Vredefort District, and then Major Damant's to Heilbron, whilst the remainder, now directed by Colonel Rochfort, were transferred to the more disturbed area on the east of the railway. Colonel Henry's column continues to operate in this district.

Cape Colony.

11. After passing the Orange River on the night of the 3rd September, Commandant Smuts moved into the Jamestown – Dordrecht district where he was engaged on the 12th of the month by Colonel Monro. On the same night Smuts eluded our pursuing columns, and, passing over the Sterkstroom – Indwe line of railway at Halseston Station, moved rapidly by Putter's Kraal in the direction of Tarkastad. He was followed south by Colonel Gorringe, Lieut.-Colonel Doran, and the 17th Lancers, whilst Colonel Scobell's column moved to Cradock to try to intercept him from the west.

On the 17th September, Smuts's Commando arrived at Modderfontein, 18 miles north-west of Tarkastad, where the Boers made a most determined attack upon a squadron of the 17th Lancers, under Major Sandeman, posted to close all egress to the south. The enemy being dressed in khaki were taken for our own troops, and got to close quarters with the advantage of ground before the mistake was discovered. Thus taken at a great disadvantage our men offered a most gallant resistance, and worthily maintained the traditions of their regiment. The losses of the squadron were very severe, 3 Officers and 20 men being killed, and 2 Officers and 30 men wounded. The Boers, who had evidently made the attack in order to elude the close pursuit to which they were subjected, also suffered heavily, before the approach of another squadron of the 17th Lancers compelled them to break off the engagement.

After this encounter Smuts rapidly continued his movement to the south for several days. The pursuit, however, was never relaxed, and the troops under Lieut.-Colonels Gorringe, Doran, and Scobbel responded cheerfully to the great exertions demanded of them. The enemy's route lay through Paling Kloof, Bankview (18 miles N.N.E. of Bedford) to Mount Prospect, and thence across the Mancazana at Koonap's Drift, along the Fish River to a point near Sheldon Station, where they crossed the Port Elizabeth line to the west on the night of the 27th September. Lieut.-Colonel Gorringe next engaged him at Oud Murazie in the Zuurberg Mountains, and here succeeded in dividing his force, driving one-half south towards Glen Connor, and the other west towards Darlington. The Boers subsequently re-united at Diep Drift, 10 miles south of Darlington, but again attacked on the 3rd October by Colonel Gorringe, were driven north, with a loss of three men killed and five wounded. Our columns in close contact still maintain the pursuit in this direction.

In the north-eastern portion of Cape Colony the operations against Myburg and Fouché, the latter of whom has recrossed the Orange River, have been continued by the columns under Colonel Monro, Colonel Pilcher, and Lieut.-Colonel Western; Major-General Hart, with Lieut.-Colonel Hon.

A.D. Murray's troops and the Connaught Rangers remaining in observation of the river line between Bethulie and Herschel.

On the 10th September an attack upon Ladygrey was easily driven off. On the 15th, Colonel Pilcher's columns were south and west of Jamestown, Lieut.-Colonel Western between Jamestown and Ladygrey, and Colonel Monro to the north of Dordrecht. Smuts with his column had already gone south, but about 400 Boers, most of whom had returned from the Transkei, remained scattered in small parties throughout the district.

Early on the 20th September a determined effort was made by Commandant Kruitzinger near Quaggafontein, north of Herschel, to force a passage over the Orange River at a point covered by 80 men of Lovat's Scouts under Lieut.-Colonel Hon. A.D. Murray. The attempted crossing failed, but the loss sustained by our small force was very heavy, Lieut.-Colonel Murray, his Adjutant and 16 men being killed, and 1 Officer and 85 men wounded. I much deplore the death of Lieut.-Colonel Murray, an Officer of great promise, who has led Lovat's Scouts with gallantry and distinction throughout the campaign.

At the end of September, Colonels Monro and Pilcher were watching the passes over the Drakensberg, across which most of the enemy had again withdrawn into the Transkei, and Lieut.-Colonel Western was near Ladygrey. From these positions Colonel Pilcher and Lieut.-Colonel Western were recalled to the south-eastern portion of the Orange River Colony; Colonel Monro, supported by local troops, being in charge of this area.

In the southern sphere of operations, it will be remembered that early in September Commandant Scheepers had made several unsuccessful attempts to cross to the west of the Cape Town – De Aar line near Matjesfontein. On the evening of the 9th September, General Beatson, who was directing the operations in this district, hearing that a party of the enemy had outspanned at Driefontein about 12 miles east of Laingsburg, despatched Colonel Crabbe's column on a night march from his camp at Waggon Drift. At daybreak of the 10th, Colonel Crabbe completely surprised the Boers under Commandant Van der Merwe. During the short resistance offered by the enemy, Commandant Van der Merwe and one of his followers were killed, and several burghers were wounded. 37 prisoners (including Field-Cornet Du Plessis), together with a good deal of ammunition and equipment, were captured. After this blow to his detachment, Scheepers turned east, and, passing to the south of Ladismith and Oudtshorn, reached Klip Drift with the remainder of his commando on the 20th. From this point he took a northerly direction, closely pursued by the columns under Colonels Crabbe, Atherton, and Major Kavanagh.

After constant changes of direction, Scheepers narrowly escaped capture on the 5th October, at Adam's Kraal, 20 miles S.S.W. of Ladismith, where he was successfully attacked by Major Kavanagh.

On the 8th September, Commandant Theron was moving rapidly west from the direction of Willowmore, with the apparent intention of joining Scheepers. On approaching Heidelberg and Swellendam, however, he suddenly turned northwest and, making for the railway, crossed to the north of the line between Triangle and Touw's River Stations. After passing the railway, Theron was opposed by a force under Lieut.-Colonel Capper, who pursued him into the northern portion of the Ceres District. The troops under Lieut.-Colonels Alexander and Wyndham joined in the pursuit, and Theron was driven well away to the north-west, after which our columns moved back to the railway line to co-operate once more in the chase after Scheepers.

In the Philipstown and Hanover districts, small columns under Lieut.-Colonel Sprot and Major Lund have had frequent encounters with parties of Lategan's men, who reappeared once more to the south of the Orange River. Field-Cornet Louw, an influential rebel, and seven of his followers were captured by Major Lund on the 23rd September.

I must also make allusion to a very gallant stand made on the 17th September by nine men of the 3rd Bn. Grenadier Guards, under Lieutenant M. Gurdon-Rebow, who found themselves attacked by some 30 to 40 of the enemy near Cyferkuil, 10 miles north of Riet Siding. A summons to surrender was refused, and it was not until Lieutenant Gurdon-Rebow and one man had been killed and two others dangerously wounded, as the result of 3 hours' fighting, that the remaining men were overpowered and captured. The Serjeant of the patrol was drowned in a gallant attempt to cross the Carolus River in search of help.

12. Throughout the period covered by this despatch, the movements of our columns have been somewhat impeded by the prevalence of rinderpest amongst the cattle. This first made its appearance on the Thabanchu line 3 months ago. For some time it was kept more or less under control, but in spite of every exertion the disease has now spread, and is likely to make itself felt in every district in turn. It is consequently necessary to inoculate all cattle, a process which throws them out of work for a fortnight or more, and considerably reduces the efficiency of the ox transport for at least a month. The bulk of our oxen have been, or are now being, subjected to this treatment, but some time must elapse before its effects on the whole transport will have completely passed off, and very considerable losses must occur meanwhile.

It is a matter of great consideration to note that, in spite of all the difficulties that have presented themselves, there has been no falling-off in the results which the mobile columns are able to show in return for their hard work during the month of September; 170 Boers have been killed in action, 114 have been wounded and are prisoners in our hands. We have taken 1,385 unwounded prisoners, and 393 burghers have surrendered. Our columns have captured in addition 798 rifles, 119,000 rounds small-arm ammunition, 770 wagons, 11,000 horses (most of which are practically useless), and 41,500 cattle.

It cannot be expected, even under the most favourable conditions, that in the presence of ever-diminishing numbers opposing us in the field, these figures can be maintained, but I feel confident that so long as any resistance is continued no exertion will be spared either by Officers or men of this force to carry out the task they still have before them.

Recommendations for Good Service.

13. I beg to forward herewith the lists of Officers, non-commissioned officers and men whom I wish to bring to notice for good services during the past two months.

I have, &c.
KITCHENER, General.
Commanding-in-Chief, South Africa.

*2 guns 69th Battery, Royal Field Artillery; three companies Mounted Infantry.

Index

(1) Index of Persons

(2) Index of Military and Naval Units